COLOSSIANS:

THE CHURCH'S LORD AND THE CHRISTIAN'S LIBERTY

COLOSSIANS:
THE CHURCH'S LORD AND THE CHRISTIAN'S LIBERTY

An Expository Commentary with a Present-Day Application

by
Ralph P. Martin, M.A., Ph.D.

Professor of New Testament, Fuller Theological Seminary, Pasadena, California

ZONDERVAN PUBLISHING HOUSE
A DIVISION OF THE ZONDERVAN CORPORATION
GRAND RAPIDS, MICHIGAN

COLOSSIANS: *The Church's Lord and the Christian's Liberty*
Copyright © 1972 The Paternoster Press

The Bible text used in this Commentary is the
Revised Standard Version, copyright 1946 and 1952
by the Division of Christian Education of the
National Council of Churches of Christ in the U.S.A.,
and is used by permission.

Library of Congress Catalog Card Number 72-95516

Library of Congress Cataloging in Publication Data

Martin, Ralph P.
  Colossians.

Bibliography:
  1. Bible N.T. Colossians — Commentaries.
I. Bible N.T. Colossians. English. Revised standard. 1973
DS 2715.3.M37 1973 227 '.7'077
Isbn 0-85364-125-0

This printing by special arrangement with
The Paternoster Press

First American printing 1973

Printed in the United States of America

TO

FREDERICK FYVIE BRUCE

TEACHER, COLLEAGUE, FRIEND

CONTENTS

PREFACE

THE COMMENTARY THAT FOLLOWS ATTEMPTS TO MEET THE NEEDS of those readers who wish to understand a little more clearly the background and message of Paul's letter to the Colossian church. Its primary aim has been the clarification of the text of the epistle, taking the Revised Standard Version translation as a starting-point. Paul's Greek in this epistle often contains shades of meaning which are important, so for that reason the Greek words are quoted in their English characters and an effort is made to throw some light on their particular nuance in the context.

This commentary, of course, builds on the fine heritage of its predecessors and is grateful to what is already available in the justly commended works of J. B. Lightfoot, E. F. Scott, C. F. D. Moule and F. F. Bruce. One of the ways in which it may offer a reason for its existence is simply that it tries to express in popular form the insights and helps which abound in these larger works and in some significant articles in recent journals.

Two other reasons have guided the writer in his task. Since the last full-scale commentary on this epistle appeared, Kittel's *Theological Dictionary of the New Testament* has reached its seventh volume in translated form, and there is now placed at the disposal of all who seek a full lexical treatment of the main New Testament words this invaluable storehouse of interpretative material in English. This is a great boon to serious students, and no apology is needed for the ample use made of the *Dictionary* in the following pages.

Then, the large commentary of Eduard Lohse (in the Meyer Kommentar series) appearing in 1968 gave access to the most recent discussions of the Pauline text in German-speaking circles. Though the present writer is by no means persuaded by Lohse's arguments for a placing of the epistle in the Pauline school, he has been enriched and stimulated by this commentary. The subsequent pages will show frequent places where he has been glad to follow Professor Lohse's lead, particularly in those verses which bear upon the nature of the Colossian crisis and the epistle's cosmic christology.

Every commentator hopes that his efforts will be rewarded by the close attention of the readers as he tries to share what he has found in pursuit of the exegetical task. The present commentator is no exception. He has tried to make plain the setting of Paul's argument in the context of certain historical circumstances at Colossae in the hope that the relevance of what Paul wrote long ago may become apparent for the present day. He has sought to help those who came to a commentary for guidance in their calling as ministers of the word or who have responsibility to teach others, in church or school. With this pedagogical interest, he has not avoided a certain amount of repetition so that each part of the commentary might be complete in itself.

Above all, he believes that the letter to the Colossians has still a meaningful message to us in the modern age. It shows the person of Jesus Christ as the answer to man's questions about the cosmos of which he is such an insignificant part. Insignificant he may be, and terrified by vast reaches of outer space, yet his life has meaning. For our human life was once owned and dignified by the coming of God into our world in His Son. Henceforth the character of God is spelled out in terms of that human life. And the pattern of human existence is set by Him as the "new man" in whose image a renewed humanity is born.

So far, much of the epistle's teaching on incarnational theology and the nature of the Christian life is clear and pertinent. A more vexing problem comes when we try to understand and apply Paul's statement of Christ's rôle in creation and His relations as lord of and victor over all spiritual super-beings and cosmic forces in the universe. Notions of dualism and demonism do not come easily into our modern world-view. Even more baffling to the sensitive reader of this epistle is what may appear at first sight to be a separation of the person of Jesus of Nazareth from true human experience. He seems a remote figure, cast in a transcendental mould and far removed from the prophet of Galilee.

Two observations may be made as we seek an easement of the difficulty. Paul is deliberately combative and argumentative as he addresses himself to the situation at Colossae. It may well be that, in order to make his line of reasoning clear and more pointed, he is employing, if not the language of his opponents, at least the cosmo-logical ideas which were very much "in the air" at Colossae. He is driven to formulate his understanding of Christ's rôle in creation by the need to speak a language which will go home to those in the church who were impressed by this theosophy. His terms may seem strange and forbidding to us, but that is not the point. The point is that Paul as apostle of Jesus Christ is primarily here writing in a pastoral context and concerned with a specific set of historical and cultural circumstances. What he writes has a timeless validity, but in its original form it is dressed in garments of its own day and age.

For a second reason Paul's presentation of Jesus Christ in our epistle takes on a deeper meaning than the homely picture of the Jesus of popular imagination. Paul lived on the other side of the resurrection from that of those who saw Jesus in His homespun Galilean clothes. The Christ he knew was the Lord of glory. This is not to deny his intense interest in a person who became truly incarnate; but it is to assert that Paul never saw Jesus except in the light of the glory and majesty of Easter day and the Damascus road encounter.

We need the witness of the first three Gospels today with their story (especially so in Mark's Gospel) of a truly human life in which the divine is bodied forth. But this picture can never be sought at the expense of the transcendental dimensions of the Christ who is Lord of creation and vanquisher of evil. Somehow we must strive to hold the two facets together, which is another way of saying that the clearest affirmation of the present day must be that of continuity between the Jesus of history and the Christ of apostolic faith. What that latter figure was becomes classically clear in the letters to the Colossians.

At least one footnote reference carries allusion to the Festschrift volume *Apostolic History and the Gospel* which Dr W. Ward Gasque and I had the pleasure of editing in honour of the sixtieth birthday of Professor F. F. Bruce. It so happens that the present commentary is reaching its final stages of preparation during the period which marks the publication of this Festschrift, and I would like, as seems fitting, to offer the pages which follow in tribute to F. F. Bruce on this happy occasion.

Pauline studies have been greatly enhanced by the many books, commentaries and articles which have come from his pen. I know that he will take pleasure in receiving and reading the birthday volume in his honour; and since it was not possible for the present writer to include an essay of his own in that book, his hope is that at least some of the subsequent pages will not be unworthy to stand alongside the many fine contributions to the Festschrift.

I am indebted to the Faculty secretary, Mrs. Charmian Pugh, for her ready co-operation in preparing the typescript.

RALPH P. MARTIN

INTRODUCTION

A. The Church of The Colossians

I

THE CITY OF COLOSSAE LAY IN THE VALLEY OF THE LYCUS RIVER a tributary of the Maeander, in the southern part of ancient Phrygia which would be located in the west of modern Turkey. As the city was situated on a main trade route from Ephesus to the east, it is not surprising that ancient historians refer to it in their descriptions of the military movements of such generals as Xerxes and Cyrus. When Herodotus tells how the army of Xerxes was stopped in its march on Greece, he speaks of Colossae as "a great city of Phrygia" (*Histories*, vii. 30). A century later, the chronicler Xenophon described it as "a populous city, both wealthy and large" (*Anabasis*, i. 2, 6). Its commercial importance was due largely to its place as an emporium of the wool and weaving industries.

But the importance of Colossae became diminished in Roman times, largely because the city's neighbouring centres, Laodicea and Hierapolis had expanded and grown more prosperous. At the beginning of the Christian era, the geographer Strabo (xii. 8, 13) could describe it as only a "small town" (Greek *polisma*) and this tribute is confirmed by the virtual disappearance of Colossae from history's page, though the evidence from inscriptions and coins belonging to the second and third centuries AD attests the continuance of its civic life (see J. L. Houlden's commentary, p. 119). The present-day site is uninhabited.

At the time when Paul lived, the commercial and social importance of Colossae was already on the way down. What effect this depression might have had on the Colossian townspeople or the Christians among them, we have no means of knowing. What does seem certain is that, in Lightfoot's words, "Colossae was the least important church to which any epistle of St Paul is addressed" (*Commentary*, p. 16).

When Paul wrote to the Christians living at Colossae, the city's population consisted mainly of indigenous Phrygian and Greek settlers. But Josephus, the Jewish historian (*Antiquities*, xii. 149) records the fact that Antiochus III in the early part of the second century B.C. had brought several thousand Jews from Mesopotamia and Babylon and settled them in Lydia and Phrygia. Colossae, in Paul's day, was thus a cosmopolitan city in which diverse cultural and religious elements met and mingled. This is quite possibly a serious factor in the total situation which provoked what P. Benoit calls the Colossian crisis, which followed the emergence of a religious and theosophical teaching which threatened to engulf the church there. As we shall observe, the nature of this teaching is composite and was made up partly of Jewish elements and partly of ideas belonging to the world of hellenistic religious philosophy and mysticism. Colossae was a cultural centre where this pot-pourri might well have been expected; so it is not surprising that it was the Colossian congregation in a city partly Jewish-oriental and partly Greek-Phrygian that became the target of an assault in the name of a syncretistic "fancy religion." To judge from 1:21,27; 2:13, however, the composition of the Colossian church was predominantly Gentile-Christian.

II

The Christian gospel was introduced to Colossae during Paul's ministry based on Ephesus. According to Acts 19:10 Paul exercised a preaching ministry in the capital city of proconsular Asia with a result that "the whole population of the province of Asia, both Jews and pagans, heard the word of the Lord" (NEB). This description, which is not followed by an intimation that Paul did further itinerant preaching in the province, must mean that, while he was based on Ephesus, he sent out his representatives to carry the message to outlying cities and districts in the province. The letter to the Colossians itself affirms that Paul was not personally responsible for evangelistic work in the Lycus valley region eighty miles or so from Ephesus. In two places (1:4, 2:1) there are indications that Paul had not, at the time of writing, visited the church nor any Christian communities in the area including Laodicea. His hope to meet them personally may have been realized later, if the request of Philemon 22 was made good in the fulfilled desire he had to be released from prison and to spend some time in the home of Philemon.

The most likely person to have carried the good news of Christ to Colossae was Epaphras. He was a native of that city (4:12: "one of yourselves"), and stood in a special relation to the believers there as well as to the apostle (4:13). Tribute is paid to him (1:7) as a "faithful minister of Christ" who as Paul's personal delegate had evidently evangelized the Lycus valley district and later had come to visit Paul in his captivity. Indeed, he had, either voluntarily or because of his arrest by the authorities, shared Paul's imprisonment (Philemon 23), and so was not free to return to the congregation when the letter was sent. It was entrusted to Tychicus as its bearer (4:7, 8). He is commissioned to carry also the news of the apostle's prison experience and to bring some encouragement to the Colossian church over the detention of their leader, Epaphras. From him the Colossian Christians had "heard and understood the grace of God in truth" (1:6, 7), and it is only natural that they were concerned about their pastor's well-being, especially since he would not be returning along with the delegation (Tychicus, Onesimus) which brought the letter. Other members of the Colossian church included Philemon and his family (Philemon 1, 2) including Archippus (4:17) and his fugitive slave Onesimus (4:9. Philemon 10) who is to be welcomed as a fellow-believer and new church member (Philemon 16, 17).

III

When Epaphras came to seek Paul in his imprisonment, he was able to report that the Colossian church was responding well to apostolic instruction, both in growth (1:6) and determination to stand firm in the faith (2:5-7). The tenor of these verses and others has suggested to some interpreters, notably H. J. Holtzmann (*Kritik der Epheser- und Kolosserbriefe*, 1872) and C. R. Bowen (*Journal of Biblical Literature*, 43, 1924, pp. 189ff.), that the Colossian church was a young community, only recently established at the time of Paul's writing to them. Bowen's appeal is especially made to some 18 verses (1:4, 5, 6, 7, 8, 9, 21f., 23; 2:1f. 5, 6, 7; 3:7f., 9f.) in which, he maintains, there are some 14 direct allusions to the Colossians' conversion. He concludes: "All this is the language of fresh and vivid reaction upon that happy event. . . . at the time the letter is written the Colossian church has been in existence only a period of weeks or of months at most" (p. 190).

This inference of the church's being of recent foundation is a matter which cannot really be confirmed or confuted. It is in the best sense a matter of conjecture. But the consequentials, if the proposal is true, are of greater importance. Two other issues which form the background of the letter hang on our decision about this suggestion, for Epaphras also brought news to Paul about a threat to the church's faith. This called for his intervention, couched in the plain warnings of 2:4,8 and 2:16. The first question is, Is the nature of this false teaching such as would appeal to a newly formed church? Indeed, what can we say about the speculative and practical issues involved in this Colossian "heresy"? The second matter concerns the dating of the epistle, which in turn is settled by our answer to the question, Where was Paul in captivity (4:3,18)? To which part of his apostolic career does this "epistle from prison" belong?

These are two questions which have excited scholarly interest for some time, with no clear consensus emerging. But plainly they do throw light on the epistle and are important for our fullest appreciation of its message and meaning.

The two issues are, however, not of equal importance. For an understanding of the letter far more depends upon what we can make of the nature of the Colossian errorists' teaching than upon the matters of Paul's imprisonment and the epistle's date and authenticity.

For that reason, we consider the more important question in the pages immediately following. Chapters on the provenance and authorship of the letter are relegated to an Appendix after the commentary (pp. 154ff.).

B.   THE THREAT TO FAITH AND THE COLOSSIAN CRISIS

Perhaps quite unconsciously the church at Colossae was being exposed to a false teaching which Paul regarded as both subversive of the faith and inimical to it. Part of the occasion of his letter may be traced to the presence of this threatened danger and the need to rebut the error which lay at the heart of the aberration. The letter to the Colossians is thus "Paul's vigorous reaction to the news of the strange teaching which was being inculcated at Colossae" (F. F. Bruce, *Commentary*, p. 165). But, as H. Chadwick has shown, Paul's defence of the apostolic faith goes hand in hand with an apologetic statement of that faith to the intellectual world of his day ("All

Things to All Men," *New Testament Studies*, i, [1954-5, pp. 270ff.).
In this sense his letter to the Colossians is one of the earliest Christian
"apologies," or defensive statements of the faith over against its
rivals and competitors, that we possess.

What was the exact nature of the error which Paul combats?
Nowhere in the letter does Paul give a formal definition of it, and
its chief lineaments can only be detected by piecing together and
interpreting his positive counter-arguments. There are, however,
some crucial and combative passages where he seems to be actually
quoting the slogans and watchwords of the propaganda, and these
form invaluable clues in our attempt at literary detection. The hope
is that these citations will enable us to build up a sort of identi-kit
picture of the teaching against which Paul sets his face. The verses
in question are:

1:19 "For in him all the fulness of God was pleased to dwell"
2:18 "insisting on self-abasement and worship of angels"
2:21 "Do not handle, do not taste, do not touch" (the clearest
    instance)
2:23 "rigor of devotion and self-abasement and severity to the
    body"

And, quite possibly, the allusions to "elemental spirits of the
universe" (2:8,20) pick up terms which were being advocated as an
important part of the strange theosophical cult.

Even from this short list we are able to see that the threat to
apostolic faith and life was both academic and practical. Part of the
teaching was related to a theological matter and centred on the
big question, Where is God's true presence to be found and how
may mortal man gain access to that presence? The answer came back
from these Colossian teachers: God's fulness is distributed throughout a series of emanations from the divine, stretching from heaven
to earth. These "aeons" or offshoots of deity must be venerated and
homage paid to them as "elemental spirits" or angels or gods
inhabiting the stars. They rule men's destiny, and control human
life, and hold the entrance into the divine realm in their keeping.
Christ is one of them, but only one among many.

The other question was intensely practical. How may a person
prepare himself for a vision of heavenly realities as part of his rite
of passage into the divine presence? The reply was given in terms
of a rigorous discipline of asceticism and self-denial. Abstinence

especially from food and drink; observance of holy seasons for
fasting and affliction of the soul (2:16); possibly a life of celibacy
and mortification of the human body (2:21,23)—all these exercises
and taboos were prescribed as part of the regimen to be accepted if
the Christians at Colossae were ever to gain "fulness of life" (2:10).

In brief compass, this is the sketch or "cartoon" boldly brushed
onto the canvas in deft strokes by these verses. Can we now fill in
the vivid lines and add more colour and distinctiveness to the picture
of this doctrine and way of life, so alien to Paul's gospel? But before
we get down to fill in something of the cultural and intellectual
background, we should pause to enquire why Paul was so vehe-
mently opposed to this system of thought and practice. Three reasons
are offered:

I

Paul quickly discerned that such a wrong-headed theology *meant
a derogatory attitude to Jesus Christ*. If his teaching on the person and
place of Jesus Christ has any meaning at all, it is emphatic on the
point that He is unique and without peer. Both His relationship to
God the Father and His value as revealer and redeemer are stamped
with a finality and completeness which cannot be compromised. To
Paul any suggestion that Christ was one mediator in a series of
intermediaries between heaven and earth would be effectively to
rob Him of His dignity and to paralyse Christian salvation at a vital
nerve-centre. Nor could he tolerate any thought that Jesus Christ
had only partially revealed God or imperfectly secured the church's
redemption. This would open the door to the need for various
supplemental contributions to human reconciliation, and so introduce the element of uncertainty into the Christian's fellowship with
God. If Christ's reconciling work were incomplete, what assurance
has he that he has placated the right angel-spirit or sufficiently understood the apparatus needed to gain a full salvation—on the errorists'
principle that Christ's achievement is not sufficient by itself?

This setting explains much of the insistence Paul gives to the
cosmic and reconciling rôle of the church's Lord, especially in the
impressive diptych of 1:15–20. Here the two sides of Christ's office
are fully described. He is both cosmic agent in creation (1:15–17)
and the church's reconciler through whom God restores harmony
between Himself and His creation (1:18–20). No loophole is left for
any intruding aeon to come between God and Christ on the one

hand, or between Christ and the world and the church on the other. In Him (and not in any spirit or angel or other intelligence) the totality of the divine fulness dwells, at the pleasure of God (1:19) and for the security of the church, which is assured thereby of fulness of life in Him (2:9,10).

The comprehensiveness of His reconciling work is such as to include even those alien powers which the hellenistic world thought of as hostile to man. The risen Lord is both their creator and ruler. He engineered their coming into being (1:16) in the beginning; and by His victory over death He has taken His place as "the head" or ruler over all cosmic forces, angelic and demonic (2:10). In the new beginning which is marked by His resurrection, He takes His rank as the pre-eminent one (1:18), having gained the victory over all the evil powers which first century man most feared (2:15).

In a strange way the syncretistic theological teachers not only cast a rôle for Jesus Christ which demoted Him from His pinnacle as God's image and Son; they seem to have doubted the reality of His manhood also. Yet this was part of their general understanding of God and the world. In their view, God was remote and inaccessible except through a long chain of intermediaries. Jesus Christ was one of these, but He was sufficiently related to God to share the divine abhorrence for any *direct* contact with matter. To the gnostic mind God was pure spirit, and the world stood over against Him as something alien and despicable. On this assumption, no incarnation —a veritable coming of the divine into human life—was thinkable, and the net result was the rise of docetism. This term says (it comes from the Greek verb "to seem," "to appear") that Jesus Christ came from the divine side of reality but only dressed Himself in human nature as a token appearance. It was a piece of play-acting when God wore a mask of humanity on the stage of human history, giving the appearance of being a man but really being still God-in-disguise.

Is there evidence of this teaching of a divine charade at Colossae? We cannot say so definitely, but Paul has some verses which seem directly to oppose what looks like this type of heretical teaching. At the head of the list are those texts which anchor Christ's incarnation in an acceptance of our "flesh," that is our human nature, weak, frail and exposed to temptation (1:22; 2:11). His death on the cross is vividly pictured by the reference to His blood (1:20), and His afflictions are mentioned (1:24).

His work of reconciliation was accomplished at great cost, we read. It was not by some wave of the hand that God took action to forgive our sins (1:14) and trespasses (2:13). It required His coming to our deepest levels of human experience—Christ's taking a human body (2:9) and being subject to demonic powers which sought to overcome Him and hold Him prey (2:15). They succeeded in so far that they put Him on a cross (2:14) where His blood was spilt (1:20) and He died a real death (1:22). Moreover, His sufferings were real and those who continue the work He came to achieve— Paul himself is His representative in this enterprise, 1:24—must expect also to tread a path of tribulation. So the apostle is a prisoner (4:18) as "apostle of Christ Jesus by the will of God" (1:1) and not in spite of being such.

Possessing Christ as the repository of "all the treasures of wisdom and knowledge" (2:3) is the sufficient antidote to this sub-Christian teaching which casts a slur on the church's Lord and God's very essence (2:2). Moreover, losing one's grip on Him as the Head (of God? 1 Cor. 11:3; of the church? 1:18) is to forfeit one's only hope (2:19). But what lies at the basis of this uncompromising statement? Is Paul simply opposing the Colossian errorists in his own name and arrogantly anathematizing all who do not choose to agree with him? Clearly not in view of the contrast he draws between "human tradition" (2:8,22) and the deposit of apostolic teaching concerning Christ which he adheres to and has passed on to the Colossian church *via* Epaphras. It is the contrast between human "philosophy" and divine revelation committed to the apostles.

The key-verses here are 2:6,7. Paul is reflecting on the past experience of the readers' Christian standing. From Epaphras they had learned of God's grace (1:7) and he in turn came to their city as Paul's proxy and missioner. What he taught was the "gospel" and this was clearly certified as "the word of truth" (1:5), that is, it carried the ring of truth as a God-given message. The Colossians had accepted it as such and had been drawn to "faith in Christ Jesus" (1:4).

Paul can therefore express his deep gratitude to God for this ready reception and cordial acceptance of the saving word. Now (in 2:6) he recalls this in the statement that the Christ they had received as Lord was the Christ of apostolic proclamation. It was no human tradition they had assented to; rather they had been "taught" the true word and had begun to build their lives on Christ, to take root in the soil of divine truth and to bear fruit in Christian living (1:6). They had come to know God's grace *as it really is* (1:6) and not in reliance on any human tradition.

There is a subtle play on words here, which it is difficult to see in the English versions. It is the contrast Paul has in view between acceptance of "human tradition" (Greek *paradosis*, 2:8) and "teaching" (Greek *didaskalia*, 2:22) and the obedience to apostolic tradition, represented in 2:6: "as you received" (Greek *parelabete*: the complementary verb is "what was handed on to you"—*paradidonai*—as in 1 Cor. 11:23; 15:3; Gal. 1:9–14) and 2:7: "as you were taught" (Greek *edidachthēte*). It is the stark contrast between a man-made religion, both cleverly contrived and laying claim to a kind of wisdom ("philo-sophy") but *ersatz* and ineffectual, 2:23, and the true word which is entrusted to the apostolic preachers and which centres in Christ, the mystery and relevation of God (2:2; 4:3).

II

Paul's theology was always closely connected with the need to live the Christian life in this world. Theology for him was not an intellectual game making its appeal to the curious-minded or offering a pastime to fill the vacant hour. Theology was a matter of life and death. What God is and has done in Christ and is doing by His Spirit in the church and the world are all matters of vital concern because they impinge directly upon our understanding of life and human destiny. Paul can intertwine profound theological interest and pressing ethical claims in an amazing way, as he does memorably in Philippians 2:1-12. At Colossae, the dangerous speculation about God, angels and access to the divine takes on a fearsome aspect because *it robs the church of its Christian liberty.*

The connecting "therefore" in 2:16 is a good illustration. Precisely because Christ has overcome the church's enemies in the heavenly world by divesting these spiritual forces of their power to tyrannize over human life, the Colossians are bidden to accept their freedom from the bondage of bad religion.

The Colossian propagandists made much of dietary taboos and ascetic practices. Paul sees these as a threat to the Christian's charter of freedom in Christ, already secured in Him by His death and risen life. The call he sounds is one to a new quality of Christian living, unencumbered by false inhibitions and man-made regulations

(2:22; cf. Gal. 5:1). These prescriptions and rules belong to the shadows (2:7). He asks, Why remain in the dismal half-light of fear and uncertainty when the sun is high in the sky, filling the world with light? Seek a life which draws on Christ's own risen power (3:1-3), as those who share an inheritance in light (1:12) with all God's people, since you have died with Him to those agents of demonic powers which tried to get rid of Him on the cross (2:20). Have no truck with their authority since it has been once-for-all broken, and don't compromise or forfeit your Christian liberty (2:8) by surrendering to a specious philosophy which is deceptive and to a type of religion which can only be branded as man-made, and therefore fake (2:23: see commentary on this verse).

Paul clearly does not mince his words or hold back in his forth-right judgment. The reason can only be that what is at stake is something vital and precious. And for this apostle nothing would be more central to the Christian life than his and his people's freedom in Christ in which what counts is not observance of human tradition (2:8,22) or man-devised rules (2:20) or a way of life which ignores the tremendous difference Christ has made (2:17). For him the essence of "religion" is Christ, and the mainspring of morality is a death-and-resurrection experience (signified in a believing response in baptism) in which the old nature dies to self and sin, and the new nature is received as a gift from God (2:11-13; 3:9-12). It is that new humanity, which is Christ-living-in-His-body, the church, which provides both the sphere in which Christian morality is defined and also the motive-power by which Christians are able to live together in the one family of God. This has been called the *koinonia* motive (in A. M. Hunter's phrase) by which is meant that Paul's ethical norms are found by following the call, "Act as members of Christ's body." His counsels in chapter 3 of our epistle include a teaching on the true self-discipline as well as a much fuller statement of what life is to be like among Christian men and women in their church relations and in contemporary society, who are called into the "one body" (3:15) with love giving coherence to all the ethical qualities which characterize that new life-style (3:11,12).

The contrast is seen at its clearest by setting side-by-side two verses. In 2:20 Paul asks in amazement how the Colossian believers have so readily given hospitality to false teaching and so yielded their freedom: "Why do you submit to regulations?"—rules which impose false demands which have been met in Christ's cross (2:14).

At the opposite end of the spectrum to this restrictive code is the vocation of the Christian man whose entire life, in word and deed, is one of dedication to the Lord Jesus who came to give him life in its fulness (2:10). It is small wonder, then, that he will show his gratitude to God for such an expansive attitude to life, world-affirming and full of *joie de vivre* (3:17; cf. 3:23).

III

A third reason why Paul writes so incisively against the false doctrine, decrying its value (2:4) and labelling it no better than "empty deceit" (2:8) is seen in what he says about the spirit of those who are its self-appointed teachers. The promoter of this cult is a man who is "puffed up without reason by his sensuous mind" (2:18). Literally translated the last phrase would run: "by the mind of his flesh." This is the hallmark of the unregenerate man (Rom. 8:7), and Paul is quick to identify the false prophet as a teacher who has no place in the church. J. B. Lightfoot thinks that Paul is making use of a claim put forward by this man who insisted that he was directed by his "mind," i.e. he was excogitating his novel teaching by drawing an inference about divine truth from his visionary experience. Paul caustically remarks that, if his mind is at work in this fantasy, it is a mind still held captive to his "flesh" (Greek *sarx*), his own conceits and pride. "Flesh" here carries "the sense of natural man in his selfishness" (E. Percy). It is pride which lay at the root of this claim to esoteric knowledge (cf. 2 Cor. 10:5). And for that reason Paul opposes this current teaching *because it ministers to human boasting and a haughty, exclusivist spirit.*

We should find a similar judgment in 2:23 (see commentary) where the regime of ascetic restrictions is misdirected and serves only to increase the devotee's sense of false security. It offers no remedy to keep him humble and dependent on God's grace; on the contrary, it inflates his pride in self-achievement and gives him a wrongful sense of self-congratulation that he is numbered among the fortunate ones who are better than the average run of Christians.

Paul's way of self-mastery is held out to all men, not restricted to a favoured few. This epistle constantly returns to the theme of the universality of the gospel in the Pauline mission churches, and there is no mistaking the way this accent sounds a counter-blast to heretical exclusiveness (see 1:6,23,28,;3:11).

Again, we may point to a contrast. What passes as a species of "humility" (2:81,23) is little better than a mock piety because the motive is wrong. It is a desire to make a proud claim and to belong to a select group of élite that governs these advocates at Colossae. The church members are warned to see the danger in this pretended religion's aspiration, to turn away from it, and to seek the true "humility" (3:12, same Greek word) as God's elect, who are no esoteric group in a self-contained circle but are co-extensive with all Christian people throughout the world (1:23).

IV

On every count, Paul has a low opinion of the novelties which lurk at the threshold of the Colossian congregation. He sees in their appearance a threat to faith and a dangerous deceit. He can entertain no serious discussion with such an *outré* religion and such an offering of theosophical mishmash. The more eccentric and out-of-the-way this false cult seems to be, the greater danger he senses. For this first-century scientism is being advocated with enticing words (2:4) and in the name of what claims to be serious-minded and highly "intellectual" (2:8). The apostle calls it an empty delusion. This designation has suggested to W. Bieder (*Die kolossische Irrlehre und die Kirche von heute*, 1952, pp. 62ff.) how we should understand 2:4. A deliberate design on the part of the Colossian innovators is to be read into these words. They purposed to trick the Christians inside the church as part of a manipulative process of clever rhetoric, and "the art of persuasion" (so Bieder translates the text in verse 4). In fine they made false promises, offering a call to wisdom (2:23) which turns out to be, in Paul's estimation, nothing more than specious make-believe.

Yet name-calling is not enough. Paul will consider its nature and claim. He will expose its shallowness and peril. And he will fortify his Colossian friends to take their stand against this spurious religion.

It is time to examine its nature more closely.

C. The Colossian "Philosophy"

Two terms are used to fasten an identity-label on the false teaching introduced at Colossae. They are "philosophy" (2:8) and "forced piety" (2:23, NEB). The latter term is not easily translateable (Greek *ethelothrēskia*) and of the various possibilities (see commentary) we prefer the rendering: "fake religion."

What are the elements which went to make up this teaching?

I

Much was made of *astrology* which centred on the importance accorded to "elemental spirits of the universe" (2:8,20). This is a controverted phrase. The Greek phrase runs *ta stoicheia tou kosmou*, and the key word is *stoicheia*.

The basic meaning of *stoicheia* is "objects which stand in a row or which form a series." The most natural example of these objects is letters of the alphabet, which stand together in a line to make continuous writing. From this idea it is an easy step to reach the notion of "elements of learning," or, as we say, ABC, meaning rudiments or basic principles. This is the sense of Hebrews 5:12: "the elementary truths of God."

The translation "elements" came also to be applied to physical substances, as again in our modern speech when we talk of the "elements" as everything which goes to make up the natural world or the weather conditions! A New Testament reference to the physical components of the universe is 2 Peter 3:10,12; and the ancients spoke of four such elements—earth, fire, water, air.

In later Greek religious and philosophical thought the parts of the universe were placed under the control of spirit-powers, and there was a tendency to divinize if not the parts of earth then the heavenly bodies. Diogenes Laertius speaks of "the twelve *stoicheia*" in regard to the signs of the zodiac, and the constellation of heavenly bodies is placed under the description of "immortal *stoicheion*."

The final stage of this development is reached when the stars themselves are dignified with being not only dwelling-places of the gods but divine in their own right, and so requiring to be venerated. This startling transition came about mainly because of the advent of oriental astrology and occultism which "with its accompanying astral religion and dominant fatalism, lay like a nightmare upon the soul"[1] of first-century man whose vacuum (caused by disillusion over the collapse of the Homeric gods who were like magnified men and women on Mount Olympus) was quickly filled with an

---

[1] The documentation for this quotation from P. Wendland and some original texts of hellenistic religion will be found in my book *Carmen Christi: Philippians 2:5-11*, 1967, pp. 306ff.

all-embracing fatalism. Men who came under the spell of star-worship were made to feel that all things were ruled by "fate." The particular conjunction of the stars or planets under which a person was born was of decisive importance and settled irretrievably his destiny. Hence the central place of the heavenly bodies in popular hellenistic religion was established once the astrologers had capitalized on this yearning for a "religion" to fill the void.

What hope was there for a man in this setting of religious determinism and inevitability? One way of salvation was offered in a placating of the star-deities, and by ascetic practices a possibility was held out for a person to escape from the mesh of inevitability and the hopeless round of uncertainty. Also some deities were hailed as protectors of men and women on earth, and fellowship with these gods and goddesses raised the devotees above the circle of fate and iron-clad determinism. In that way the *stoicheia* could be overcome and their victims set free.

The question before us is simply one of choice. In this context and given the total situation of the Colossian errorists' teaching, which meaning of *stoicheia* seems most likely? Two alternatives form the main possibilities.[1]

Either, Paul is regarding the false system as "elementary teaching" either by Jewish or pagan ritualists in the sense that it is materialist at heart and exclusively tied to this world and so infantile. By contrast, Paul's gospel invites men to accept the freedom of Christ and to remain no longer in a kindergarten stage of religious taboos and restrictions (so Moule). Alternatively, Paul is branding this cult as false because it was under the control of powerful spirit-intelligences which held men prey and which needed to be placated. Many reasons are forthcoming to support the second interpretation:

[1] The entire field is canvassed in A. J. Bandstra's book, *The Law and the Elements of the World. An Exegetical Study in Aspects of Paul's teaching*, n.d. His conclusion is that by this phrase "Paul specifically means the law and the flesh as operative in the world of humanity before and outside of Christ" (p. 173). But his reasoning is hampered by an (unproved) assumption (p. 174) that the term is Paul's own coinage and not part of the cosmological speculation in contemporary thought. The conclusions of two recent discussions of the term "the elements of the world" may be mentioned. In *TDNT* vii, pp. 670ff. G. Delling denies any connexion of the Pauline phrase with spirit powers and especially the star gods and gives the term a neutral connotation.

E. Schweizer, "Die 'Elemente der Welt'," in *Verborum Veritas* Festschrift Gustav Stählin, 1970, pp. 245–59 thinks that the four physical elements had been drawn into a system of Jewish-hellenistic mystery-teaching and given a sort of personal significance in cultic worship. This explains the heavy emphasis on ritual abstentions which forbad contact with material objects and bodily functions. His essay is rich in documentation.

(*a*) The tenor of other polemical parts of the letter indicates Paul's belief in Christ's victory over demonic agencies (2:15 especially; 2:20).

(*b*) Only this view explains his repeated insistence that the divine "fulness" dwells in Christ, not in these cosmic forces (1:19; 2:9). They, on the contrary, owe their existence to Him (1:15-20; 2:10).

(*c*) The references in 2:16,17 to calendrical observances link up with the Jewish notion of angels who mediated the law (Acts 7:38,53; Gal. 3:19, 4:9f.). Further, the relapse of the Galatian Christians to "the weak and beggarly elements" (Greek *stoicheia*) must mean a return to the gods of paganism from which they had been converted (4:8-10). Paul can hardly mean that they were relapsing to simplistic forms of religion and that the effect of a superstitious evil-eye of bewitchment (3:1) was calculated to match their yearning for an uncomplicated faith!

(*d*) E. Percy[1] has argued cogently that Paul sets the *stoicheia* in direct antithesis to Christ (2:8) and this suggests that "for him the contrast lies not between spirit and matter . . . but between this age ruled by spirit-forces and Christ. It is the contrast between Greek and early Christian understandings of existence."

(*e*) The practice of asceticism was encouraged by these teachers (2:20-23) as part of their discipline. It is likely that such was a preparatory exercise calculated to overcome hostile spirit-powers and to induce a trance-like visionary experience (2:18).

(*f*) "Worship of angels" (2:18) must be related to the cultus, and the homage paid to these heavenly orders suggests that it is part of the same "philosophy" or theosophical system which venerated the star-deities.

Our conclusion is that Paul's evidence suggests that the Colossian "philosophy" was concerned to give a prominent place to angelic orders as custodians of human destiny. In current hellenistic thought this was closely related to the stars and their patron deities. But Paul will have none of this in his insistence that all cosmic powers are dependent upon the pre-existing Christ who entirely fills the universe and leaves no room for comₜeting agencies, now that they are defeated and subservient to Him. He alone gives meaning to the universe which coheres in Him (1:16,17); and so He alone gives meaning and purpose to life (2:10).

[1] E. Percy, *Die Probleme der Kolosser- und Ep heserbriefe*, 1946, p. 167.

II

But there was another tenet championed by the innovators at Colossae. They evidently held a *dualism* which separated the high God from creation and taught that to attain to God man must be delivered from the evil influence of material things. This "liberation" in later gnostic religion was achieved along two quite diverse routes, one starting from the premise of matter especially the human body as evil, the other treating matter as indifferent.

One path to gnostic salvation was (as we have indicated) asceticism, which summoned the devotee to a life of abstinence and self-punishment. Paul preserves the actual wording of the slogans which were being advocated at Colossae (2:21,23) and retorts that such denials—"Don't handle" (or possibly, "don't engage in sex relations");[1]
"Don't taste" wine;
"Don't touch" food (cf. 1 Tim. 4:1-4)—are of no value to counter "the indulgence of the flesh." That is, when these ascetic pratices are used simply to prepare an initiate to enter a trance-like state and thereby to gain a vision of heavenly things (2:18), they serve only to inflate him with pride and fill him with vain knowledge and so bolster his "flesh"—his unrenewed ego, which is puffed up by this experience (cf. 1 Cor. 8:1).

Coupled with these ascetic practices was a code clearly influenced by Jewish legalism, with its observances of the Sabbath, feast-days and new moon celebrations (2:16), possibly the practice of circumcision (2:11) and Jewish dietary laws (2:21f.). Various suggestions have been made to pinpoint the cultural milieu of these practices. Lightfoot drew a comparison between these restrictions and the taboos and practices of the Essenes; and recently the Qumran texts from the Dead Sea area have shown that similar calendrical details were highly regarded among the Essene monks in that community. But it is doubtful if Essenism had penetrated to the Lycus valley, and there is a singular absence of debate over the Mosaic law in the Colossian controversy.

More interesting is the suggestion of a link between the prohibitions in Colossians and the type of heresy countered in the epistle to the Hebrews.[2]

---

[1] This prohibition is given a sexual connotation by A. R. C. Leaney, "Col. ii. 21-23", *ExpT.* 64, 1952-53, p. 92.
[2] T. W. Manson, "The Problem of the Epistle to the Hebrews," *Studies in the Gospels and Epistles,* ed. M. Black, 1962, pp. 252ff.

F. O. Francis argues that Paul's opponents appealed to Exodus 19 which is used in Hebrews 12 as a foil to advance the idea of worshipping in heaven with the angels (12:22,28). Colossians 2:17 presents a contrast: shadow-substance, which plays a decisive rôle in Hebrews. But Francis' view that the Colossian errorists stressed a sharing in heavenly worship *led by angels* is contradicted by 2:23 (see commentary). See his article, "Visionary Discipline and Scriptural Tradition at Colossae," *Lexington Theological Quarterly*, II. 3. July 1967, pp. 71–81.

The type of Judaism reflected in these chapters is a matter for continuing discussion. Clearly it is not the orthodox Judaism of the Palestinian rabbis, nor is it indubitably a sectarian wing of Essenism or Qumranism. A body of continental scholars prefers to speak of a "Jewish Gnosticism" which combined with Christian elements to form the substance of the Colossian heresy (so Kümmel) or "a Jewish or Judaistic gnosis, most thoroughly infected with Iranian ideas" (so G. Bornkamm).[1]

For the sake of precision, the terminology is important and R. McL. Wilson's essay, "Gnosis, Gnosticism and the New Testament," *The Origins of Gnosticism*. Colloquium of Messina 13–18 April 1966, 1967, pp. 511–527 rightly calls attention to the impropriety of using "gnosticism" for "gnosis." His preference is for "pregnosis" (p. 515 n. 3). But see Kümmel, op.cit., p. 240.

Other attempts to delineate the nature of the heresy are: "a piece of pre-Christian gnosis, perhaps of Iranian origin. But Paul's controversy at Colossae is not with paganism but cosmological speculation" whose Jewish dress had made it appealing to the members of the church (Dibelius-Greeven, p. 39); "a kind of 'theosophy'—in this instance, a 'gnostic' type of Judaism or a Jewish type of 'gnosticism'" (Moule, p. 31); "when the gospel was introduced to the area [of Phrygia], a Jewish-Hellenistic syncretism would find no great difficulty in expanding and modifying itself sufficiently to take some Christian elements into its system, and the result would be something like the Colossian heresy as we may reconstruct it from Paul's treatment of it" (Bruce, pp. 166f.). If these options seem wide-ranging the conclusion of J. Lähnemann's section (*Der Kolosserbrief*, [1971], pp. 82–100) takes in an even more extensive

[1] W. G. Kümmel, *Introduction to the New Testament*, 1965, p. 240. His term actually is Gnosis in the German original, p. 244; G. Bornkamm, "Die Häresie des Kolosserbriefes," *Das Ende des Gesetzes*,[3] 1952, p. 150.

group of possibilities as he traces the roots of the Colossian false teaching to Phrygian nature-religion with elements drawn from ecstatic rigorism, Iranian myth and hellenizing Judaism. The title "philosophy" linked it with Greek wisdom and as a mystery religion it acted as a unifying influence and proved an attractive power exerted over the Colossian believers.

The measure of success in finding in a Jewish gnosis the key to the Colossian heresy will be judged by a threefold presentation in the epistle itself.[1]

(a) The importance Paul gives to religious "knowledge" (Greek *gnōsis*) seems to indicate that he has to deal with a situation where the acquirement of esoteric knowledge needed to be refuted, as the apostle does in his repeated teaching (1:9,10; 2:3; 3:10,16) on God's gift of knowledge and wisdom. But these terms are filled with a new connotation based on the Old Testament meaning of "to know God" = to obey His will and walk in His way.

(b) The cosmological rôle ascribed to Christ is a highlighted feature of chapters 1 and 2. In the commentary we shall investigate the different lines of interpretation possible in regard to 1:15–20, and argue that Paul is not adopting gnostic terminology in his ascriptions to the cosmic Christ of such titles as "image of God", "fulness of God," and "first-born," but stands in the tradition of the wisdom scholars in hellenistic Judaism. Of course, it is open to possibility that these terms may have been used in a gnosticizing fashion at Colossae; but who can tell what their original use was? We can say that *pleroma* seems to have been a technical term for both Paul and his readers, and that later it became extensively used in the classical gnostic cosmology of Valentinus. E. Best submits that the process of transition by which "the Hellenistic philosophical conception of the universe as filled by God was at this time passing into the Gnostic conception of a divine *pleroma*, at once the abode of the aeons and the aggregate of them" was already begun in Paul's time.[2]

(c) The principal argument in favour of a first century gnosticism in existence at Colossae and refuted in our letter is found in the polemic against an angel cult and a dualistic system. This takes us to the heart of the gnostic world-view. Again we are hindered in

[1] I draw here on S. Lyonnet, "Saint Paul et le Gnosticisme. L'épître aux Colossiens" in *The Origins of Gnosticism*, 1967, pp. 538–551, but with different conclusions.
[2] E. Best, *One Body in Christ*, 1955, pp. 140, 148; referred to by R. McL. Wilson, *Gnosis and the New Testament*, 1968, p. 57, whose words are cited above.

our effort to press back behind Paul's words to what must have given rise to them in the Colossian church. Clearly there was a practice of angelic worship (2:18) and Paul goes out of his way to accentuate the teaching on cosmic reconciliation, with no part of the universe unaffected (1:15-20) and no hostile power unsubdued (2:15). The angelic super-beings are reduced to impotence and are led in triumph. Some transcendental engagement between Christ and an enemy is envisaged, and peace is proclaimed after the armistice is declared (1:20).

What is the type of dualism implied here? Lyonnet insists that it is a moral tension, not an ontological gulf which sets Christ in opposition to His rivals. *Evil* spirits are not mentioned as such, but their existence is implied. What may be the case is that it is Paul who has set these angelic powers against Christ and given them the character of rivals to Him, because he cannot tolerate any lasting dualism between good and evil.[1]

Then these powers have become only a foil to display the unrivalled excellence and wide embrace of Christ's reconciliation and victory—and are not like the "opposites" in the second century systems which had a permanent character and were invested with a quasi-metaphysical function.

Our conclusion concerning this part of the error runs as follows: Evidently Paul had to face tendencies and teaching at Colossae which set God and the world in some sort of opposition. God was distanced and made remote; the world was spurned and the human body held in contempt and its physical appetites held on unnaturally tight rein. Possibly some teachers had argued from the premise of a dualism between God and matter, that asceticism should be replaced by its opposite. The trend would then flow towards libertinism. If matter has no relation to God (the argument ran), then the material body has no relation to religion. Therefore, a man can indulge his body without restraint or conscience (cf. the false teaching combated in 2 Pet. 2:4-22; 3:3; Jude 4, 7, 8, 16; 1 John 3:4-18, and Rev. 2:14,20).

To be sure, there is no explicit reference in this epistle to an antinomian strain. But it may well be in the background and explains Paul's vehement and stringent moral warnings in 3:5-8.

---

[1] Cf. R. M. Grant, *Gnosticism and Early Christianity*, 1966, p. 160. "The Colossians actually seem to have been less dualistic than Paul himself. Perhaps this lack of dualism was due to a lack of concern for apocalyptic eschatology."

III

Conclusion

The soil of Phrygia was fertile ground for the luxuriant germination and growth of strange religious practices.[1] The synagogues had a reputation for laxity and openness to speculation drifting in from the hellenistic world. In the Colossian church we appear to be in touch with a meeting-place and melting-pot where the free-thinking Judaism of the dispersion and the speculative ideas of Greek religion are in close contact. Out of this interchange and fusion comes a syncretism, which is both theologically novel (bringing Christ into a hierarchy and a system) and ethically conditioned (advocating a rigorous discipline and an ecstatic visionary reward). On both counts, in Paul's eyes, it is a deadly danger to the incipient church and on both counts it is remorselessly exposed.

---

[1] W. L. KNOX, *St Paul and the Church of the Gentiles*, 1939, pp. 146–49; W. M. Ramsay, *The Cities and Bishoprics of Phrygia*, i, 2, 1897, pp. 667ff. For a recent discussion of Phrygian syncretism in antiquity, see Lähnemann's study, *Der Kolosserbrief*, 1971, ppp. 38ff.

ANALYSIS OF THE EPISTLE

I

OPENING GREETING

1:1,2. Paul, an apostle of Christ Jesus by the will of God, and Timothy our brother, ²To the saints and faithful brethren in Christ at Colossae: Grace to you and peace from God our Father.

THERE IS A REMARKABLY CLOSE SIMILARITY BETWEEN THE OPENING lines of this letter and the introduction of 2 Corinthians. In both epistles Paul lays claim to his apostleship as a special messenger of Christ Jesus. This is no idle claim, moreover; for his office as apostle has been conferred upon him "by the will of God." And he goes on to associate Timothy as his "brother" with himself, though he does not extend to his colleague the title of "apostle."

Paul was introducing himself to a Christian community to which he was personally unknown (2:1) and which he had not founded (1:4,9). We cannot suppose that his apostolic authority had been challenged or denied at Colossae and account in this way for his explicit reference to his status as Christ's apostle, for there is no evidence of this possibility. Yet the rest of the letter shows that the Colossian believers were facing the threat of false teaching and needed some corrective instruction. Paul does this in two ways. Negatively he warns his readers of a menacing danger to which they must on no account succumb (2:8,16,18); and positively he sets out the teaching on the person and place of Jesus Christ as an antidote to heretical claims (e.g. 1:15ff.). Paul is thus exercising a teaching office throughout the epistle as "a teacher of the Gentiles" (1 Tim. 2:7), and invokes his apostolic authority as a credential at the outset.

Timothy's name appears most probably because the apostle wished to show that he was not alone in his place of imprisonment. He regarded Timothy, as we learn from 1 Thessalonians 3:2; 1 Corinthians 4:17; Philippians 2:19ff., as a trusted agent and collaborator, and almost at times as an extension of his own personality. It would be tactful, therefore, to include his name in the superscription. There may be another reason if we understand 4:18 to mean that Paul at that point took the pen from the scribe and

personally wrote a final greeting. It could be that Timothy was the
scribe up to that part of the letter, and Paul mentions his name at
the frontispiece because of his rôle as amanuensis.

These points of connexion with 2 Corinthians are interesting, and
it is just as remarkable that Paul should refrain from his normal
practice of using the word "church" when writing to the Colossians.
The same omission is found in Romans and Philippians. Instead in
all three instances he turns to an equivalent title with his appellation,
"the saints." This word may be understood in one of two ways.
If we retain its form as an adjective (carrying the meaning "the
holy ones"), it could agree with the noun "brethren" along with the
middle term translated "faithful." This construction would then
produce the translation: "to the holy and faithful brethren." Alternatively, the word "holy" (Greek *hagioi*) may be seen as a technical
expression which when used with the definite article denotes
Christians as the holy people of God. They stand in succession to
ancient Israel who were also called God's holy nation, and elect
race (Ex. 19:5,6; Lev. 19:1,2; Deut. 7:6; 14:2). "The saints" in the
New Testament church can stand for the Jewish–Christians at
Jerusalem, as in the phrase "the collection for the saints" (2 Cor. 9:1;
cf. Rom. 12:13; 15:26), but when the term stands at the head of a
Pauline letter it clearly has a wider reference and takes in the Gentile
churches as successors to Israel's calling to be a people set apart for
God and His service (e.g. 2 Cor. 1:1; Phil. 1:1; Eph. 1:1). On this
view Paul's opening greeting will be sent to "the holy people of
God at Colossae, who are faithful brethren in Christ." This latter
translation places an emphasis on the fidelity of the Colossian
Christians, and significantly it is just this quality of steadfastness in
the face of false teaching that Paul commends in his subsequent
letter (1:23; 2:6,7).

1:2 *Grace to you and peace from God our Father.* The coupling of grace
and peace is a characteristic trait of Paul's style. The Greek word
charis which means "grace" has a similar sound to the normal
greeting used in letter-writing (*chaire*) but it is far richer in content.

Grace is the undeserved favour of God reaching out to men who
need His pardon because they are sinners. It is divine love expressed
in the forgiveness of sins (so Masson); and so it is not surprising
that the partner of "grace" is "peace." The latter term, correspond-
ing to the Hebrew *shalom*, "is not just 'spiritual prosperity;' it is the
salvation of the whole man both body and soul" (W. Foerster,

TDNT ii, pp. 414f.) as the direct result of God's grace extended to sinful men. There is a logical sequence in Paul's thought. We enjoy peace with God and all the benefits which flow therefrom on the ground of His gracious action in Christ Jesus. The name of "Christ Jesus" as the one through whom the blessing comes is strangely omitted here, though several texts and versions expand the greeting by adding "and the Lord Jesus Christ." But this expansion can be explained by a desire to make the reading here conform to Paul's usual practice elsewhere of including the name of the Lord Jesus.

II

PAUL'S THANKFULNESS TO GOD

1:3–8. *We always thank God, the Father of our Lord Jesus Christ, when we pray for you,* ⁴*because we have heard of your faith in Christ Jesus and of the love you have for all the saints,* ⁵*because of the hope laid up for you in heaven. Of this you have heard before in the word of the truth, the gospel* ⁶*which has come to you, as indeed in the whole world it is bearing fruit and growing—so among yourselves, from the day you heard and understood the grace of God in truth,* ⁷*as you learned it from Epaphras our beloved fellow-servant. He is a faithful minister of Christ on our behalf* ⁸*and has made known to us your love in the Spirit.*

ALTHOUGH PAUL KNEW HIS READERS AT COLOSSAE ONLY AT A distance, he is in no doubt of their Christian standing. News of their true life in Christ had been brought by Epaphras who also was at Paul's side when he wrote this epistle (4:12); and it was through Epaphras' ministry that the Gospel had first been carried to that part of the Lycus valley in which the Colossians lived. Their response to the overtures of divine grace expressed in his ministry gladdened the apostle's heart, and stimulated his prayers for this infant community.

The format of ancient letters included an assurance on the part of the sender that he was praying for his friends who would read the letter. But it would be wrong to conclude that this letter-writing convention was borrowed by Paul in an unthinking way. For Paul's prayers were directly called out by what he knew of God's grace in the lives of those to whom he wrote (e.g. 1 Cor. 1:4), and his thanksgiving to God for this fact was as continual as his habit to pray incessantly for his people (see Rom. 1:8,9; 1 Cor. 1:4; Phil. 1:4; 1 Thess. 1:2; 2 Thess. 1:3).

The reason for his glad thankfulness is dictated by what follows in verses 4–6. Epaphras (v. 7) had visited their district as a representative of the apostolic mission. The RSV reads, "He is a faithful minister of Christ on *our* behalf" in verse 7; and this reading which has the clear support of P46 as well as the Alexandrian and Western textual authorities makes Epaphras one of the members of Paul's

ministerial and missionary team, presumably sent out on evangelistic tour from Ephesus. He had evangelized the Colossian region,
led men and women to faith in what may well have been his native
city (4:12) and brought back to Paul some enheartening report of
their "good order and the firmness of your faith in Christ" (2:5).
They had "received Christ Jesus the Lord" (2:6); what that implies
is now spelled out in a way which recalls the well-known triad of
graces in 1 Corinthians 13:13; "So faith, hope, love abide, these
three."

A. M. Hunter in *Paul and his Predecessors*,[2] (1961), pp. 33ff. draws
attention to the way in which these three virtues appear together in
the New Testament (1 Thess. 1:3; 5:8; Rom. 5:1–5; Gal 5:5,6;
Col. 1:4,5; Eph. 4:2–5; Heb. 6:10–12; 10:22–24; 1 Pet. 1:3–8,21–22
as well as occasionally in post-apostolic writings). This feature
"strongly suggests that the triad in Paul is not his own creation, but
something common and apostolic, perhaps a sort of compendium
of the Christian life current in the early apostolic church" (op. cit.
p. 34). Often the same order of words as in the familiar 1 Corinthians
13:13 is preserved; but at Colossians 1:4,5 the sequence runs: faith,
love, hope.[1] Faith in Christ stands at the head of the list, for it is by
faith that salvation is brought within the realm of human experience
(Rom. 5:1; Eph. 2:8). Yet faith does not stand alone, and Galatians
5:6 speaks of "faith working through love." Love is directed prin-
cipally to God or Christ; here a living faith shows itself in love which
engages in concern and help for fellow-Christians, "the saints." This
term may single out the Colossians' willingness to contribute to
Christians in distress, as in Romans 12:13, but more probably a
general allusion to Christian compassion and goodwill is intended.
It must have been something concrete, however, since Epaphras was
able to give an account of it to Paul (verse 8). As George Johnston
rightly comments, no thought of commemoration of the blessed
dead—giving to "saints" a specialized meaning which is never found
in the Pauline corpus is to be seen here. The "hope laid up for
you in heaven" does, however, reach out in the unseen world as
faith and love grasp, in anticipation of their final perfection, the
eternal life in God's kingdom.

Paul obviously attached much importance to the Christian hope
"laid up" for his Colossian readers "in heaven". Though the term

---

[1] A. M. Hunter has expounded Paul's meaning of the triad under the caption, "What is
Christianity?" in *Teaching and Preaching the New Testament*, 1963, pp. 81–84.

speaks of what is by definition set in the future, it still rings out a message of confident certainty, not wistful longing. The Christian builds upon the promises of God which are no will-o'-the-wisp produced by a fertile imagination but utterly dependable because they are grounded on the divine character.

The immediate background of this emphatic hope may be that the false teachers at Colossae were intending to rob the church of this prospect. Perhaps, like other false teachers whose names we know from 2 Timothy 2:18, they were asserting that "The resurrection is past already," and so "they were upsetting the faith of some" at Colossae as at Ephesus.[1] See further comments on p.105.

The antidote to any tendency which leads believers to "swerve from the truth" (see 2 Tim. 2:18, again) is found in a firm adherence to "the word of truth, the gospel;" a major tenet of this gospel is the assurance of hope, as the Colossians had known when they first received the good news at the time of Epaphras' evangelistic ministry (verses 6b, 7).

Paul inserts here a further description of the apostolic preaching which he calls—again opposing a false message with a statement of the truth—"the word of the truth, the gospel."[2] The gospel is almost personified, as Masson remarks, and is pictured as a personal, living force which conquers the world. But the imagery of a person who "has come to you" quickly shades off into a horticultural metaphor which uses two verbs of plant growth: "bearing fruit and growing." We may recall Jesus' teaching on the kingdom of God in Mark 4:26-29; 30-32, which in turn makes use of the Old Testament imagery in Ezekiel 17:23; Daniel 4:10-12. Once more, Paul's use of these two terms may reflect his counterblast to the heretical claim that the false doctrine boasted of world-wide success; and Masson explains the special use of the verb "you learned" (in verse 7), set as it is in the framework of a glowing commendation of Epaphras, as Paul's way of opposing the novel and pernicious

[1] An interesting sidelight on this verse and 1:23: "not shifting from the hope of the gospel" is offered by L. J. Baggott, *A New Approach to Colossians*, 1961, p. 5. He suggests that the earthquake which ravaged parts of the Lycus valley cities in AD 60–61 may account for Paul's words of encouragement and assurance concerning spiritual realities which cannot be earthquake-shaken. But this historical allusion presupposes a later dating of the epistle.

[2] RSV translates thus, giving to the words "of the truth" the sense of the objective genitive, which is then explained by "the gospel" in apposition. This is preferable to translating, "the true word of the gospel." The title *Gospel of Truth* of a gnostic work produced by the Valentinians is mentioned by the church fathers, Irenaeus and Tertullian, and its probable identification with a document discovered at Nag Hammadi in Egypt in 1945 or 1946 is accepted by many scholars.

teaching of the heretics by an appeal to Epaphras' authority and credentials, "on *our* behalf."

The background we have sketched is necessarily speculative. But what is clear is the unbounded confidence of the apostle which shines through this opening preamble of his letter. He is glad to report the good state of the Colossian church, confirmed to him by their initial response to the gospel and by Epaphras' latest bulletin which has apparently recently been brought by Epaphras' arrival. He has "brought us the news of your God-given love" (verse 8, NEB).

III

PAUL'S PRAYER FOR HIS READERS

1:9–11 *And so, from the day we heard of it, we have not ceased to pray for you, asking that you may be filled with the knowledge of his will in all spiritual wisdom and understanding,* [10] *to lead a life worthy of the Lord, fully pleasing to him, bearing fruit in every good work and increasing in the knowledge of God.* [11]*May you be strengthened with all power, according to his glorious might, for all endurance and patience with joy.*

PAUL HAS ALREADY PLEDGED THE PROMISE OF HIS CONTINUAL prayer for this Christian fellowship. What follows in this section is a summary of the content of such a prayer. The apostle's prayers for other Christians are parts of the New Testament deserving a close study, both for what they teach in themselves about the nature of the Christian life and also as a stimulus and encouragement for our own intercessions. Too often our praying is petitionary and self-centred. If so, we need the broadened horizon of the Pauline prayers and the example of the man who not only coveted the prayers of his fellow-believers (Rom. 15:30; 2 Thess. 3:1) but undertook to remember their needs and opportunities as a part of his apostolic service.

1:9 The occasion of prayer which follows is evidently Epaphras' report of the Colossians' good heart and steady progress, in spite of the threatened assaults of false teachers. And it is clearly the case that many of the key-terms which are found in the prayer belong to the vocabulary of these men. Paul seeks to disinfect these heretical watchwords by giving to them a specifically Christian content. So he asks God to supply the Colossians with a true "knowledge" (Greek *epignōsis*), wisdom (Greek *sophia*) and spiritual insight (Greek *synesis*).

"Knowledge" is explicitly concerned with God's will for human lives, and so is related directly to obedience, for it is in a practical outworking and acceptance of God's purpose for our lives that we come to know His will. Paul's teaching follows the same line as the Old Testament where a knowledge of God is never theoretical or speculative but descriptive of a personal relationship between God

and His people. He reveals Himself to them in an act of gracious
condescension; they respond to Him with a loyal obedience and
devotion. The twin poles of this "revelation and response" nexus
are thus marked out as God's grace and man's obedience.

"Wisdom" is similarly a practical application of such knowledge
of God's will as we have. "It shows to the Christian the direction
in which he is to go, the standards by which he should regulate his
actions" (Masson). The third moral term is "spiritual insight" which
has also been defined in a most down-to-earth fashion as "a right
appraisal of a situation, a clear vision of what needs to be done in
each instance" which may arise as life's decisions are reviewed. The
Christian is not, however, to be prompted simply by native prudence
and discretion; he is not governed by motives of self-seeking and
expediency, but sets the will of God as a controlling factor in every
situation he confronts. Newman once defined a religious man as
one who has a *ruling* sense of the presence of God in his life. And in
our text we must give full value to the adjective "spiritual" which,
for Paul, is no courtesy reference but an allusion to the aid which
the Christian may call upon as he seeks the help of the Holy Spirit.

1:10 The positive and practical setting of this petition is clear
from the way Paul proceeds to spell out the meaning of these
qualities. Three ethical guide-lines are laid down, to show how the
possession of a spiritually alert mind will set its sights: it will strive
(*a*) to have a style of life worthy of the Christian profession; (*b*) to
be entirely pleasing to the Lord in all things; and (*c*) to register a
consistent growth in influence by a deepening awareness of God's
will for the believer's life.

"Live worthily" is a moral maxim elsewhere used by Paul, as he
calls his converts to conduct their lives with an eye on God's own
character (1 Thess. 2:12); the gospel message they profess to believe
and to offer to others (Phil. 1:27); and their noble calling which they
have received (Eph. 4:1). Negatively, unworthy behaviour, as at
the Lord's Supper, is a disgrace because it dishonours the Lord at
whose table the Corinthians had professed to gather (1 Cor. 11:27).
C. A. Anderson Scott (*New Testament Ethics*,[2] [1934], pp. 101f.)
makes an important comment on this ethical directive: "As one
ponders these sentences, the phrase which comes into one's mind is
noblesse oblige. In the best sense of the word these people were a
spiritual aristocracy;" he goes on to quote Benjamin Jowett, "It is
characteristic of St. Paul to ask, What will the Gentiles say of us?"

Better, perhaps, would be this phrasing of the challenge, What will they say of the Lord and of His gospel? (2 Cor. 8:21).

The intention to please God in all things was an ethical counsel, expounded by William Law in his spiritual classic, *A Serious Call to a Devout and Holy Life*, 1728, which greatly influenced John Wesley.[1] Though the precise term (Greek *areskeia*) rendered "pleasing" is found only here in the New Testament, a cognate word "well-pleasing" (Greek *euarestos*) plays a significant rôle in Paul's ethical behaviour patterns as we may see from consulting the following:

> Romans 12:2: The will of God is "the noble, the well-pleasing (to Him) and the ideal" (cf. Rom. 14:18).
> 1 Thessalonians 4:1: "How you ought to conduct yourselves and to please God."
> 2 Corinthians 5:9: "We make it our ambition . . . to be well-pleasing to him."
> Ephesians 5:10: "Try to learn what is pleasing to the Lord."
> Colossians 3:20: (cf. Heb. 12:28); contrast Romans 8:8.
> And in the non-canonical literature:
> 1 Clement 2:2; 41:1: "Let each one of us be well-pleasing to God."

The third part of this passage, translated by RSV, "bearing fruit in every good work and increasing in the knowledge of God" suggests that there are two actions here. Christians become productive by lives of good will and (apparently as an independent idea) grow in their understanding of the divine will. A number of scholars (e.g. E. Percy, p. 123, n.93) accept this construction, but it is possible and preferable to keep the two participles together (as in verse 6) and to make them both depend on the church's responsiveness to its knowledge of God's will. The translation will then run: "yielding fruit in every good deed and increasing (in influence) by the ever-deepening knowledge which believers acquire of God and His ways." The application of "fruit bearing" and growth to "good works" may recall Galatians 5:22f. and so make the reference a personal one, indicating the cultivation of qualities and dispositions in the experience of individual Christians. They will become fruitful in proportion to the measure of their obedience to God's plan for

---

[1] See R. Newton Flew, *The Idea of Perfection*, 1934, ch. xviii on Law (p. 311: he cites Law's own words: "If we desired nothing by our religion but to be acceptable to God").

their lives. The wish that follows in verse 11 neatly continues the thought of personal piety, expressing the hope that the same Colossian believers may be strengthened by the accession of two other qualities in the list of the "fruit of the Spirit" (Gal. 5:22f.; cf. Phil. 1:11). Paul seeks for them the gifts of "patience" and "joy," especially when times of testing come. Paul "prays that every access of spiritual power, flowing out of His secret source, may express itself above all things in ways which shew the dethronement of self-will; in perseverance under trial, in long-suffering under provocation, and in the joy of 'a heart at leisure from itself' and occupied with Christ" (H. C. G. Moule).

But there is an alternative way of applying verses 10, 11. "Every good work" can have equally a reference to the church's missionary task; elsewhere it looks back to the activity of God's grace in conversion (as in Phil. 1:6). Frequently the same apostle can use the term "work" of his evangelistic service and preaching (1 Cor. 15:58; 2 Cor. 9:8; Phil. 2:30; 1 Thess. 5:13; 2 Thess. 1:11) as well as employ the metaphor of fruit-bearing to denote the results of his evangelism (Rom. 1:13). Then, the companion verb rendered "increasing" may well mark the church's expansion in the world as "the knowledge of God" in the gospel is made known. The following verse now becomes a plea for the church's strengthening by God "in virtue of the power which belongs to God as he has revealed himself to men" (so C. F. D. Moule translates) that it may not fail to fulfil its mission in a hostile world where the qualities of "endurance" and "patience" are required to carry through the missionary mandate.

The combination of "endurance" (Greek *hypomonē*) and "patience" (Greek *makrothumia*)—both fruits of the Spirit, as we have seen, and not native human powers to be explained psychologically or temperamentally—is found in 2 Corinthians 6:4ff.; 2 Timothy 3:10. The rough distinction may be drawn that "endurance" is used in relation to adverse circumstances while "patience" is the virtue needed when trying persons tax our self-control (so J. Horst, *TDNT*, iv, p. 384, cf. p. 587[1]). Both terms have a special nuance when they are found in an eschatological context, that is, when they have to do with the particular virtues needed at the time of trial which God's people are to undergo at the end of the Age (1 Thess. 1:3; Rev. 1:9, 3:10, 13:10: see *TDNT*, iv, p. 385): but

[1] See C. L. Mitton, *The Epistle of James*, 1966, pp. 22f.

what is characteristic in Paul's use here is the addition of "joy," which puts a new face on the type of dogged determination and perseverance which believers are to display under trial. The example of Jesus (in Heb. 12:2) is memorably described in these terms. The circumstances surrounding such admonitions and statements as Matthew 5:12; Acts 5:41; James 1:2f.; 1 Peter 4:13 show how triumphantly the early believers bore their hardships and rose above their immediate, distressing lot when they were persecuted as Christians.

IV

CHRISTIAN EXPERIENCE AND THE CHURCH'S LORD (1:12–20)

¹²*Giving thanks to the Father, who has qualified us to share in the inheritance of the saints in light.* ¹³*He has delivered us from the dominion of darkness and transferred us to the kingdom of his beloved Son,* ¹⁴*in whom we have redemption, the forgiveness of sins.*

STROPHE I
He is the image of the invisible God,
the firstborn of all creation;
  ¹⁶*For in him all things were created, in*
heaven and on earth,
    [*visible and invisible,*
    Whether thrones or dominions
    or principalities or authorities—]
  All things were created through him and
for him.

STROPHE II
    ¹⁷*He is before all things,*
    And in him all things hold together
  ¹⁸*He is the head of the body,* [*the church*];

STROPHE III
    ^{18b} *He is the beginning, the firstborn from*
the dead,
    [*That in everything he might be preëminent*]
    ¹⁹*For in him all the fulness of God was pleased*
to dwell
    ²⁰*And through him to reconcile to himself all*
things,
[*Whether on earth or in heaven, making peace*
by the blood of his cross].

THESE VERSES POSE A SERIES OF ACUTE PROBLEMS FOR OUR consideration, and they do so at different levels. For one thing, we must seek to understand the meaning of the various words Paul uses in this context, and many of them are rare terms and apparently intended to have a specialized meaning (e.g. "image of God," "all things hold together," "the fulness of God," "making peace"). Then, there is the question of the literary form of verses 15–20 which can (as above) be plausibly set out in a poetic or hymnic arrangement. It is one of the firmest conclusions of modern New Testament study that some of its key passages dealing with the person and work of Jesus Christ are in the form of early Christian hymns (like Phil. 2:6–11 and John 1:1–18, to give the best-known examples).[1] A third matter which has occupied attention in recent discussion of this passage is to explain the connexion of Paul's thought as it moves from what he says about God's redeeming acts and their application to the Christian's experience (in verses 12–14) to the recital of the hymnic tribute in verses 15–20 which contains no allusion to the Colossians themselves, and then switches back again to the application of this teaching in verses 21f. with their clear and pointed reference to the situation at Colossae.

Two deductions are in order. The first and simplest explanation of this pattern of Pauline thought is that his mind was led to the hymn by his description (in verses 12–14) of what Christians at Colossae had become by God's redeeming work in His Son. What is more natural than that he should turn to an already existing hymn and quote it to buttress his fine statement of "What it means to be a Christian" who has known God's deliverance from the thraldom of evil, His forgiveness and an entry into the kingdom of Christ? In this way he intends to exalt the Son of God through whom God's redemption was wrought and His reconciliation, not only of individuals but of the entire creation, achieved.

The other way of explaining how the extended passage holds together is to call attention to Paul's polemical purpose. He has his eye on the menacing situation within the Colossian church and is concerned to check the false teaching which had arisen.

That error had a double effect. One baneful result was a denigrating of the church's Lord and a suggestion that He was only one member of the angelic hierarchy needed to span the gulf between the high God and His creation. Paul counters this denial of the unique and solely sufficient place of the cosmic Christ as Mediator and Redeemer by a confident assertion that all the divine essence dwells in Him, not in the angelic powers and, moreover, the latter

---

[1] The present writer has discussed the layout and the meaning of some early Christian canticles in his *Worship in the Early Church*, 1964, chapter 4; and in "An Early Christian Hymn: (Col. 1:15–20)," *Evangelical Quarterly* xxxvi. 4, 1964, pp. 195–205. I have discussed some of these issues further and given bibliographical references in an article, "Hymns in the New Testament" in the forthcoming *International Standard Bible Encyclopaedia* (revised).

only exist because He wills that they should; and He holds the secret of the whole universe in His hand (verse 17). The other consequence was just as serious and followed directly from the heresy mentioned. Because the false teachers insisted that acknowledgment of a system of angelic mediators was necessary for human salvation there could be very little certainty that sufficient recognition had been paid to them and so little confidence in a Christian assurance that life was secure in the hands of a loving God and Father. This uncertainty led on inevitably to fear and hopelessness about the meaning of life in this world and a desperate craving for some prospect of life beyond death. Gilbert Murray summed up the religious barrenness of the ancient world when men fell victims to astrology and fear of angelic spirits as hellenistic man's "failure of nerve." Paul offered release from this craven submission to the star gods and unseen spiritual forces which tyrannized over first-century man by his doctrine of redemption and hope. God had disclosed His nature in His beloved Son whose victory over death was the promise and pledge of eternal life in His kingdom. Jesus Christ comprised both the "fulness of God" (verse 19) and the means by which God's name and nature could be made known to man, for He was "the image of the invisible God" (verse 15). His death on the cross opened the way for estranged sinners to come back to the Father, with the assurance that life now takes on a meaning and a purpose controlled by a loving and powerful God.

Two cardinal errors, then, troubled the Colossian church: one, a demoting of the Lord Jesus Christ to the rank of an angelic intermediary; the other, an inference that there could be no final salvation but only a vague possibility that a person had placated the correct star deities and so stood some chance of gaining entry into the divine realm. Meanwhile, life was emptied of its meaning and joy because freedom from fear and hope for the future were removed.

When these two fearful tenets are described in these terms and applied to our modern scene, it is not difficult to see that hoary heresy is still with us, both theologically and religiously. The person of Christ as the unique image of God in whose face the Father's glory shines (2 Cor. 4:4-6) and through whom alone we come to the Father (John 1:18; 14:6) is still the foundation on which the church is built. To attempt its removal or to try to build on another is to court disaster (see 1 Cor. 3:10,11) and to introduce heresy of the clearest stripe, as the mushroom growth of the sects like Jehovah's

Witnesses and Christian Science sorrowfully may testify. The litmus test of any novel teaching is bound to be the place it accords to the person and place of Jesus Christ.

> "What think ye of Christ?" is the test;
>   To try both your state and your scheme;
> You cannot be right in the rest,
>   Unless you think rightly of Him.
>
> *John Newton*

To cast aspersion on the pre-eminence of the Lord Christ is fearful in its consequence; it is equally disastrous to rob men of an assurance that God holds their destinies, both here in this world and hereafter, in His keeping. Yet this denial of God's personal interest in His creatures and concern for them would seem to follow directly from much modern teaching whose concept of God is so remotely philosophical and sterile that it exiles a personal God and casts doubt on His loving compassion expressed in His Son.

These verses carry their message to our day and speak relevantly to heresies, ancient and modern. We turn to consider the precise way in which Paul meets head-on the challenge of the situation at Colossae.

1:12 *Giving thanks to the Father, who has qualified us to share in the inheritance of the saints in light.*

The opening words are connected with what has gone before and form part of the apostle's prayer. The participle, "giving thanks" may possibly carry a special overtone and lead us to expect a "Thanksgiving prayer" in the verses which follow. This is an argument of G. Bornkamm[1] who holds that the call to thankfulness finds its natural setting at the Lord's Supper and that hymns to Christ (a specimen is found in verses 15–20) as literary forms developed in the worship patterns of the Communion service. N. A. Dahl[2] has enlarged these arguments by pointing to and drawing in the witness of the later church when, at the eucharist, prayers normally formed the same two-part scheme, divided between creation and redemption, illustrated in this passage.[3] This resemblance, he main-

---

[1] G. Bornkamm, "Das Bekenntnis im Hebräerbrief", *Gesammelte Aufsätze*, Band II, 1959, p. 196.

[2] N. A. Dahl, "Anamnesis: Mémoire et Commémoration dans le christianisme primitif", *Studia Theologica*, I, 1947, 69–95.

[3] As in Hippolytus' *Apostolic Tradition*, dated near the year AD 215. The eucharistic prayer opens with "We render thanks unto Thee, O God, through Thy Beloved Child Jesus Christ," and joins God's creative and redeeming work as a preamble to the Words of Institution.

tains, corroborates "the supposition that the Christological passages in Col. 1 were drawn up under the influence of a 'literary' form which made a memorial of Christ at the Lord's Supper" (p. 86, n. 1). While there is some plausibility in this evidence of joining together creation and redemption, it hardly seems to make the setting of the verses here in the Lord's Supper an obvious choice; and there is far more in favour of E. Käsemann's theory that the language of verses 12–14 betrays a baptismal origin. We discuss this idea in Additional Note B.

The occasion of Paul's thanksgiving is in the reverse order from that noted above. "To share in the inheritance of the saints in light" is a sentence full of Old Testament images, especially when we recall its applied meaning: "to take your share in the heritage of (God's) chosen and holy people—who live in light." The last phrase qualifies all that precedes it, for Paul wishes to make clear that while Israel was allotted Canaan as God's promised land to His elect people, the inheritance of the new Israel is no territorial possession but a spiritual dimension, the realm of light. For Paul, "the Promised Land of the Old Testament becomes the Kingdom of God in the New Testament."[1]

The correspondences in language between the two ideas of Israel's heritage in Canaan and the church's entry into God's kingdom are impressive: "qualify" (Greek *hikanoun*, found also at 2 Cor. 3:6) may be reminiscent of Job 31:2 in the LXX: "the inheritance of the Almighty (=the sufficient One) is from above;"[2] "share in the heritage" recalls the land of Palestine chosen for Israel as a nation in which each family had a share, a promise that goes back to Genesis 13:14,15. See Numbers 26:52ff.; 34:2,13; and "the saints" is precisely the Old Testament designation of God's chosen people.

1:13,14 Two parts of God's saving enterprise are descriptively mentioned here as the middle term "redemption" is explained. Negatively, God has rescued us from "the domain of darkness," that is, the realm where evil powers hold sway and from which they exercise a malign influence over men (Luke 22:53). Acts 26:18 identifies this sphere of darkness as the area of Satan's authority (as in Luke 4:6; Eph. 2:2) in which men and women were caught and held (1 John 5:19) before they knew God's liberation as a present fact (verse 14: "we *have*," as a personal experience and present fact,

[1] J. D. Hester, *Paul's Concept of Inheritance*, 1968, p. viii.
[2] As C. H. Dodd suggests, *The Bible and the Greeks*, 1935, p. 16.

"redemption"). Redemption is here expressed in terms of forgiveness of sins to show that emancipation from evil's power is accomplished by no automatic process or non-moral fiat. It may be, as
C. F. D. Moule suggests, that Paul emphasizes the moral and life-
changing content of redemption to safeguard the gospel against a
distortion, especially if the Colossian heretics were promising an
"instant" salvation of a kind which offered immortality here and
now and made no ethical demands. The other side of the coin, to
come to the positive aspect, is pictured as a transference and entry
into the kingdom of God's dear Son.

The phrase in verse 13b which speaks of Christ's kingdom is
something unusual. Normally the New Testament writers speak of
God's kingdom and only occasionally is Christ referred to as the
king of that dominion, though the awareness of His present reign in
the church and the world lies just beneath the surface throughout
the apostolic literature. Christ's kingly rule is a present reality since
He is now exalted as the risen and victorious Lord (1 Cor. 15:23–28)
whereas the kingdom of God is more emphatically the future hope
whose certain fulfilment is assured by Christ's elevation to the
Father's presence.[1] Here the Old Testament prophecy of Psalm
110:1 played a significant rôle.

Because believers are already taken into Christ's dominion where
they enjoy immunity from sin's tyranny and are given the assurance
of the Lord's present reign as they are raised with Him (see 3:1),
they need no longer suffer doubt and fear on account of malevolent
spirit-forces. They have known emancipation from past bondage,
having died with Christ to "the elemental spirits of the universe"
(2:20; 3:3). These hostile powers were forced to release their grip
as the crucified Christ overcame them in His hour of seeming defeat
(2:15) and dereliction. How much more does His triumph in the
resurrection prove that He is "the head of all rule and authority"!
And the Colossians have "come to fulness of life in him" (2:10) as
they are risen with Him (2:13).

15–20 We may pass on now to examine these verses on the
assumption that they form a compact, self-contained hymn written
in praise of the cosmic Christ, the Lord of creation and redemption.
Part of the reason for calling the passage a hymn lies in the discovery

[1] O. Cullmann, "The Kingship of Christ and the Church in the New Testament", in
The Early Church ET 1956, p. 110: "For the basileia (kingdom) of the Son the Christian can
already thank God (Col. 1:12f.); but for the coming of the Kingdom of God he must still
pray: 'Thy Kingdom come'."

of an unusual vocabulary and elevated style which betrays a rhythmic lilt when the lines are read aloud. By the same token some recent interpreters[1] have suggested that there lies beneath the surface of the passage a pre-Pauline hymnic composition which the apostle has taken over and used, suitably modifying the original by introducing additional words which interrupt the metrical symmetry of the original form of the hymn. The main suggested additions supplied by Paul's own hand are: "whether thrones or dominions or principalities or authorities" (v. 16); "the church" (v. 18); and "by the blood of his cross" (v. 20).

The effect of these insertions is explained in the following manner: In the first case Paul wishes to make clear that the whole of the created order derives from the cosmic Christ, especially the spiritual or angelic forces represented by name in the additional phrases; for it was precisely these powers which were being advocated as intermediaries to be placated at Colossae. Paul therefore meets the point by spelling out by name the parts of the invisible creation which owe their existence and continuance to Christ's upholding. Second, the result of the insertion of "the church" is to transform what was originally intended as a tribute to Christ as head over the cosmic powers into an assurance that it is not the cosmos only but the church which is His body. And because this is so, the church can escape from the mesh of determinism by which the cosmic powers had tyrannized over human life; and in consequence "the cosmic lordship of Christ is a present reality in the church" (Lohse). The third addition is a modification made by Paul in the same way as Christ's obedience, Philippians 2:8, is given pointed application by the emphatic "even the death of the cross." The reconciliation achieved by Christ's work is memorably located at the cross.

Additional Note A:
INTERPRETING COLOSSIANS *1:15-20*

The suggested backgrounds of the verses offer a bewildering variety. In the main, they may be described in a threefold way. First of all, some writers (like E. Käsemann) build on the conviction that the original form of the passage shows signs of a gnostic influence. In fact, it is claimed, it is as a specimen of the gnostic myth of the saved Saviour that the hymn finds its proper genesis.

---

[1] See, for example, E. Käsemann's discussion, "A Primitive Christian Baptismal Liturgy," *Essays on New Testament Themes*, ET 1964, pp. 149–168.

Key-phrases adduced in support of this view are (a) "image of God" which is interpreted as a reference to the heavenly Man who bore the Father's likeness, subjected himself to the powers of fate in this world and is now exalted above the "circle of the spheres." His return to this divine realm paves the way for mortal men—devotees of the gnostic religion—to follow him; (b) "first-born." This term also describes the state of the Original Man who stood in special relation to the high God and shared his throne; (c) the world in gnostic thought was imagined to be part of the Original Man who sustained a relationship to it like that of a head to a body. Hence the descriptive phrase (in v. 18): "he is the head of the body;" (d) the notion of "fulness" (Greek *plērōma*) is also a central idea in gnosticism, and Käsemann argues that the meaning to be attached to verse 19 is drawn from the idea of the "fulness" which is the name of an aeon or spirit-power in the cosmological scheme of the classical gnostic systems in the second century. The subject of that verse, he contends, is not God but the *plērōma* as an aeon which has become "incarnate" in the Redeemer. The purpose of this "incarnation," which is thought of in terms of an epiphany or emanation from the high God, is then explained; and this is precisely how the embodiment of "the fulness" in the Saviour figure is understood by the gnostic Peratae and Monoïmus according to Hippolytus (see the texts given and the use made of Col. 1:19; 2:9 in F. H. Borsch's discussion of the Son of Man in gnostic literature: *The Christian and Gnostic Son of Man*, 1970, pp. 66–69). (e) The purpose is to achieve an objective of "reconciliation." But the object of the cosmic reconcilation is the totality of the universe, i.e. all the aeons that make up the cosmos. This pacification is not to be seen as anything personal or moral. Rather it is a recognition by these cosmic forces that one aeon is Lord and they are therefore compelled to hail this one aeon as world-ruler, to whom universal homage is due. This is the finale of the hymn, according to Käsemann, as a restored and unified creation is accomplished and a new age begun. Fate is overcome; the elemental spirits are "pacified;" and the Redeemer proclaims global peace.

This reading of the text is widely accepted as correct among Continental scholars, but it is open to question. Aside from the big issue of whether the gnostic redemption saga has any bearing on our understanding of the New Testament message, and the legitimacy of appealing to second century documents for support, the main criticism to be fastened on Käsemann's theory concerns the teaching on reconciliation. Even if we grant Käsemann's point in his argument that the phrase in verse 20: "by the blood of his cross" is a Pauline addition (like the similar phrase in Phil. 2:8: "even the death of the cross"), it still remains open to serious question whether there is any non-Christian parallel to the portrayal of the Redeemer figure as one who achieves reconciliation. The message of a Redeemer whose coming to earth unites God and man remains a distinctively *Christian* motif; and this is even clearer with the amplification of verse 20c. The most recent possible exception to this statement is the evidence from Codex V in the Nag Hammadi texts. *The Apocalypse of Adam* is interpreted by some scholars (A. Böhlig, G. W. MacRae, "The Coptic Gnostic Apocalypse of Adam," *Heythrop Journal* 6, [1965], pp. 27ff.) as offering an example of a redemption myth unaffected by the Christian story of Jesus. This document is being appealed to as evidence of gnosticism as a pre-Christian phenomenon.

But this reading of the text is not without its challengers. R. McL. Wilson (*Gnosis and the New Testament*, [1968], pp. 138f.) raises some contrary points in objection, and argues that the text itself betrays some knowledge of a dependence on the New Testament, especially in its characterization of the Redeemer figure: "the narrative . . . appears too closely tailored to the figure of Jesus in the text" (p. 138) to be independent.

II

In the second place, other interpreters have moved to the opposite end of the spectrum away from a gnostic viewpoint. One alternative proposal is to find the key to unlock the hymn's language problems and religious message in Rabbinical Judaism. C. F. Burney in an article "Christ as the ARCHE of Creation," *Journal of Theological Studies*, 27, 1926, was a pioneer in this enterprise. He drew attention to the centrality of verse 15, "first-born of all creation," which, he said, veils an allusion to Proverbs 8:22: "The Lord begat me as the beginning of his way." Further, he argued that Paul was using this Old Testament verse just as the Rabbis used it, as a commentary on Genesis 1:1: "In the beginning God created." They taught that God's creative design was put into effect through his wisdom, which is the subject of Proverbs 8. He created wisdom, and wisdom became his master-workman, as the "beginning" of God's ways. Now the term "beginning" has dramatically changed its position in the sentence. From being an adverb, it has become a noun! Paul, in the typical Rabbinic manner, has followed through this line of exegetical enquiry and boldly claimed for the church's Lord every possible meaning which the Rabbis were accustomed to extract from Genesis 1:1, and Proverbs 8:22. The net effect is to make the pre-existent Lord the beginning, sum-total, head and first-fruits of creation—each title matches the successive statements in the Pauline text:

(a) Beginning: He is before all things
(b) Sum-total: All things cohere in him
(c) Head: He is the head of the body
(d) First-fruits: Who is the beginning, the first-born from the dead.

Paul then draws a triumphant conclusion: Christ fulfils every meaning which he derived from "In the beginning": "that in everything he might be pre-eminent" (v. 18).

In the background of this exercise in linguistic comparison is Paul's intention not to tolerate any rival to Christ. He wants to repel any idea that there were other mediating beings which made up the divine "fulness", and also to oppose the Jewish insistence on the place of the Law as pre-existent, an instrument in God's creative work, the ground-plan of the universe, and the embodiment of divine wisdom. All of these attributes and functions of the law were claimed by speculative Jewish thinkers, and formed a major challenge to the early expounders of the Christian faith, as we can see from John 1:1–18. Paul's response to a Judaizing claim is to deny at its base the support on which Torah (Law) religion rests and to place Christ above the authority and dignity of the Torah.

This understanding of the background of the Colossian hymn is attractively and plausibly presented by such a writer as W. D. Davies.[1] It assumes, however, that Paul's opposition at Colossae springs solely or mainly from a Jewish source, and for that precise reason it leaves itself open to criticism. The chief objection to be raised against the setting of the hymn in a Jewish milieu is that it overlooks Paul's indebtedness to hellenistic Judaism, which would make him more familiar with scriptural exegesis in Greek-speaking Judaism of the Dispersion than with the rabbinical methods of interpretation. Therefore, to cite one of the critics of this view, "it is not evident why Paul should here suddenly introduce an interpretation of Genesis into a letter to a preponderantly Gentile Christian church."[2]

III

Thirdly, we must consider the possibility of a situation at Colossae which takes seriously the character of the church as "preponderantly *Gentile* Christian." Undoubtedly there were Jewish elements in the heresy which troubled the Colossians, but these were Jewish ideas from the world of the Dispersion. Our chief authority for such is Philo, the Alexandrian Jewish philosopher and Bible exegete; and our main source-book is the hellenistic *Wisdom of Solomon*. E. Schweizer[3] has carefully noted the possibility that Colossians 1:15–20 may be part of a wider study of the indebtedness of New Testament Christology to a type of Jewish speculation which gave central place to the "wisdom of God." He argues that three stanzas of the hymn are to be discerned covering the aspects of creation, preservation, and redemption—a pattern which we can

---

[1] W. D. Davies, *Paul and Rabbinic Judaism*,[2] 1955, pp. 150–152.

[2] H. J. Gabathuler, *Jesus Christus. Haupt der Kirche—Haupt der Welt*, 1965, pp. 28f.

[3] E. Schweizer, *The Church as the Body of Christ*, 1964, p. 64–73; and the same author in *New Testament Studies* 8, 1961/62, pp. 1–11. J. L. Houlden (*Commentary*, pp. 155–173) has an excellent section which deals with the background of the hymn in 1: 15–20.

recall today from the structure of the General Thanksgiving: "We bless thee for our creation, preservation . . . But, above all, for thy inestimable love in the redemption of the world. . . ."

This line of investigation seems worth following up; and we shall adopt E. Schweizer's analysis of the text as we move into an exegetical study.

Strophe I

1:15–16 Who is the image of the invisible God, the first-born of all
  creation;
  For in him were created all things in heaven and earth,
  Through him and to him were all things created.

Two antecedents of this text are worthy of notice. Philo spoke of the Logos or word of God as His image and His agent in creation. Indeed, in several places, Philo can use the description "first-born son" (Greek *protogonos huios*) in a way that is directly reminiscent of Paul's Greek term (*prototokos*—first-born—in v. 15 is very similar in meaning).

The *Wisdom of Solomon* has numerous allusions to God's wisdom as His agent in creation (e.g. 8:6: "Wisdom is the artificer of all that is," NEB). In a famous passage (7:22–30) wisdom is hailed as God's image and sustainer of all created things: "She spans the world in power from end to end, and orders all things benignly," v. 30, NEB.

The addition of the lines

  Visible and invisible
  Whether thrones or dominions
  Or authorities or powers (v. 16)

spells out what the term "all things" implies, and is Paul's way of saying in this poetic form (by use of a special rhetorical device) that Christ's rule extends over all the cosmic forces of the universe (2:20). In Him (like the divine word of Ecclus. 24:5f. and Wisdom 18:16) heaven and earth are joined.

The heavenly Lord is here set forth as the unique Son or Image of God in whom we see the true character of God who is invisible to mortal eye. The invisibility of God is a conclusion which follows from His nature as "spirit," i.e. non-material (John 4:24). "No one has ever seen God" (John 1:18) is an affirmation of Biblical faith which rebukes the innate human desire to conceptualize God in earthly terms. Idol-making and visible representations of God in art stand under the judgment of this word which is dramatically illustrated in Moses' encounter with the living God (Ex. 33:17-23).

The glory of the Christian gospel lies here. While its teaching adds fresh emphasis upon the spiritual and invisible character of God (1 Tim. 1:17; 6:16) and the folly of all human endeavours to fashion a likeness of God in material form (Acts 17:29), it boldly announces that God's glory may be seen in the face of Jesus Christ (2 Cor. 4:6) and His nature is revealed in one, perfect human life (John 14:9). For at the heart of this claim is the confident assertion that Jesus Christ is the true God and true man, and so able adequately and finally to reveal God's hidden name and secret nature to those who confess Him as Son and Christ of God (Matt. 11:25-27). He is the "image" or visible manifestation of God not simply in that He is "like God" or brings news from God or even a message of God. Rather it is because He is the objectivization of God in human life, a coming into visible expression of the invisible God[1] that the church hails him, "Thou art the King of glory, O Christ" and sings:

> Our God contracted to a span,
> Incomprehensibly made man.

"First-born of all creation" is a phrase which requires some elucidation. If it is taken in the strict sense demanded by Proverbs 8:22—which is how the Arians took it, to be followed by the Jehovah's Witnesses in the more recent history of Christendom—it would make Christ a creature of God, although "first-born." But this sense is not required by Paul's Greek and is flatly denied by what he goes on to say. In the next verses he attributes to Christ the work of creation as the one through whom God brought the universe into existence. If the pre-incarnate Lord was the agent of all creation, and pre-existed before everything, it leads to the conclusion that only God can satisfactorily account for Christ's being.

Against the Arian appeal to Proverbs 8:22 Athanasius drew attention to the meaning of the title "first-born" in the light of Colossians 1:16 and added: "But if all the creatures were created in him, he is other than the creatures, and he is not a creature but the creator of the creatures" (*Orations against the Arians*, ii, 62, cited by T. E. Pollard, *Johannine Christology and the Early Church* [1970], p. 213, who has a full discussion of Athanasius' many-pronged

---

[1] This is the meaning of "image" in Biblical thought as distinct from the popular use of the term. See present writer's *Carmen Christi: Philippians 2:5-11*, 1967, pp. 112f.

attack on the Arians' use of proof-texts, like Proverbs 8:22 and Colossians 1:15). What is said of Arius (op. cit., pp. 143f.) would hold equally well against more recent heresies which use the Colossians text to infer that Christ was a creature: "He uses a number of carefully selected biblical texts chosen to fit his philosophical presuppositions, and uses them as premises on which to develop his argument, and it is only as a system built on extra-biblical foundations that Arianism can be understood."

It is Paul's purpose in these verses to show that Christ is Lord of creation and has no rival in the created order. Therefore, the NEB rendering is in every way to be preferred: "his is the primacy over all created things". He is first-born before all creation, and so responsible, under God the Father and fount of deity, for all that came into being "in the beginning."[1]

Strophe II

1:17–18a He is before all things,
  And in him all things hold together
  And he is the head of the body [the church].

The first line recapitulates the entire previous stanza by re-asserting that the Lord of glory antedates all creation as "first-born of all creation." Then Paul proceeds to develop the notion of His cosmic rôle by hailing Him as upholder and sustainer of the created order.

Again there are parallels drawn in the Wisdom literature (Wisdom 1:7: "For the spirit of the Lord fills the whole earth, and that which holds all things together . . .;" Wisdom "pervades and permeates all things" [7:24]; Thy almighty Word . . . "his head touching the heavens, his feet the earth" [18:16]). In these texts wisdom or God's spirit or His word—they seem to be equivalent—is a divine agency which binds all things together and unites heaven and earth. We may also compare Ecclesiasticus 24:5f. for a similar picture of wisdom. But is this what Paul is saying in regard to Christ's cosmic task?

The answer cannot be affirmed; and it is more likely that for the thought of wisdom as the cohesive force which binds the scattered parts of the universe we should go to Proverbs 8:30. The text here is an exegetical crux, and many possibilities of meaning for the

[1] For the sense, "Archetype of all creation," see N. Turner's section in *Grammatical Insights into the New Testament*, 1965, pp. 122–24.

Hebrew word '*āmôn* are viable. A recent study by-passes the suggestions of "masterworkman," "child" (NEB "darling"), "guardian" in favour of "principle of coherence". R. B. Y. Scott[1] thus translates,

"Then I was at His side, a living link or vital bond," uniting creation—which is precisely Paul's thought in our text.

The thought of the cosmic Christ as holding the universe together as its principle of coherence is a staggering one indeed. Did Paul have some quasi-scientific world-view in mind? This is unlikely, though it cannot be denied. More probably he is at pains here to assert that Christ is the sole and rightful Lord of creation who not only set the universe in motion at the beginning of time but is responsible for all that appears since then. No new cosmic force can take Him by surprise and no power which arises subsequent to the first creation "in the beginning" can usurp this sovereign right—and all this is cast in polemical form with Paul's eye set on the Colossian errorists.

So, in summary, He is "head of the body," the universe. This is how the original statement of the pre-Pauline hymn ran. Paul inserts the words "of the church" to modify the first draft of the hymn, and the phrase is as unusual in Greek as in English, so that we should suspect a powerful motive which moves Paul's pen to make this alteration. The reason must be that he wishes to correct an implied notion that the world was physically the body of Christ and permeated by Him in a crassly literal sense. Moreover, Paul is anxious to stress that Christ's lordship over the church means that it is emancipated from evil powers which, in the current pagan thought, were believed to control the cosmos. Indeed, their rôle in both creation and the lives of Christians is now brought to an end as they are subjected to the crucified and victorious Christ (2:10,15) who is "head of the body, *namely the church*."

Headship then signifies Christ's rulership over the celestial powers and denotes His supremacy (so Benoit). By implication, Paul adds by his insertion, He rules over the church which by His overlordship is freed from astral tyranny.

[1] R. B. Y. Scott "Wisdom in Creation: the '*Amôn* of Proverbs viii. 30," *Vetus Testamentum*, 10, 1960, pp. 213–223. The same conclusion is reached by A. Feuillet in his study *Le Christ Sagesse de Dieu*, 1966, p.246, who sees one of the leading themes of Colossians 1:15–20 to be Christ (= Wisdom) as the principle of cohesion of the universe, though he prefers (p. 77) to translate '*āmôn* as master-workman. He finds the exegetical key to Colossians 1:15–16 in Proverbs 8:22 (p. 270).

Strophe III

1:18b–20 Who is the beginning, the first-born from the dead;
　For in him all the fulness of God was pleased to dwell
　And through him to reconcile all things to himself.

It is more or less certain that with this strophe a new background is to be sought. Nothing in the teaching on wisdom adumbrates the theme of redemption, whether cosmic or personal (except perhaps the references in Proverbs 8:35,36, which however seem remote), nor is there any suggestion that Hebrew wisdom was reborn or resurrected from death to life.

Death—life form a contrast which recalls man's own personal history. Moreover, Adam was God's image (Gen. 1:26,27) and God's son as king of paradise. He was the beginning of the old order, doomed to sin and death and decay. Christ is the second Man, whose coming marks a new beginning as a new segment of humanity is brought into existence. As Adam's sin brought ruin and death, so Christ's resurrection heralds a new age of life and hope. He is the first-born of many brethren (Rom. 8:29); the first-fruits of a harvest yet to be reaped (1 Cor. 15:20); a life-giving spirit (1 Cor. 15:45), who promises life for all His members as they are united to Him (1 Cor. 6:17).

The meaning of "fulness" (v. 19) seems settled by the use of the same word in 2:9 where Paul locates the totality of the divine essence in the incarnate Christ, and not in the angelic mediators. Perhaps this Greek term for "fulness" (*plērōma*) was the heretics' word which Paul boldly appropriates to his own ends. More likely it is his term,[1] used to assert the very truth the heretics were doubting or denying, namely that Christ is the Lord of all cosmic authority by divine appointment and that no spiritual power has independent existence outside of his control.

The additional lines, "that in everything he might be pre-eminent" and "whether on earth or in heaven" are designed to drive home the conviction concerning the totality of Christ's sphere of influence. No element in the universe stands outside the regimen of the lordly Christ, whose reconciliation draws together heaven and earth into a unity. Ephesians 1:10 says the same thing by asserting that God's plan is to unite under a single head all that is both in the heavenly regions and on the earth. Both passages are directed against the

---

[1] See the article "Fulness" in the *New Bible Dictionary* (ed. J. D. Douglas), 1962, pp. 442f.

contrary heretical idea that human destiny lies at the mercy of the astral gods which control the inter-stellar space and exercise malign influences on the earth-dwellers. Paul's message is simply to rebut this false teaching by denying that no part of the universe lies beyond Christ's control and lordship and that no fate can tyrannize over human life and strike fear into the human heart.

That much is common between the two passages. But there is a notable exception. There is no suggestion in *Ephesians* of alien powers which need to be reconciled by Christ, or at least of hostile forces whose enmity needs to be overcome and pacified. In *Colossians* that need is both stated and met. In fact, in 1:20c Paul has evidently spelled out the rationale of cosmic reconciliation in a way he had not done before: it is *by the blood of his cross* that he has made peace between heavenly cosmic powers and God. The non-human, transcendental dimension of the work of Calvary here receives a vivid treatment. And, as before, we must pose the question, Why does Paul emphasize this aspect of the reconciliation by seeking to tie it in with the atoning deed? Thereby he has ensured that the reconciliation, while affecting cosmic relations, shall not be thought of as a physical miracle that merely changed the state of the cosmos outside of man. By the insertion of a reference to the cross into the hymn itself and by expanding that reference in 1:21,22 in clearer terms to include the Colossian believers, he has anchored the work of Christ in a historical event. Paul has made luminous its moral effect as bringing salvation from evil (which the gnosticizing teachers were not recognizing, as is clear from references in the later parts of the letter). And he has memorably clarified the application of a "theology of the cross" by showing that "it does not work like, to use a Gnostic image, a magnet put in heaven and drawing those who are brought into its magnetic field irresistibly after it. The effect of Christ's death is the effect of a deed of love bringing its fruits in a human life which is touched by it."[1]

Additional Note B:
THE SETTING OF COLOSSIANS 1:15–20 AND ITS APPLICATION

From the foregoing sketch of how Colossians 1:15–20 has been interpreted, it is clear that it is possible to look at the passage at different

---

[1] E. Schweizer, *The Church as the Body of Christ*, 1964, p. 70. Further discussion along this line marking the difference between the gnostic and Christian understanding of "reconciliation" is offered by Schweizer in his article, "Die Kirche als Leib Christi in den paulinischen Antilegomena," *Theologische Literaturzeitung* 86, 1961, pp. 241–256, especially p. 249.

levels. We may label these (a) the verses as a christological statement; (b) the verses as a confession of faith set in a liturgical or sacramental context; (c) the verses in a pastoral context as a call to ethical action.

At this point we deal with the verses as we have them and seek to understand the purpose of the final redaction. Whatever may be the hypothetical original of the hymn, it has come down to us in its final form and set within the pastoral context of an apostolic epistle. We should therefore expect some paraenetic (i.e. hortatory) and practical purpose, and this expectation is confirmed from the two sections by which it is flanked (vv. 12–14; 21f.).

(a) These surrounding verses pose a problem for the traditional interpretation which sees the text of 15–20 simply as a doctrinal and dogmatic statement in reply to the problems raised by the Colossian error. To be sure, what was needed in terms of an avowal of Christ's primacy and authority in creation has been supplied, and the thrust of heresy that Christ was one of a number of inferior aeons making up the *plērōma* has been successfully deflected. His office as pre-existent image of God—and so the archetype of creation—has been established. He is the one through whom all created life sprang into being, including the angelic hierarchies of verse 16. In Him all things including these powers hang together and He is their sustainer. Moreover, He is the final goal towards which the whole creation tends, so that Christ becomes (in A. M. Hunter's words, *Interpreting Paul's Gospel*, [1954], 60) "the key to creation, (*Paul*) declaring that it is all there with Christ in view." And finally, hostile cosmic powers, inimical to man, have now been pacified and brought under the domain of the cosmocratic Christ, Lord of creation (v. 20). All this is memorably and magnificently stated.

The problem is to relate this Christological poem to the human scene, and to enquire how Paul was led into the hymn from verses 12ff. and why he should resume his pastoral counsel by proceeding immediately to include the readers within the scope of that universal reconciliation (vv. 21, 22).

(b) It is the merit of E. Käsemann's treatment that, as with a parallel case in Philippians 2:5–11, he has addressed himself to this question of the "life-setting" of the passage. There are two elements in this approach:

First, an axiom among recent Continental interpreters is that the false teaching at Colossae is *not* the chief purpose of this hymn which had an existence independent of and prior to its inclusion in the Pauline letter. This is put clearly in Käsemann, loc. cit. p. 164, "The alleged allusions to the Colossian heresy . . . are rendered untenable by (our) interpretation." As Ch. Masson puts it, the purpose of the citation of the hymn is not as an antidote to heresy but in praise of Jesus Christ. The hymn is an aretalogy and its content *as such* has no eye on the situation in the Lycus valley though its use by the apostolic writer is clearly related to his purpose. But that purpose cannot be discerned in the hymn *per se* but only in the *application* which may be detected from the neighbouring verses.

Secondly, the surrounding verses, especially vv. 12–14 give the substantial clue to the reason why the hymn is cited; and Käsemann has here picked out the salient features which betray a *baptismal setting of the introit*: (*i*) The attribution of Sonship to Christ ("of his beloved Son") is reminiscent of the synoptic account of Jesus' baptism in Jordan, especially in the common use made of "beloved" (Mark 1:11 etc.). Cf. "I am well pleased" and "was pleased" (1:19).

(*ii*) As a footnote to this piece of evidence which betrays a baptismal context, we may call attention to G. Bornkamm's discussion of "Confession (*homologia*) in the epistle to the Hebrews" (represented in *Studien zu Antike und Urchristentum*, 1959, pp. 188ff.) and in particular to his demonstration that "recognition of the 'Son of God' formula can have no other meaning than that which is found in the divine announcement of the 'Son' in the story of Jesus' baptism" (loc. cit. p. 193). It is true that from this premise Bornkamm draws some surprising conclusions to which we may return later.

(*iii*) The verbs "to deliver" and "to transfer" are placed in contrast in the context of "deliverance from the power of darkness" (cf. Acts 26:18 which shows that "darkness" and "Satan" are synonyms; and other comparative material—Luke 22:53; Ephesians 2:2; Luke 4:6; Mark 16:14 [W]—indicates that *exousia* carries the sense of "realm," "sphere" where Satan's power holds sway. Cf. Qumran's *Community Rule* I, II and IQH xii. 6). Hence Bauer's *Lexicon* [Amdt-Gingrich) gives correctly: "the domain of darkness"; and deliverance from evil and transference into the realm of God's beloved Son are strictly parallel, and are to be located in the Christian's experience following baptism, linked (as the next phrase goes on to relate) with the forgiveness of sins (as in Mk. 1:4; Lk. 3:3; Acts 2:38).

(*iv*) The third group of terms suggestive of a baptismal motif is "light," "share," and "inheritance" (in v. 12). All these words speak of the new existence of the baptized Christian and denote the effect of "the sacramental action of incorporation into the new sphere of jurisdiction" (Käsemann, loc. cit. p. 160). We may query whether the English translation of "in den neuen Herrschaftsbereich" really does justice to Käsemann's idea here (cf. his discussion on Phil. 2:6–11 in the same volume, of original essays, pp. 93–95). What is needed is the idea of the Christian's passage, through baptism, to a new domain of lordship so that he is no longer under the regime of Satan but passes into the domain of Christ's control, receiving "a heritage of the saints in light"—a comprehensive term which is now illumined by the Dead Sea scrolls. The references in that literature are as follows: 1OS xi. 7, 8: "God has given them to His chosen ones as an everlasting possession, and has caused them to inherit the lot of the Holy Ones" (Vermes' translation, p. 93); 1 QH xi. f. "Thou hast purified man of sin . . . that he may be one [with] the children of Thy truth and partake of the lot of Thy Holy Ones" (Vermes, p. 186) opposed to "lot of darkness" (1QM xiii. 5f. "Truly they are the company of Darkness, but the company of God is one of [eternal] Light" (Vermes, pp. 140f.). See too 1QM 1:5: "This shall be a time of salvation for the people of God, an age of dominion for all the members of His company, and of everlasting destruction for all the company of Satan" (Vermes, p. 124). Cf. i:11 and iv:2: "The Wrath of God is kindled against Satan and against the Men of his Company" (Vermes, p. 128).

(v) But the baptismal milieu here is far more obvious once we have regard to the close tie-up between 1:12ff. and Colossians 2:9-15. The common element is the teaching on the new creation: on a cosmic scale, the hymn describes the universal reconciliation; the later chapter applies this to the church in terms of the "new man" re-made in the likeness of Christ in baptism. That there are many verbal similarities between the two passages is obvious, with the "middle term" found in the use of *apekdusis*="putting off" (1:15; 2:11; cf. 3:9 for the paraenetic application in the participle *apekdusamenos*).

On the cross Christ divested himself of the "principalities and powers" in His triumph over them (2:15). This is the meaning of the line of the hymn which proclaims a universal pacification of those cosmic powers (1:20). But the same technical term is used (2:11; 3:9) for the appropriation of Christ's victory in the Christian "circumcision"; and the same imagery of "putting off" and "putting on" comes easily to be applied to the baptismal rite, as the baptizand takes off and then puts on his clothes (Gal. 3:27). The baptism is likened to a death (Rom. 6:3ff.) in which the believer dies to those very powers which sought to enslave his Lord (Col. 2:20; 3:3). His new life is akin to a re-birth as (here again with the employment of the *apekdusis* imagery) he puts off the old nature (3:9: "the old Adam") and puts on the new nature which is being renewed after the second Adam, in the image (*eikōn*) of its creator (3:10; 3:12 "put on").

The interconnexion of thought and explanation is so subtle and close-knit that it is hardly credible to follow Bornkamm's lead and think of a eucharistic setting for these verses in chapter 1. The eucharist is certainly a "foreign body," alien to the context. "There is no allusion to the Lord's Supper in the epistle as a whole," Käsemann correctly observes (loc. cit. p. 159); and "the hymn itself in its present form contains nothing that could be construed as a reference to it." See *Evangelical Quarterly*, xxxvi. 4, 1964, pp. 203-4 for Bornkamm's study and a critique thereof.

(c) We come finally to the passage as a summons to ethical endeavour; and this presses us back to the original sense of Colossians 1:15-20 in its pre-Pauline form, i.e. before its incorporation into the Colossian letter. In its first draft the hymn represents a christological statement of Christ's office as First Man and Bringer of cosmic peace. But we have to ask now for the intention of the apostle in the additions he has made; here E. Lohse[1] has made some important observations, namely:

(i) These two additions are: "of the church" which turns a cosmological reference into an ecclesiological/eschatological insistence, in verse 18: and, "by the blood of his cross" (in v. 20) which fixes the *locus* of the reconciliation in the historical event of the Crucified's obedience unto death. And both play a very significant rôle. They sound a new accent distinguishing both the theological standpoint of the author of this letter and serving his particular purpose (loc. cit., p. 162).

(ii) He also, loc. cit., p. 164, concludes that it is wrong for Ernst Käsemann to suggest that these additional interpolations may go back not to the editor as the author but to the tradition which he found already to hand; for they represent a meaningful addition which constitutes the author's response to the Colossian heresy.

By the transformation of Christ's headship over the powers to the application of this to the church, he has underlined the victory of Christ for His people. Thus there is proclaimed the conquest of fate, with the clear *application* that the church may rise above the tyranny of the "elements" to whose malign authority Christians have died in baptism (2:20). At baptism they enter into the fruits of the Lord's triumph when they die and are re-born into a world of freedom and joy and set free from the restrictions and fears of hellenistic "philosophy" which has been robbing the Colossians of their heritage as sons of light and of God. "For baptism proclaims: 'You are reconciled and the cosmos pacified, because the powers which swayed it have been despoiled and now follow in the train of the triumphal progress of Christ. They have lost their lordship and their position as mediators. For you are "translated" (*metastenai*, 1:13), you have entered into an immediate relationship to the Christ, you are his body'" (Käsemann, loc. cit., p. 168).

The second amplification, by the insertion of "by the blood of his cross," picks up the teaching on baptism which proclaims the offer of divine forgiveness (1:14) as the basis of personal reconciliation to God (1:22). And baptism is a vital element in Christian *paraenesis* of a summons to newness of life as Christians are reminded that they are no longer members of the old Adam who was tyrannized over by the demonic rulers of this Age (so Käsemann, *Leib und Leib Christi*, [1933], pp. 140ff.) but are called to "become what they are," to accept the privileges of their baptized status as children of God and members of the new man, the ultimate Adam whose image they are meant increasingly to share and reflect in ethical deportment (Col. 3:10,11). As He was the elect Son (Lk. 9:35) so they are the elect community (2:13) and summoned to live

---

[1] E. Lohse, "Christologie und Ethik im Kolosserbrief," in *Apophoreta: Festschrift for E. Haenchen*, 1964, pp. 156ff.

in the world as God's freeborn sons who rejoice in a forgiveness which
has forever broken the spell of malevolent forces and set them free.

The content of this ethical call is rooted and shaped by baptismal
catechesis, which in turn depends upon the Head-body relationship of
Christ and His members (Lohse, op. cit., p. 166). The setting of 1:15–20
within the pastoral context of 1:9–11 makes this clear, with the insistent
summons in the earlier text to live "worthy of the Lord." Lohse has
shown the correspondence between the ethical terms, "knowledge,"
"wisdom," "understanding," and Qumran's rule as part of "the counsels
of the spirit to the sons of truth in this world" (1QS iv. 3f.); and the
Teacher of righteousness rejoices in this possession: "I the Master know
Thee, O my God, by the spirit which Thou hast given to me, and by Thy
Holy Spirit I have faithfully hearkened to Thy marvellous counsels. In the
mystery of Thy wisdom Thou has opened knowledge to me. . . ."
(1QH xii. 11f.); "Thou hast favoured me, Thy servant, with a spirit of
knowledge" (1QH xiv. 25).

The Judaeo-Palestinian *paraenesis* which Lohse traces here is the pattern
(he argues) of how the new man lives as a member of the realm of God's
Son, "set free for a new life of confession and obedience" (p. 168).[1]

Conclusion

We may now attempt a summing-up. Admittedly notions of literary
structure and growth are speculative and tentative, and it is unwise to
build too much on "stages of production" by which Käsemann seeks to
account for the three forms of Colossians 1:15–20 (see p. 50 earlier).

What can be affirmed, however, is that in our Colossian epistle,
1:15–20 is not being used to check incipient gnosticism by countering
one cosmological speculation by another, as though "fulness" was
taken by the heretics to mean the totality of spiritual forces and by Paul to
suggest that all the aeons exist only in the cosmic Jesus Christ. That
would reduce Paul to the level of a speculative thinker.

Paul, on the other hand, roots his cosmology in Christian experience.
But this must not be taken to imply that his doctrine of creation is to be
reduced to an anthropocentric and existential level, which is what
N. Kehl, *Der Christushymnus im Kolosserbrief*, 1967, seems to infer. See the
critique passed on this conclusion by M. Barth, *Catholic Biblical Quarterly*,
30, 1968, p. 110. The full study of J. G. Gibbs, *Creation and Redemption*,
1971, (pp. 93–114) makes the point that Christ's lordship in the created
order does not depend upon human experience. However, the dichotomy
is artificial since "Christ's mediatorship in both respects is dependent on
the redemptive purpose of God the Father" (p. 109). We may say that

---

[1] E. Lohse has recently contributed an essay in English on the theology of Colossians in
New Testament Studies, 15. 1969, pp. 211–220.

Paul's chief concern is with the new creation, actualized in conversion and Christian baptism. The epitome of this experience is forgiveness; and forgiveness is possible not by indulgence in cosmic speculation but by Christ's atoning death (1:20,23). Redemption does not consist in knowing the cosmic secrets of the universe but in the experience of sin's release and cleansing.

Sin in the world (Paul argues) is traceable to a cosmic disorder, for it is the evil intelligences which goad men into disobedience and wickedness. They do this because they are themselves rebels against their Creator and reconciliation is needed to annul their hostility to God and men (1:20; 2:15). "Now no one reconciles or triumphs over what is not opposed to him; i.20 and ii.15 make no sense unless we may suppose that powers that were created for subordination to the heavenly Man have rebelled, and deserted their appointed rank."[1]

Now it is but a short step—still pressing backwards—to say that these cosmic authorities belong to Christ not only by reconciliation but by creation, since it is He who pre-existed them and so brought them into being. The line of Paul's argument runs from redemption to creation, not vice versa; and this piece of hymnody in praise of the Creator-Redeemer is just one further token of the functional christology—Christ-for-us (*pro nobis*)—which runs through the New Testament literature. But it was a short step to accord Him a status vis-a-vis God, as a later part of this letter seems to indicate. See p. 126.

---

[1] C. K. Barrett, *From First Adam to Last*, 1962, p. 86.

V

A PERSONAL APPLICATION

1:21–23 *And you, who once were estranged and hostile in mind, doing evil deeds,* ²²*he has now reconciled in his body of flesh by his death, in order to present you holy and blameless and irreproachable before him,* ²³*provided that you continue in the faith, stable and steadfast, not shifting from the hope of the gospel which you heard, which has been preached to every creature under heaven, and of which I, Paul, became a minister.*

THE OPENING WORDS OF VERSE 21, "AND YOU," ARE AS EMPHATIC in the Greek of Paul's letter as they appear to be in our English translation. He resumes at this point the pastoral concern of his letter which had been interrupted by the insertion of the lengthy section of verses 15–20. In that hymnic portion the theme was the universal character of Christ's reconciling work which touches every part of creation. Paul now applies this truth to the local church situation at Colossae. Christians there too are included in the "all things" of verse 20. In fact, there is a second reason supplied for this reference to the Colossian readers: in their old, pagan life they stood in desperate need of restoration to God. Formerly they were "once . . . estranged and hostile in mind" with a consequence that their conduct was associated with "evil deeds."

The Colossians' alienation from God in their pre-Christian state is described in this threefold way. They were continuously and persistently out of harmony with God (this is the force of Paul's unusual and roundabout Greek construction, as in Eph. 4:18). They stood defiantly opposed to Him as rebels, "enemies" whose thoughts and actions were a sign of that proud independence which is the tap-root of sin.

Nor was it just their disposition and religious life which displeased Him. They offended Him by their wicked ways, a term which suggests a combination of idolatry and immorality, as in Romans 1:21–32. Ephesians 2:3 shows the close connexion between a man's thought-life and his overt behaviour when he yields to the down-grade pull of "the flesh," his unregenerate self.

As the opening of verse 21 is emphatic, so too is the glad

reminder which stands at the head of the next verse. "But now" matches the earlier allusion to "once;" and this is a contrast, "once you were that, now (by the grace of God) you are this," which Paul loves to reiterate, perhaps because it mirrored his own experience (1 Cor. 15:9,10; 1 Tim. 1:13-16). The Colossians' old life finds its secret of transformation in what God has done through His reconciling deed in Christ who both became incarnate (taking a "body of flesh") and died on the cross to secure this reconciliation. And what that restoration to God's fellowship means is spelled out in a statement of purpose: "to present you holy and blameless and irreproachable before him."

The general drift of the Pauline teaching is clear. But some ambiguities remain, partly compounded by a textual problem.[1] We may ask, even on the basis of the English translations, who is the subject of the verb, "he has now reconciled" (v. 22). The quick answer would be, God who is the prime author of reconciliation in verses 19,20 where the Son is the agent through whom the work is achieved. This construction entails the necessity of seeing a change in reference half-way through verse 22, for "his body of flesh," "by his death" can only relate to Jesus Christ. NEB clarifies the meaning by inserting the names "God," "Christ's death."

Perhaps the best explanation is to see the words "in his body of flesh by his death" as Paul's after-thought, supplied to demonstrate that God's reconciliation of the church is accomplished only at the cost of a veritable incarnation and a realistic death. By the use of these phrases, Paul may well have been pressing home his teaching as a denial of the heretics' claim that reconciliation was an automatic or necessary achievement not requiring or involving any incarnation in the real sense of that term since the divine (by nature) cannot suffer.

The phrase "body of flesh" certainly looks cumbrous, though an exact parallel to it is found in the Dead Sea scrolls (1 QpHab ix:2: "And they inflicted horrors of evil diseases and took vengeance upon his body of flesh." Other references to a similar phrase, suggesting a man's physical nature, are given by K. G. Kuhn, in

---

[1] The problem is whether to read an active meaning of the verb, "he has reconciled" (so RSV, following the bulk of the MSS) or a passive indicative (attested by B and P46: see Lightfoot, pp. 249f.). The latter reading involves a repunctuation different from the usually accepted text (see C. F. D. Moule, p. 72). One way of resolving the problem is by an appeal to a Hebraistic type of sentence structure; for details see C. C. Oke, *ExpT* 63, 1951/52, pp. 155f.

The Scrolls and the New Testament, ed. K. Stendahl [1958], p. 107).
But it is just the right expression needed to underline the physical
cost of the church's redemption, which is achieved not by a wave
of the hand or some automatic process, but by the coming of God
in the person of His Son to our world, His clothing Himself in
our humanity and, then, suffering the bitterness and shame of a
death on the cross because of His close identity with humanity in
its need. Romans 8:3 provides a good parallel (cf. Phil. 2:6–8).

The purpose of God is then described. It is that His restored
children should be presented before Him—as the tribe of Levi
was in Old Testament days (Deut. 10:8; 18:5,7; 21:5)—displaying
a moral fitness and acceptance which delights His heart—as the
Old Testament sacrifices are so described in language which runs
parallel with Paul's adjectives "holy and blameless and irreproachable" (Ex. 29:37f. LXX; cf. 1 Pet. 1:19). Paul, however, spiritualizes
the cultic terms, as he does in Romans 12:1. The last term in the
list, rendered "irreproachable" (Greek *anenklētos*, literally, "not to
be called to account") has suggested to some scholars (e.g., E. Lohse,
C. Masson, Dibelius-Greeven) that the thought in the verse is
juridical rather than ceremonial. The presentation is not one of
sacrificial animals, "without blemish or spot" but of an accused
person who is acquitted of the charge brought against him and
presented to the court as a man free from the penalty of guilt.
The court is the divine tribunal before which the Christian believer,
now forgiven and reconciled, is declared blameless (Rom. 8:33f.).
If this interpretation holds good, it prepares for a similar understanding of 1:28 where the task of Paul's mission is to "present
every man" perfect in Christ, i.e. acceptable to God at the tribunal
of His judgement (Rom. 14:10).

Paul never wearies of introducing moral considerations. The
Christian is already a justified man, acquitted at the bar of God's
righteous judgement on the ground of Christ's vicarious work
(Rom. 5:1, 9–11; 2 Cor. 5:19–21). But *simul justus et peccator*—at
the same time an acquitted man and a sinner—is a Lutheran formula
of which Paul would have approved. For his salvation, while
complete and final on the Godward side, needs his diligence and
perseverance, in the manward aspect. Hence "provided that you
continue in the faith" (v. 23) is a needful addition which saves
Christian salvation from slipping into an experience inalienably
guaranteed and certified to any who once professes the faith and

imagines that thereafter he can live as he pleases. This is obviously a travesty of the elemental truth enshrined in the popular dictum, "once saved, always saved." Paul's conditional clause, "*provided that* you continue" is needed to give the full perspective, true to experience.[1]

The call here is to steadfastness in the face of a seduction which would draw the Colossians away from the Pauline gospel. "Stable and steadfast" suggest metaphors of strength and security drawn from the picture of a house. It is settled on firm foundations (the Greek word for "stable" indicates this clearly. It is the same root, *themelioun*, as in Rom. 15:20; 1 Cor. 3:10f.; Eph. 2:20). And the house is erected with strong supports and buttresses (Greek *hedraiōma* which is the word used in 1 Tim. 3:15 of the Church as the bulwark of the truth). Paul's summons to this quality of steadfastness is sounded elsewhere (1 Cor. 15:58)[2] and his teaching on the church as a holy building of God is equally attested.

The opposite of a house's firm foundation and security is its exposure to danger through landslide and earth-tremor. Colossae in A.D. 60–61 was to feel the effect of an earthquake in the Lycus Valley (see above p. 27). "Not shifting from the hope of the gospel" is another call to the same purpose. Paul's verb is found only here in the New Testament, though there are several places in the Old Testament where it means "to be put to flight" (e.g. Deut. 32:30 LXX). He calls his readers to remain loyal to his teaching and not to yield to the speculative notions which have been imported into their church. Rather, let them stay committed to their first allegiance which gave them "hope" (a term frequent in the opening chapter and used to signify the content of the gospel as preached by Paul to the Gentiles and embodied in Christ Himself whose salvation embraces them in its scope, 1:5,6,27). Why should they cut themselves off from the source of this new life and so forfeit the very reality which had transformed their lives? This is the tenor of Paul's appeal.

---

[1] The construction (Greek *ei ge* translated "provided that") needs to be seen in the light of other Pauline uses (Gal. 3:4; 2 Cor. 5:3; Eph. 3:2; 4:21). On the first reference Lightfoot comments: "*ei ge* leaves a loophole for doubt." But this concession can hardly be true of the other texts, as Lightfoot grants in regard to Colossians 1:23: the particles "express a pure hypothesis in themselves, but the indicative mood following converts the hypothesis into a hope." The same conclusion, namely that the use of the particles "would appear from [the] contexts to be confident rather than doubtful" is endorsed by M. E. Thrall, *Greek Particles in the New Testament*, 1962, pp. 87f. 90. See, for a somewhat different presentation, I. H. Marshall, *Kept by the Power of God*, 1969, p. 118.

[2] The need for adherence to the gospel is felt and expressed especially in times of assault from heretics. Both Ignatius and Polycarp use Paul's word (*hedraios*=firm) in this sense.

But could they be sure that Paul's ministry was valid? Or that his message carried a seal of divine authentication? Or be certain that the innuendoes of the false teachers may not have some truth in them? Paul seems to be countering all these suggestions in his statement (v. 23b) that his gospel has reached out to all the Gentiles, breaking down barriers of nationality and social status (see 3:11) and so clearly carrying the hall-mark of God's approval, as in verse 6 where "in the whole world" has the same sense. The universal outreach and effectiveness of the Pauline gospel stands in stark contrast to the heretics' concern to restrict *their* message to a select coterie of initiates (so Masson). And Paul's obviously successful Gentile mission includes the Colossians who may be feeling somewhat disappointed that he had never personally visited their city. But he and Epaphras and Tychicus who will carry the letter have a common title ("minister", vv. 7,23; 4:7) and that should be enough to dispel any chagrin that the great apostle to the Gentiles had neglected them. To reinforce the point Paul moves from the plural "we" to a personal pronoun "I." The term he uses is "minister" (Greek *diakonos*) partly to show its common property shared by other Christian preachers including Paul himself (Rom. 15:8) and partly because he will use this term as a transition-point into his discussion on the ministry entrusted to him. Seen in this way, this reference cannot really prove that Paul's apostolate is being appealed to by a later generation of his followers in the sub-apostolic age who want to tie-in the Pauline gospel with his apostolic office.[1]

---

[1] As E. Käsemann (*Essays*, pp. 166f.) argues; and E. Lohse, p. 111 concurs with this idea. The singular absence of the term "apostle" or "apostleship" in this section clinches our objection. Moreover his choice not only of *diakonos* ("minister") but of the word *oikonomia* (rendered "office" in verse 25) is significant, if we grant the cogency of John Reumann's conclusion. After a detailed study of this term ("*Oikonomia*—terms in Paul in comparison with Lucan *Heilsgeschichte*," *New Testament Studies* 13 (1966/67), pp. 147–167) he writes that *apostolos* "emphasizes his commission and authority and mission from God, through revelation. *Oikonomos*, like *doulos* and *diakonos*, emphasizes with great humility the compulsion and grace which marked his special case" (p. 167).

VI

PAUL'S MISSION AND PASTORAL CONCERN

1:24—2:5 *Now I rejoice in my sufferings for your sake, and in my flesh I complete what is lacking in Christ's afflictions for the sake of his body, that is the church,* ²⁵*of which I became a minister according to the divine office which was given to me for you, to make the word of God fully known,* ²⁶*the mystery hidden for ages and generations but now made manifest to his saints.* ²⁷*To them God chose to make known how great among the Gentiles are the riches of the glory of this mystery, which is Christ in you, the hope of glory.* ²⁸*Him we proclaim, warning every man and teaching every man in all wisdom, that we may present every man mature in Christ.* ²⁹*For this I toil, striving with all the energy which he mightily inspires within me.*

2. For I want you to know how greatly I strive for you, and for those at Laodicea and for all who have not seen my face, ²*that their hearts may be encouraged as they are knit together in love, to have all the riches of assured understanding and the knowledge of God's mystery, of Christ,* ³*in whom are hid all the treasures of wisdom and knowledge.* ⁴*I say this in order that no one may delude you with beguiling speech.* ⁵*For though I am absent in body, yet I am with you in spirit, rejoicing to see your good order and the firmness of your faith in Christ.*

PAUL PROCEEDS TO ENLARGE UPON THIS TOPIC OF HIS GENTILE ministry and his concern lest the Colossians should feel in any way neglected by his remoteness from them. Underlying this sensitivity is his passionate desire to warn them not to give way to seductive teaching which would destroy the work of his *alter ego*, Epaphras, in their midst by a turning away from his gospel. He clearly spells out the danger in 2:4.

This section is devoted to a number of important pastoral themes. The apostle expounds his understanding of the stewardship to which God has appointed him (vv. 24-25); then, he defines what this "mystery" involves and how he has fulfilled his task (vv. 26-29); finally, he offers a sort of restrained appeal to Christians whom he does not know on a man-to-man basis by assuring them of his interest and his gladness at their loyalty to his message as though he were personally present among them (2:1-5).

a. Paul's ministry to the Gentiles (1:24, 25)

The sufferings of Paul were evidently a source of embarrassment to the Asian congregations. He alludes to them more than once (Col. 4:3,18; Eph. 3:1,13; Philemon 1). Possibly his being a prisoner was being exploited by his enemies and the false teachers who sought to subvert his teaching. They would stress that he was hardly to be trusted as a God-honoured teacher if the best he could do was to write letters from a prison-cell and not come to visit the Colossians in person. Or perhaps they made much of Paul's sufferings which would destroy any claim to be an accredited religious teacher like the "divine men" of hellenistic religiosity or like the semi-divine gnostic "apostle" (see W. Schmithals, *The Office of Apostle in the Early Church*, ET 1969). So Paul has to give some rationale. The afflictions are not self-chosen nor are they deserved; they are endured "for your sake" (cf. 2 Tim. 2:10). This means not "because I love you," but rather "to your advantage." But how? they might ask.

Paul's answer is less than clear. In fact, verse 24 has laid a cross on would-be interpreters so that the term "exegetical *crux*" is no idle phrase. What is meant by "filling up what is deficient in the afflictions of the Messiah?"

Two preliminary remarks are in order. First, Paul's confession "in my flesh" relates to his bodily sufferings endured in the course of his apostolic ministry on behalf of the churches. A good illustration would be in 2 Corinthians 7:5: "For even when we came into Macedonia, our bodies (literally, our flesh [*sarx*]) had no rest but we were afflicted [same root word as in Col. 1:24] at every turn—fighting without and fear within." The second observation is that his sufferings are calculated to benefit the church, Christ's body. No hint is given that Paul enacted the rôle of saviour or, in some mystical way, identified his own afflictions with the unique, atoning suffering of Christ. The setting of this verse seems determinative and would indicate that Paul's thought is related specifically to his work as pastor rather than to his experience as a "private" individual. To be sure, in that latter capacity he can speak about yearning to enter into the sufferings of Christ (Phil. 3:10),[1] and it is the combination of these verses which has given rise to the idea of Pauline "Christ-mysticism" or the close identity between Christians

---

[1] There is an extended comment on this verse in the present writer's *Epistle to the Philippians* (Tyndale Commentary series), 1959, pp. 49f.

and their Lord in the experience of dying and rising again. But in the present context it is Paul's ministry to the churches which is at the forefront of his mind. The nearest parallel would be in 2 Corinthians 1:4ff., 4:11 which verses pick up the thought that Paul has a special destiny as the apostle to the Gentiles. This was made known to him at the commencement of his missionary service (Acts 9:15,16) and confirmed in the bitter crucible of his labours (e.g., 1 Thess. 3:3f.). But there is a divine purpose in his suffering which is borne for the gospel's sake. Thereby the cause of Christ is advanced (so Acts 14:22) and the church with whom Christ is intimately linked through the apostle as His personal agent is strengthened.

The background of this verse is not easily found, but we may note how Paul's thought about Christ and the church is closely interwoven with his own person and mission. On the Damascus road he came to realize how Christ and His people were one in a most realistic fashion, so that the voice from heaven charged him with attacking the risen Lord Himself (Acts 9:5). Paul never forgot that stinging rebuke, as is evident from 1 Corinthians 8:12; 12:12. On the other side, Paul views both his own ministry and that of his coadjutors as in some way extensions of the Lord's own person— see 2 Corinthians 8:23: "as for our brethren, they are messengers of the churches, the glory of Christ." And see also 1 Corinthians 5:4 where his personal presence by the Spirit among the Corinthian congregation is an actualization of Christ's presence there too.

The application to our verse is given in terms of Paul's sufferings as Christ's special messenger to the Gentile churches. Christ is one with them in their tribulations and hardship in a pagan and hostile world; and Paul as His envoy bears on his heart the pastoral needs of these congregations, supplying "what is lacking in your faith" (1 Thess. 3:10) and in that sense complementing the tally of Messianic sufferings which Christ-and-His-people as the corporate Messianic community have to endure in the world of persecution and duress.

It is a pastoral concern which moves Paul to write thus. Anxious to remove any misunderstanding on the part of the Colossian believers, he offers a justification for his sufferings as a prisoner and his remoteness from the Lycus valley at a time of pressing need. They must see God's hand in these events and perceive that his captivity is for their good in that the Messianic afflictions which

Christ and His people must undergo before the end-time are being carried by him *in persona Christi* and so he is advancing the day of final victory (3:4) which is linked with the success of the Pauline mission (Rom. 11:25f.).[1]

1:25 Paul's determination to show the close link between himself and the Colossian church is continued in verse 25. The key here lies in the noun rendered "divine office" (Greek *oikonomia*). The unusual element of this designation of Paul's ministry is twofold: (a) he entitles himself a servant (*diakonos*) of the universal or ecumenical church and (b) uses a term for his calling which elsewhere is applied to God's saving purpose for the world (Eph. 1:10; 3:9). As in Ephesians 3:2 the high dignity of his mission is here elaborated in a way which can only mean that Paul's summons to be a minister is in keeping with God's plan for the world and he is bidden to execute that plan by the grace which has been conferred upon him. The Colossians are those who have a share in that ecumenical ministry; hence a transferred honour accrues to them as they stand in the shadow of that service to which Paul has been appointed (so Masson, followed by J. Reumann, *NTS*, 13, [1966/67], p. 163). A more effective way of (a) answering charges that his ministry was self-devised, and (b) repelling any idea that the Colossians stood outside the embrace of his interest, could hardly be imagined.

b. Paul's message (1:26–29)

His chief task was "to make the word of God fully known" which is perhaps better rendered by a more literal translation: "to fulfil the word of God." That is, Paul is charged to carry out the divine plan in his life by extending the gospel to the Gentile areas (as in Rom. 15:19). Just what is meant by God's word which he is commissioned to proclaim and obey is then mentioned in a kind of digression (in Dibelius' word).

That Pauline message is expressed in terms of a "mystery," formerly "hidden" but now "revealed." This language may be a conscious borrowing of terms which were being bandied about in Colossae as the false teachers excited the congregation with this

[1] For the Jewish background in terms of Messianic birth-pangs to be suffered in anticipation of the final vindication of God's saints, see E. Best, *One Body in Christ*, 1955, pp. 132–136. G. Delling, *TDNT*, vi, p. 307, interprets the verb *antanapleroun* "to complete" similarly: "Predominant here [in Col. 1:24] is the thought of vicarious filling up with reference to the measure of eschatological affliction laid on the community in a non-mystical but soberly realistic fellowship of its destiny with Christ."

esoteric talk. But there is no need to insist upon this because Paul's earlier writings contain the same group of ideas: I Corinthians 2:6-10; Romans 16:25-27, notably. Indeed there are Jewish examples, both within the Old Testament canon (Dan. 2:28f.) and outside it (1QpHab vii. 4f. The text "concerns the Teacher of Righteousness, to whom God made known all the mysteries of the words of His servants the Prophets: 1QH iv. 27f. "For Thou hast given me knowledge through Thy marvellous mysteries").[1]

1:27 The essence of the mystery in this context is Christ's presence among the Gentiles (v. 27). These people were formerly spiritually under-privileged and separated from God both by their addiction to idolatry and by lying outside the scope of His immediate purpose (Eph. 2:11ff.). That purpose concentrated upon Israel which was a nation "elect for the sake of mankind"·(J. Skinner). But now what was previously concealed is made public—at least to the "saints," i.e. believers (Lohse) who are part and parcel of the Pauline mission. To them has come, through Paul's preaching and ministerial labours, the inestimable knowledge of Christ's presence in their midst, making them no longer outcasts and aliens but "fellow-heirs, members of the same body, and partakers of the promise in Christ Jesus through the gospel" (Eph. 3:6).

Moreover, these converts to Christ through Paul's Gentile ministry are the sign and token that God's saving design is being fulfilled and made real in the world. The Gentile mission is another proof that Paul is God's true servant. Nor need the Colossians feel that Paul restricted his ministry to an élite group within their ranks. The heavy emphasis is verse 28 on the inclusive "every man" (three times repeated) shows how Paul viewed the range of his pastoral interest, and is an overt rebuke to an implied claim by the gnosticizing errorists that religion was restricted to a favoured few, the "perfect ones" (Greek *teleioi*). On the contrary, Paul's declared aim was to "present every man" *teleios* in Christ, that is, to lead him to full acceptance with God on the ground of divine redemption and spiritual maturity and progress. A similar phrase is found in Ephesians 4:13, "a fully grown man," but there the reference is to the full complement of Christians who make up the body of Christ. In the Colossians verse Paul's desire and design is to secure for all the readers the realization of God's purpose for their lives,

---

[1] For a discussion of the Qumran background of "mystery" and its Pauline usage, see J. Coppens in *Paul and Qumran*, 1968, pp. 132-158.

for which both he (verse 29) and Epaphras (4:12) strain every nerve in pastoral solicitude. The verbal connexions between these two sections[1] would confirm our earlier plea that Paul's ministry, while unique as "apostle to the Gentiles," is not an unshared responsibility. Rather both he and the preachers of the Gentile mission are collaborators in a common enterprise.

1:28 The ministry of Paul is described in verse 28 by the employment of three related terms: proclaim, warning, teaching. The object of the first verb is Christ Himself as the Lord of the non-Jewish peoples among which Christ has come to live as the divine glory of the Presence of God (the Shekinah) dwelt among the ancient Hebrew people. In that sense Christ is "the hope of glory"; "glory" meaning the visible presence of Israel's God. That presence is now seen in the face of Jesus Christ (2 Cor. 4:4–6) who embodies and actualizes the invisible God (1:15; cf. John 1:14). The stress here falls on "Christ *in* you." The Greek preposition (*en*) may carry this sense (so Lightfoot) but recent interpreters are agreed that a second meaning, "Christ *among* you" is much to be preferred, as in the identical use of the preposition in John 1:14: "the Word dwelt in our midst, and we beheld his glory." Paul will have more to say on the special character of this revelation in 2:2,3. It is clear, however, that Christ's personal presence is the theme of his Gentile preaching.

"Warning" (Greek *nouthetein*) is a word belonging to New Testament pedagogy, sometimes of a general character (Acts 20:31; cf. 1 Cor. 10:11) and sometimes specifically related to the training of children in the Christian family (Eph. 6:4). Paul's use is directed chiefly to a ministry of admonition, criticism and correction, whether by himself, as at Corinth (1 Cor. 4:14f.) or by church leaders, as at Thessalonica (1 Thess. 5:12, cf. 14). At least one reference is to the disciplining of those who espoused heterodox beliefs (Tit. 3:10), and it may well be that we should discover this background for the present verse, though 3:16 shows how the word can be more generally used of congregational edification.

"Teaching" (Greek *didaskein*) plays a more significant rôle in the epistle. It is used "in a pastoral and ethical sense as a function of Christians in their mutual dealings [in 1:28; 3:16]" (K. H. Rengstorf, *TDNT*, ii, p. 147), though 2:7 gives another side of the coin.

---

[1] 1:29: *agōnizomenos*, as in 4:12;
   1:28: *teleion*, as in 4:12 (*teleioi*);
   2:2 *plerophorias*, as in 4:12 (*peplerophoremenoi*)

Perhaps too 1:28, as it related to Paul's own ministry, carries a more authoritative tone and speaks of his instruction "in all wisdom" as a God-inspired "teacher of the Gentiles" (1 Tim. 2:7). His claim to the possession of "wisdom" may reflect a polemical stance as he opposes the Colossian errorists who were boasting of their superior wisdom.

1:29 Paul's ministry was undertaken in no easy-going spirit. Some emphatic verbs are word-pictures of the cost of his ministry. "I toil" is sometimes found in the setting of his resort to manual labour (1 Thess. 2:9; 1 Cor. 4:12). In the present context the verb is figurative and powerfully denotes the intense concern of Paul in his pastoral attitudes and actions.

An even stronger term follows. "Striving" (Greek *agōnizomenos*) is a verb sometimes used of physical combat (John 18:36: cf. 1 Cor. 9:25) but here again the sense must be metaphorical.[1] It speaks of the need Paul consciously reflects to make every effort in his ministerial responsibility, straining every moral sinew in an exertion which, however, is energized by God's help. The energy for his labour is supplied by God in Christ who gives His servant the strength he needs. Philippians 4:13 is a similar confession, while Philippians 2:13 also blends the twin notions of divine power and human effort which can only hope to succeed as it draws upon that God-given resource.

c. Paul's call to the church (2:1–5)

Paul drives home the lesson of his pastoral involvement in the state of the churches in the Lycus valley of Asia Minor. Though he is physically removed from them by reason of his confinement in prison, he wants to impress upon his readers the seriousness of the situation (v. 4), the need he sees to promote a full understanding of his message (v. 2) and a closing of the ranks in the face of threatening heresy (v. 5). He wants to express his concern in these churches' well-being and to remind them of his continuing care for them (v. 1).

He has spoken generally up to this point. His ministry to the

[1] See V. C. Pfitzner, *Paul and the Agon Motif*, 1967, who argues that (p. 110) "whereas the verb refers to the intensity of all Paul's labours in the service of the Gospel, the noun [in 2:1] introduces the added thought of conflict and struggle against opposition, the new side of his Agon which arises out of his position as a prisoner (4:10)." But this view seems unlikely, as there is no hint in Colossians comparable with Philippians 1:12–30; 2:17, which would suggest that Paul has in mind some personal enemies against whom he has to wrestle. Even more unlikely is Lohmeyer's submission that Paul is conscious of his fate as a martyr.

Gentile churches included the Colossians (1:24a,25b). Now he makes the allusion more pointed and unmistakable. By the use of an introductory form he borrows from the letter-writing conventions of his day—"I want you to know"—he wishes to enforce an important matter (as in 1 Cor. 11:3). This is simply that his pastoral solicitude extends not only to the Gentile congregations he has personally founded and visited, but also to other groups whom he does not know at first-hand. The Colossians fall into the latter category. It is equally for them that Paul expends his energies— by his care, his prayers (he strives [verse 1] as Epaphras does, in a ministry of intercession, 4:12) and by his letters. Hence the reason for the letter he is at present dictating and sending to them.

The Colossian church, however, is not the only congregation in the region. Nearby Laodicea is included, and this church will receive a separate communication (4:16) which will be circulated to the Colossians. They in turn are to pass on their letter to Laodicea. Little is known of that church, though one other letter addressed to them has survived in Revelation 3:14-22. Still other congregations are in Paul's mind, expressed in the phrase "all who have not seen my face." The Greek adds "in the flesh," but this simply underlines the statement that these churches, like the Colossians and Laodiceans, were personally unknown to Paul. Perhaps a church at Hierapolis (also in the Lycus valley, twelve miles distant from Colossae) is in mind in view of 4:13 and indeed some copyists add this place to the text of 2:1; but the phrase is evidently intended to take in all the Gentile churches not of direct Pauline foundation.

2:2,3 Paul wishes for all these Christian groups a true unity in love and a firm adherence to truth, especially concerning the central Pauline doctrine of the real being of God in Christ. That seems to be the main thrust of these verses.

There are several textual and translation problems to complicate the issue. "Knit together" is one way in which the Greek verb *symbibazein* may be taken, and its correctness here is supported by 2:19 where the unity of the church is pictured as the inter-connectedness of the tissues of a human body which is under the control of its head. Love, says the apostle, is like that network of ligaments and tendons which binds all the various members into a unity (so 3:14). On the other hand, the verb can carry a didactic meaning, with the sense of the Vulgate *instructi in caritate* and this meaning of being taught in love is paralleled by the use of the verb in 1 Corinthians 2:16, Acts 9:22; 19:33. It also paves the way here for the transition into "understanding" and "knowledge," which follow. On balance, however, the first-mentioned translation is preferable in the light of the later verses in the letter (so Lohse, Bruce).

There is an appeal to clear-sighted appreciation of theological truth in the second part of Paul's pastoral concern. The object of this "assured knowledge" is given as knowledge of "God's mystery, of Christ." Textual witnesses are divided over the exact wording[1] but the sense is hardly affected. Christ as the image of God (1:15) unlocks the secret of the divine nature and provides the key to the riddle of deity. He stands as the "explanation" (John 1:18; the Greek verb rendered is literally "has given an explanation" of God) of God the Father, as His name stands in grammatical apposition to "God's mystery" in our text. A stanza of Josiah Conder's hymn accurately conveys the rich meaning:—

> True image of the infinite,
> Whose essence is concealed;
> Brightness of uncreated light;
> The heart of God revealed.

To say more about the way Christ reveals the Father, verse 3 continues: "in whom are hid all the treasures of wisdom and knowledge." "Wisdom" and "knowledge" are given in Romans 11:33 as the two constituents of the divine character which human redemption and God's control of history bring into play. There they are coupled, as in verses 2,3, with the word for "riches," and the whole train of ideas and words suggests a conscious indebtedness to the figure of wisdom in Proverbs 2:3ff. (cf. Ecclus. 1:25). Paul is then remarking "that Christ has become to Christians all that the Wisdom of God was, according to the Wisdom literature, and more still" (Moule). He is using an appeal to Jewish sources partly because the false teaching at Colossae on its Jewish side was insisting that Jesus Christ was only one mediator and one source of revelation among many. His counter-insistence is to place an emphasis on "all," declaring that Christ embodied in His inmost being ("hidden" in the sense of "deposited", "stored up") the totality of the divine

---

[1] See for a recent discussion, B. M. Metzger, *The Text of the New Testament*, 1964, pp. 240–242 [1968², pp. 236–36]. The RSV translates the most difficult reading of the text, witnessed by p. 46, B and Hilary. The other variants are evidently attempts at improving this text.

attributes which are represented by those elements in the divine nature in its manward relation: "wisdom" and "knowledge." *2:4* Paul's polemical intention in so naming Christ as the sole repository of what men may know of God's character is all but proved conclusively by the words which follow. "I say this *in order that* no one may delude you." We prefer this way of rendering to that which gives the sense, "What I mean is, nobody is to talk you into error" (Moule, Bruce) or to that which makes the antecedent to "this" the whole paragraph from verse 1 to verse 3 (Masson). The warning against being tricked (a verb found again in the New Testament only at James 1:22: "deceiving yourselves") is clearly one to be heeded in the presence of a determined attempt to do just that by errorists who would employ "beguiling speech," i.e. the power of persuasion (Lohse). For the first time in his letter Paul puts his probing finger on the false notions which were being introduced into the Colossian assembly and identifies their presence. *2:5* If Paul were present in Colossae, he would spare no pains to deal with the menacing situation (as he wished to be at Galatia for a similar purpose, Gal. 4:20). But his imprisonment renders this out-of-the-question and his responsibility for this church is not a direct one. Nonetheless, he has such a vivid sense of his kinship with these readers that he can speak of actually being among them "in spirit." 1 Corinthians 5:3 shows that this is no empty expression but speaks of a presence charged with power. He views approvingly their steadfast intent to close ranks and stand firm, with no yielding to erroneous propaganda. The language he uses is drawn from military formation ("order", "firmness"). So "the apostle is 'with them' as a general standing before his troops and reviewing the battle-lines" (Lohmeyer). And he has much to say by way of commendation and hope that they will not break ranks and lose their oneness (v. 2) in the face of an intruding enemy. This verse suggests that the heresy has not gained much secure ground at Colossae, and that Epaphras' report has been more of a danger on the immediate horizon than of a serious problem already entrenched in the church. But Paul will take no chances, and so launches into a full rebuttal.

VII

THE ANTIDOTE TO ERROR

2:6–15 As therefore you received Christ Jesus the Lord, so live in him, *⁷rooted and built up in him and established in the faith, just as you were taught, abounding in thanksgiving.*

⁸See to it that no one makes a prey of you by philosophy and empty deceit, according to human tradition, according to the elemental spirits of the universe, and not according to Christ. ⁹For in him the whole fulness of deity dwells bodily, ¹⁰and you have come to fulness of life in him, who is the head of all rule and authority. ¹¹In him also you were circumcised with a circumcision made without hands, by putting off the body of flesh in the circumcision of Christ; ¹²and you were buried with him in baptism, in which you were also raised with him through faith in the working of God, who raised him from the dead. ¹³And you, who were dead in trespasses and the uncircumcision of your flesh, God made alive together with him, having forgiven us all our trespasses, ¹⁴having cancelled the bond which stood against us with its legal demands; this he set aside, nailing it to the cross. ¹⁵He disarmed the principalities and powers and made a public example of them, triumphing over them in him.

THESE VERSES TAKE US TO THE HEART OF THE LETTER IN EVERY sense. They lie in the central portion of the text. More importantly, they contain the urging of Paul to allow no room for erroneous ideas (v. 8, which will be elaborated in the paragraph of vv. 16–23) and they offer a full exposition of the Pauline teaching which is an effective counter-attack on the false positions. Paul's pastoral strategy is worth a comment. He goes to the root of the trouble deftly at v. 8, which is then followed by a lengthy statement of the gospel message, both doctrinal (vv. 9,15) and practical (vv. 10–14), in which the answer to error will be discovered if only the Colossians will take time to reflect upon it. Let them recall what they were taught (v. 7) and re-settle their roots in Paul's teaching on Christ the Lord, true God and victor over all evil; and on the nature of the Christian life as an experience of death to evil powers and a rising with Christ to new life, which is not to be compromised by a reversion to pagan ways. Before actually spelling out the precise terms of the heresy, Paul gives a magnificent positive

statement of what the true instruction is, and our interest focuses
with him on worthwhile and eternal truth rather than on some
ephemeral manifestation of error. For this reason, while today the
exact form of the Colossian error is no longer with us, Paul's
positive declarations hold an undiminished fascination and offer a
statement of Christian doctrine which will never become dated.
We learn, too, that defenders of the faith should be more concerned
to accentuate the positive elements in the gospel than to spend their
energies in detecting every slightest flaw and defect in a rival
system.

The appeal in these verses is a double one: Paul recalls the
foundation of the Christian life in the person and work of Jesus
Christ the Lord; and he bids his Colossian friends to apply the
elemental truth they learned in their baptismal instruction (v. 12)
to everyday experience of the life in Christ. These are the two
headings, brought together in v. 6, under which his expostulation is
gathered. He begins by remarking on what "according to Christ"
(v. 8) implies and uses this summary as an antidote to ward off
the perils arising from false teaching, "philosophy . . . according to
human tradition" (v. 8). The two phrases are strictly parallel, as
their common construction shows.

2:6 Tradition can be good or bad. Verse 8 uses it in a pejorative
sense, as something alien to the true word. But its good sense lies
behind the terminology of v. 6. The Colossians had "received"
what had been transmitted to them—in the kerygmatic tradition
of Paul (see 1 Cor. 11:2,23; 15:1,3; Gal. 1:9,12; 1 Thess. 2:13;
4:1; 2 Thess. 3:6 for these verbs which Paul uses as semi-technical
expressions of the way in which the statements of the faith were
communicated from teacher to learner). That tradition was
essentially christological. It spoke of the person and place of Jesus
Christ, His relationship to God and His lordship over the world,
including the church; and it claimed the allegiance and devotion
of those who in faith yielded their lives in an act of commitment,
viz. in baptism.[1] The reason for this emphasis seems clear. "If the
heretical teaching really cast a slur on the universal primacy of
Christ (1:15–20), it was extremely important for the apostle to
remind his Colossian brethren of the lordship of Jesus Christ"

[1] The present writer's *Worship in the Early Church*, 1964, contains chapters on early
Christian confessions and baptismal procedures. "Christ Jesus the Lord" recalls the formula
of Philôippians 2:11, also justifiably credited to a baptismal context.

(Masson). And the appropriate response to that lordship is obedience to Paul's teaching.

The summons—and it is noteworthy that Paul's language changes gear at this point and shifts into the mood of command and exhortation—is: "so live in him". In fact, the verb is one of movement. "Walk" (Greek *peripateite*) is a term often found in Paul of the outworking of the new life in Christ, especially in a baptismal context (Rom. 6:4: cf. 8:4; Gal. 5:16), though the metaphor comes ultimately from the Jewish world ("walk" = conduct your life, as in 1:10). The inference then is clear: you have begun the Christian life by a commitment to Christ Jesus 'as Lord, having confessed him as such (Rom. 10:9; 1 Cor. 12:3). Now make good that profession and shape your life by living under this lordship, which excludes all lesser rival loyalties, especially to alien principles. *2:7* Further allusion to the baptismal instruction ("you were taught") reminds them of the need to be firmly attached to their first vows. Paul mixes his metaphors by switching from the language of horticulture ("rooted" as a tree sending down strong roots) to that of building ("built up," a present tense to denote continuous growth in contrast to the perfect participle of "rooted," meaning "once for all" settled in a fixed spot, not to be up-rooted). He makes the same swift transition of thought in 1 Corinthians 3:9: "you are God's husbandry, you are God's edifice." A third verb adds to a pardonable confusion of thought, "established" (as a legal agreement is confirmed and ratified by both parties: for this background, see H. Schlier, *TDNT*, i, p. 602) "in the faith," or by your faith. This confirmation as it is ratified gives proof of the believers' firm roots and solid structure. Abraham's case (in Rom. 4:19,20) is a good example of a believer whose faith grew strong and reached the level of conviction (21: the same verb as underlies Paul's noun in 2:2, translated "*assured* understanding").

One final admonition rounds off this stirring call to Christian stability. Somewhat surprisingly Paul invites them to overflow with thankfulness. Yet on reflection we may add that this is an important part of the Christian's response to the grace of God. His hold on divine realities is not the full picture. He holds firm because he is grasped by God's power and love; hence, the most appropriate attitude is not one of firm determination not to yield nor of foolish self-confidence that imagines it can never fall (1 Cor. 10:12), but a grateful acknowledgement of God's goodness and protection.

Another possible interpretation is offered by E. Lohse. This would read into Paul's term *eucharistia* not so much the notion of general thanksgiving as the praise of Christ expressed in hymnic confession to Him as Lord. Paul is thereby calling his Colossian brethren to abide firm by the confessional statement directed to the exalted Christ which he has quoted in 1:15-20 (1:12 uses the verb expressing "praise"). This is suggestive, but our reserve is demanded by Paul's word "abounding" which is strange-sounding as a call to remain attached to a hymnic creed.

2:8 This verse sounds the warning note in clearest terms. Up to this point in the letter, Paul has been hinting that there is an insidious false teaching which needs to be resisted. Now he comes out into the open, and unmasks it. His warning is not directed to a general situation only; rather he pinpoints the menace in an individualizing way by the use of a construction which singles out a particular teacher: "See to it that a certain individual (Greek *tis*) does not capture you. . . ." He would be known to the Colossian readers, though Paul does not precisely name him (cf. Gal. 5:10).

The Colossians are put on their guard against his attempts to carry them off as a prize of war (so Arndt-Gingrich render the verb). The expression is a dramatic one suggesting a violent assault which would rob the church of a most precious commodity, the truth of God, though Paul writes of the Colossians themselves as being carried away. The rival teaching which is offered in exchange for the gospel is branded by Paul as "philosophy." The apostle uses it first in its neutral sense (literally, "love of wisdom") but proceeds immediately to pass judgement on the word by the phrase "empty deceit." So, that phrase is not something different from "philosophy," but it is Paul's way of exposing the folly of a teaching which would oust his gospel by proclaiming a system which is man-devised and which exalts the celestial powers ("the elemental spirits of the universe") to a rank of mediatorship and worship. The effect of this teaching would be to set up a rival to Christ as the sole way of access to God and to lead the victims of this pernicious propaganda to venerate these angelic spirits as a means of securing salvation (2:18). For Paul this is deadly heresy. He has already indicated the error of it in his earlier insistence (1:16,20) that these angelic hierarchies and astral powers were both created by the cosmic Christ and brought into subjection to Him by His reconciling work. There is therefore no justification whatever for a continued recognition to be given to them—and certainly no valid reason why they should rob the Colossians of their hope in Christ. The precise sense to be given to the phrase "elemental spirits" (Greek *ta stoicheia*) is discussed in the Introduction.

2:9 On the contrary, if the Colossians wish to be reassured about the sufficiency of Christ in His office as mediator between God and the world, the answer lies in Paul's next statement. It is "in him"—and not in angelic intermediaries—that the divine fulness dwells in its totality. Nor is the Christ simply another spiritual aeon or cosmic cipher. He embodies the fulness of God in His human person; the fulness dwells in Him "bodily," whether in the sense "really, not symbolically" (cf. 2:17) or "really, not apparently"— as though Paul were rebutting a denial of Jesus' full humanity by insisting on His "complete manhood and not a manhood which is simply a cover for deity" (E. Schweizer, *TWNT*, vii, p. 1075) or "corporeally, as the head of the universe and the church, not in a way which would make Him one repository of deity among several others." The latter view seems preferable in the light of Paul's subsequent remark that the fulness of God is both found in Christ as the head and shared by the church, His body which has come to fulness of life in Him.

Paul is using strong language here to assert the uniqueness of the cosmic and the church's Lord. "Fulness" (Greek *plērōma*) was evidently a term in current vogue at Colossae, where a major item in the novel teaching was the practical solution to the problem of crossing the gap between the high God and the universe. A system of intermediate links between the two made up the *plērōma*. Paul accepts this premise and the need for mediation, but quickly demolishes any spurious claims to a hierarchy of intermediaries (the aeons) by roundly asserting that all the *plērōma* is in Christ; and moreover this fulness is one of the divine essence so that Christ's office as go-between is perfect since He is true God, true man. His unique relationship to God is expressed by "deity" (*theotēs*, not *theiotēs* used in Rom. 1:20. The latter means divine qualities over against the stronger term meaning divine essence, God in himself "an abstract noun for God himself" [Arndt-Gingrich]). On the other side, His real sharing our humanity in a sense which does not make the incarnation a charade is indicated by one meaning attached to "bodily." The fulness of the Godhead came to live in a truly human life which was lived out in our world as the perfect "image of God" in a human person (1:15).

2:10 What Christ's office is as the embodiment of "all the fulness of God" is now revealed. He stands as head over both the universe ("the head of all rule and authority") and the church whose members as His body have entered into the realization of His unique work as mediator and reconciler. The same double reference is found in 1:15–20, especially at verse 18.

Paul is obviously making capital out of the words for "fulness:" "fulness of life" answers to "fulness of deity"; and "bodily" is the link-term uniting what He is in Himself and what He has become to His people, His body. It is not easy to comment further to draw out this play on words. Paul is saying: Christ bodies forth the divine *plērōma;* and you as His body have a share in that fulness. Together He and the church form one indissoluble entity, the whole Christ.

2:11–15 This paragraph elaborates the theme of "fulness of life in him" and shows how the Pauline readers came to its conscious realization. Certain steps are clearly marked out, and to that extent the author's thought is clear. It is when we press the details that our exegetical troubles begin.

In simplest outline, Paul is directing attention to such memorable experiences of the Christian's life as baptism (**vv. 11,12**), new life in a spiritual awakening from death (v. 13), forgiveness and a new standing before God (v. 14), because Christ overcame all our enemies and accusers (v. 15).

The key-phrase in this entire section lies in verse 11: "but putting off the body of flesh." This is Paul's way of recalling the Christian's initiation to his new life in Christ. The noun rendered "putting off" (Greek *apekdusis*) suggests a clean break with a past life, though the metaphor is one of disrobing and stripping off an unwelcome set of garments. *"Put off* the old nature with its practices" (3:9) shows the practical side of this transformation, using the cognate verb and in reference to Christians' new way of life. The background allusion to a baptismal action when the new convert divested himself of his clothes for baptism and re-clothed himself after the rite is very suggestive, especially in the light of Galatians 3:27. Moreover, Paul elsewhere makes the contrast between "circumcision" (in the Old Testament) and its replacement in the New Testament by Christian faith-response (Rom. 4:9–12) certified in baptism, which is explicitly mentioned at verse 12 of our chapter.

So far the thought is clear, and our interpretation requires that we take "the body of flesh" to mean the believer's unregenerate nature which would tyrannize over him and hold him in bondage. On this view, "body of flesh" is virtually the same as "body of this death" (Rom. 7:24) or "body of sin" (Rom. 6:6). From this tyranny deliverance is promised by a cutting free from bondage, a release symbolized in the Christian counterpart of circumcision, a "circumcision made without hands", i.e. one which is wholly the work of God. He sets the believer loose from the fetters of his old nature as the believer enters into a faith-union with Christ, dies in baptism to his old nature (Rom. 6:4–11) and rises to newness of life in Him. Christians henceforth are called to yield themselves to God "as men who have been brought from death to life" (Rom. 6:13), a life which is Christ's risen life now made available to check the downward pull of the old nature whose dominion has been broken when they responded in faith to God's call and sealed that response in baptism.

On another showing, however, a more subtle cross-movement of the apostle's thought is possible. This view (championed by C. A. Anderson Scott, *Christianity according to St. Paul*, [1927=1961], pp. 36f.) is governed by two preliminary convictions: first, it wishes to give full value to the Pauline phrase "in the circumcision of Christ." This is held to mean, not a spiritual counterpart to circumcision which belongs to the Christian dispensation, but the circumcision which Christ Himself underwent. To the question, when did this occur? the answer (a second point) is discovered in 2:15. The RSV disguises the presence of the verb from which "putting off" in verse 11 derives. "He disarmed (lit. stripped off: Greek *apekdusamenos*) the principalities and powers." By His death on the cross, Christ dealt a mortal blow to His spiritual foes and passed from under their control by forcing them to submit to Him after they had "engineered" His death; and so He "reconciled" them by drawing the sting of their hostility (1:20).

This reading of the text is dramatic and exciting. Paul is consciously appealing to what Christ did in His saving work. He stripped off all alien tyranny represented by the spiritual forces of the unseen world which tried to hold Him captive (1 Cor. 2:6–8). In that submission to them at death and victory over them at the resurrection, Christ also represented His people. In that sense when He was victorious over His enemies, they were victorious over the same set of alien spirit-powers. The sacramental means by which His victory becomes theirs is baptism, in which personal faith is a vital ingredient (v. 12 it is "*by* faith" and "*in* baptism" that the believer's new life is begun, as Masson aptly remarks). And the risen Lord imparts His own life and plenitude to His church which is risen with Him (3:1), and as such called to make a daily affirmation of freedom from the evil powers which work on frail human nature to pull it down (3:9). This second interpretation coheres with this apostle's thought throughout the letter, and should be preferred, however strange the drama seems to us as a cosmic, dualistic struggle. See further Additional Note C, pp. 82–87.

More easily comprehended is the second picture of conversion: it is a passage from death to life (v. 13). "Dead in trespasses" matches a similar, if longer, expression in Ephesians 2:1. But the addition "the uncircumcision of your flesh" will mean that the Colossians were Gentile and before their incorporation into God's people lay outside the scope of His covenant mercy (as in Eph. 2:11,12). Such was their plight. Two areas of need are covered. Morally they were cut off from the life of God as alienated sinners; and religiously they stood afar off from God's presence as an outcast and disadvantaged people.

Now all this has changed, and a new order has been introduced with Christ's coming. Ephesians 2:5 repeats the same idea, that God has raised the Gentile people to new life with Christ; our text adds in the explanatory clause that He has forgiven us all our trespasses. The latter is evidently Paul's personal comment since he identifies himself ("us all") with his erstwhile pagan readers (contrast Eph. 4:32, though the textual authorities oscillate between "you," and "us").

The meaning of forgiveness is illustrated by the use of vivid picture-language. The "bond" is that of an I.O.U. signifying a debt to be paid.[1] In that regard it stood "against us." What exactly does Paul have in mind? How does the next phrase "with its legal demands" fit in? And how is Christ's action in setting aside the bond by nailing it to His cross to be related to the general picture? If we work backwards from the reference to the action of removing the legal document, it would appear that it was not the law *per se*

---

[1] One familiar example of a *cheirographon* as an I.O.U. promising repayment is Paul's note to Philemon (verse 19). Other examples are given by A. Deissmann, *Light from the Ancient East*, 1927, pp. 334ff.

which Christ abolished (Paul never so speaks; the nearest he gets to this is Rom. 10:4 or Gal. 2:19) but that aspect of the law which was against us, i.e. its denunciation of the law-breaking sinner. Of this aspect he speaks in Galatians 3:13 under the phrase "the curse of the law."

The content of the phrase "which was against us" is then to be read as the "legal demands" (Greek *dogmata:* so E. Percy, pp. 88–90). It was by these strict requirements that the law became an instrument of condemnation. But the obedient Christ endured that curse on sinners' behalf (Gal. 3:13; 2 Cor. 5:21) and so "cancelled the bond" in its judgemental aspect. This sense of the law's demands which bring condemnation is seen in 2:20 where judgement is being passed on the Colossians for their failure to measure up to the heretics' code of rules and regulations.

The way in which Paul can closely identify Christ's self-sacrifice with the body of flesh, representing human sinfulness, has suggested to some recent interpreters[1] a new line in regard to our understanding of the bond (Greek *cheirographon*) that was inimical to us. There is a difficulty with the traditional view, viz. that it is awkward to equate a certificate of indebtedness signed by men with a divine exhibition of condemnation in the bond which is nailed to the cross.

There is evidence, drawn from the Old Testament and Jewish literature, to show that the idea of a book of works kept by God and recording all men's sins was familiar. The actual term *cheirographon* is used of this book in an anonymous Jewish apocalyptic writing, dated in first century B.C. Here the book is held by the accusing Angel who notes down all the seer's sins. The seer asks that they may be wiped out. There is another book containing the seer's good deeds; and Paul's addition of "which was against us" may serve as an identification of the book of evil works.

If this notion of a book of indictment presented by a grand inquisitor at the heavenly court lies in the background of our text, it paves the way for the view that the bond was not a certificate of debt signed by men but one presented by malevolent spirits. Then the "legal demands" may have nothing to do with the Mosaic law, but may stand for the ordinances (Greek *dogmata*) which form

---

[1] O. A. Blanchette, "Does the *Cheirographon* of Col. 2,14 represent Christ Himself?" *Catholic Biblical Quarterly* 23, 1961, pp. 306–12; A. J. Bandstra, *The Law and the Elements of the World. An Exegetical Study in Aspects of Paul's Teaching*, n.d. [about 1964], pp. 158ff.

the basis of the angelic indictment, viz. that man is fleshly and unspiritual and out of harmony with the divine, a typical gnostic indictment of mankind.

Christ assumed a human body in His incarnation and took that body to the cross, also bearing our sins and becoming identified with man the sinner in His death (2 Cor. 5:21; Gal. 3:13; Rom. 8:3). This is Blanchette's argument to link *cheirographon* with Christ's body bearing our sins. The gnostic *Gospel of Truth*—20:23ff. speaks of Jesus taking (? wearing) that Book as His own; being nailed to a cross where He affixed the ordinance of the Father to the cross. Bandstra rightly supports the sense "wearing" since the text goes on to say: "Having divested himself of these perishable rags (His flesh), he clothed himself with incorruptibility, which it is impossible for anyone to take away from him" (20:34 R. McL. Wilson's translation).[1]

The association of "wearing" and "setting aside" recalls the previous verse (v. 11) where Christ divested Himself of His body of flesh on the cross (2:15). Christians repeat this experience sacramentally when they accept the "circumcision of Christ" and are united with Him in His death and victory. The result is the same as that given in Romans 6:6: "Knowing this, that our old nature was crucified (with Christ) that the body of sin may be done away"— a possibility whose antecedent must be that Christ became one with our sin, "wore" it as a garment in His human body and so accepted responsibility for it on our behalf when the angelic accuser levelled its charge against us. His body was nailed to the cross; our debt was discharged by Another; and the accusing voice of evil powers (cf. Zech. 3:1ff.; Rev. 12:10) silenced.

H. C. G. Moule quotes the following poem:
> He gave me back the bond;
> It was a heavy debt;
> And as He gave, He smil'd, and said,
> "Thou wilt not Me forget."
> He gave me back the bond;
> The seal was torn away;
> And as He gave, He smil'd and said,
> "Think thou of Me alway."

---

[1] For a recent assessment of the evidence from the *Gospel of Truth* (20:22–28) as it bears upon Jesus' redeeming work in gnostic understanding, see now Cullen I. K. Story, *The Nature of Truth in "the Gospel of Truth" and in the writings of Justin Martyr*, 1970, pp. 128–134.

It is a bond no more,
But it shall ever tell
All that I owed was fully paid
By my Emmanuel.

Cancelling the certificate of indebtedness and nailing it to His cross go together, though it is not certain just how the latter action referring to the historical crucifixion of Jesus bears upon the wiping out (the Greek verb *exaleiphein* means to rub out, wipe away and so obliterate from sight, as writing on wax or a slate was removed) of sin's debt. Dibelius-Greeven suggest that the bond is like the *titulus* or sentence of condemnation which was posted over the criminal's head as he died on the gibbet (John 19:20). So the crucified Christ assumed our tale of guilt and made it His own responsibility in His sinless and so vicarious death. Against this, "there seems to be no evidence for the alleged custom of cancelling a bond by piercing it with a nail" (Moule).

The effective action seems more to lie in the removal of a list of sins by wiping it clean. For this the Septuagint version of Isaiah 43:25 provides some anticipation: "I am the one who wipes out (Greek *exaleiphōn*) your iniquities and I will not remember them." In the Jewish service for New Year there is a preparatory litany of ten days during which the prayer *Abinu Malkenu* is recited. This takes its name from the opening invocation: "Our Father, our King!" and two consecutive lines run:

Our Father, our King! blot out our transgressions,
    and make them pass away before thine eyes
Our Father, our King! erase in thine abundant mercies
    all the records of our guilt.

The nailing of this document, now wiped clear of all its accusations, is then a subsequent action suggesting "an act of triumphant defiance in the face of those blackmailing powers" (F. F. Bruce) who were threatening the Colossians in the heretics' system.

Paul continues with the message of Christ's triumph. The spirit-forces which accused you (he is saying) Christ has finally defeated, having divested Himself of their clinging attack. He stripped away their rule and showed them up for what they were—usurpers and tyrants, domineering over human beings and making them the plaything of fate and iron necessity in subservience to an astrological cult. His cross was the scene of the public exposure—and of Christ's resounding triumph.

This line of interpretation gives full weight to this Greek participle rendered, "He divested" (*apekdusamenos* cf. verse 11). The voice is middle, suggesting that He stripped off these powers from Himself. Other translators (notably RSV) follow another line of explanation. This gives a different sense to the verb, now rendered "disarmed" (Arndt-Gingrich), the middle voice being used in a figurative way to denote the personal interest of the one who acts (so A. Oepke, *TDNT*, ii, p. 319). E. Lohse objects to this translation on the score that the evil powers have been stripped of their rule and so exposed to ridicule, the verb indicating the "divestment of dignity rather than despoiling of weapons" (so *TDNT*, ii, p. 31 n. 2).

One further action also high-lights the way in which Christ's victory-in-death disgraced the would-be conquerors. He not only made a public spectacle of them but led them in a triumphal procession as the defeated enemy. "Triumphing over them in him" is a phrase which uses a verb by which Roman writers describe the victory march of a returning general. Behind him, in chains were dragged the enemy captured in the war. In this bold picture Paul is recalling the utmost degradation of these evil forces which conspired to bring Christ to His cross. In a surprising reversal of fortune, He turned the tables on them and led them bound as He mounted the cross. "The paradox of the crucifixion is thus placed in the strongest light—triumph in helplessness and glory in shame. The convict's gibbet is the victor's car" (Lightfoot).

Additional Note C:

INTERPRETING COLOSSIANS 2:11–13

The few verses which are contained in the section which begins at 2:8 are worthy of separate treatment. 2:11–13 have assumed a prominent place in recent discussions because they pose certain exegetical difficulties for the Pauline expositor; and also they are frequently appealed to in treatises which deal with the apostolic teaching on baptism and Christian initiation. In the following note we will attempt to indicate what the problems and possibilities of solution are, though all commentators confess that it is an intricate passage.

There is a clearly demonstrated continuity in Paul's thought which begins at verse 9 with a statement of Christ's person as the exclusive embodiment of the divine fulness; then (v. 10) he goes to declare that the Colossians have entered upon an experience of "fulness of life" by their union with Christ, since they are "in Him" and so set free from the tyranny of all evil spirit-beings ("every rule and authority" in the celestial regions). Now comes the third term in the series, linked by "in whom" (v. 11) and intended to show how, on an experimental basis, the Colossian Christians escaped from the mesh of their past bondage and came to be united with Christ who set them free.

To explain the nature of the new life, Paul makes use of three figures of speech: circumcision, burial, and resurrection. As the climax and outcome of this transcript of Christian experience, he describes the awakening to newness of life which accompanied the readers' being raised up "with Christ" (v. 13). In this way he is preparing the ground for the statement in 3:1–4 which makes ample use of the same prepositional phrase. In that sense, as R. Schnackenburg (*Baptism in the Thought of St. Paul*, ET 1964, pp. 69–73) notes, the phrase "with Christ" is the exegetical key to the present passage.

Each of the three terms mentioned above has presented its own problem, and together they stand in some sort of relation to the transformation wrought in Christian conversion, the rite of baptism and the exercise of faith. How to relate these concepts and to draw them into a composite picture is exactly the issue before us.

(a) Circumcision

This term refers to the Jewish ceremony, involving a minor surgical operation which came to play an important rôle in the nation's self-awareness as the people of God. It seems originally to have been a puberty rite, connected with pre-marriage customs (Gen. 34; Ex. 4:24–26). But later it took on the meaning of a sign of incorporation into the life and identity of the Jewish community (Gen. 34:14–16; Ex. 12:47,48). Above all, it took an honoured place as the token and seal of the covenant which God made with Abraham and his family (Gen. 17:9–14; Rom. 4:11). At the time of the Babylonian exile when Israel lived among a pagan people, circumcision served as a badge of identification, and still later extreme measures of Maccabean zeal in proselytizing among surrounding nations (e.g. Edom) made much of the rite by forcibly circumcizing the captive peoples, according to Josephus' record. Conversely, Syrian persecution of the Jews in the second century B.C. showed itself in expressly forbidding the practice of the rite among the faithful pietists in the land. A final chapter in the history of circumcision came to be written in the way that, in New Testament times, unusual importance was ascribed to the blood shed at the ceremony. In this Rabbinic tradition Exodus 4:24–26 played a decisive part, and the Rabbis set the blood of circumcision alongside the blood of the Passover as of equal importance. Thus they brought together the idea of entering into the covenant community and the sacrificial value of blood in a way that, according to G. Vermes ("Baptism and Jewish Exegesis: New Light from Ancient

Sources" *NTS* 4 [1957–58], pp. 308–319) anticipated Paul's linking of circumcision/baptism and redemption in the Colossian texts.

But (we may enquire at this point) what is the reason for Paul's appeal to circumcision which, though given a new meaning ("made without hands"), is used as a term to denote and describe the reality the Colossians had found in their new life in Christ? Various answers are forthcoming.

(i) For some (R. Meyer, *TDNT*, vi, p. 82; G. Delling, *Die Taufe im Neuen Testament*, [1963], pp. 124f.; J. Jeremias, *Infant Baptism in the First Four Centuries*, [ET 1960], pp. 39,47) the equation of circumcision and baptism is the point of transition in Paul's thought. In this view he is arguing that Christian baptism as the rite of initiation into the new Israel as a covenant community replaces the former ceremony, and the "circumcision which belongs to Christ" is consciously set over against the circumcision that belongs to the old dispensation (so Lightfoot).

There is every reason for refusing this identification as has been demonstrated by such writers as H. H. Rowley (*The Unity of the Bible* [1953] pp. 157ff.) and G. W. H. Lampe (*The Seal of the Spirit* [1951] pp. 56,62,85). The latter comments that circumcision is not likened to baptism by New Testament writers, but contrasted with it (p. 83). There are additional arguments against this view drawn from the ceremonies of Jewish proselyte admission which included both circumcision and baptism, and from the New Testament practice itself (1 Tim. 6:12; Acts 16:1–3; Timothy was both baptized and circumcized). Besides which, Paul never says to his Jewish opponents, "Our baptism is a more effective ceremony than your circumcision" (J. D. G. Dunn, *Baptism in the Holy Spirit* [1970] p. 154).

(ii) A much more convincing case can be made for the view that Paul is contrasting the outward, physical rite of circumcision with that to which it pointed forward, viz. a spiritual renewal of the heart. The middle term is then the prophetic anticipation and pledge (in Deut. 10:16; 30:6; Jer. 4:4: contrast Jer. 9:26) that God would in the future offer His people a new covenant in which His law would be written on the human spirit (Jer. 31:31–34; Ezek. 36:26,27) and in which the motive power of obedience would be supplied by the Holy Spirit (cf. *Odes of Solomon* 11:1–3 "The Most High circumcized me by His Holy Spirit"). This is the "inward circumcision of the heart" as in Romans 2:28f. and Philippians 3:3 (so Lampe, p. 56) which is "experienced by the initiate when he becomes a Christian" by "participation in the circumcision of Christ" (Dunn, p. 153) or by "putting away the flesh" (i.e. by God's action in destroying the tap-root of sin, so Masson, p. 125f.). Paul's intention is to expose the hollow mockery of any promise made to give man deliverance from evil which does not depend on the renewal of his inner life, the gift of the Spirit's dynamic and the conquering of the gravitational pull of the "flesh". his unredeemed self-life. Baptism is the symbolic and sacramental witness to this spiritual renovation by which a believer's old nature is renewed as it expresses visibly his inward and spiritual union with Christ and so marks the commencement of his membership in the new covenant of grace.

(iii) An extension of this interpretation centres upon the objective saving reality to which both circumcision (as a promise) and baptism (as the fulfilment of that to which the inward circumcision pointed forward) bore witness. This is G. R. Beasley-Murray's line of reasoning (Baptism in the New Testament [1962], pp. 152f.). For him the allusion in the phrase "the circumcision of Christ" is meant to draw attention to Christ's death as the God-appointed way through which believers are set free in their conversion experience. Baptism is not in view; indeed, he argues, it does not come into the picture until verse 12 ("buried with him in baptism"). This view is hard to accept, chiefly because it provides no reason for Paul's recourse to the strange phrases he uses. Would the Colossian readers make the intended connexion of thought, "circumcision of Christ" = His death; "you were circumcised" = you shared in the benefits of that sacrifice, unless there was some reason hidden in the background of the Colossian situation?

(iv) We may submit that Paul' coinage of the terms he employs and his appeal to circumcision is explicable on the assumption that the heretics (on the Jewish side) were advocating the necessity of circumcision and possibly making much of a sacrificial element in their cultus. They may even have devised a baptismal or initiatory rite to rival that of apostolic practice, and promised to those who accepted it a way of life based on the features mentioned in 2:23. Paul counters this mock sacrament by asserting that Christian baptism has no need to be supplemented or replaced in this manner. When the Colossians responded to the Pauline preaching and fastened their hopes on Christ they became united to Him in an experience which combined both "the objective relation of Christ's death to baptism and the believer's subjective confession thereto in the consigning of his 'old nature' to death" (G. R. Beasley-Murray, "Baptism in the Epistles of Paul," Christian Baptism, ed. A. Gilmore [1959], p. 140) And this new beginning stands in direct antithesis to its rival claim. The contrast is made by A. W. Argyle, "'Outward' and 'Inward' in Biblical Thought," Exp T, 68, 1956-57, p. 198 between "baptism regarded as a physical rite in which the use of hands was prominent . . . and inward baptism, spiritual, regenerative, which is made without hands and infinitely more important than the outward rite considered by itself." This would support the suggestion of a rival initiation-rite at Colossae, which Paul has in view in his polemic.

(b) Burial

The reason for the unrivalled excellence of the promise of new life made in the apostolic announcement lies in the profound significance of baptism as a burial with Christ in His death. Paul has to remind the church at Rome of this teaching (Rom. 6:4ff.) as a counter-statement to the false deduction that the Christian is free to sin at will but here his purpose is different. Indeed, the present text may well be an earlier statement of what Romans 6:3: "Do you not know . . .?" acknowledges to be traditional teaching in the churches, intended to draw out and accentuate some salient features which needed emphasis in view of the special situation at Colossae. In particular Paul stresses the death of Christ as a basic theological datum needful as a protest against an incipient denial of a real incarnation and a historical death. Redemption, Paul avers, is accomplished by His acceptance of a "body of flesh" (1:23) and a death on the cross (1:20). But in that hour of seeming defeat He triumphed over His enemies (2:14,15); and believers who are thus identified with Him in that death re-presented and re-enacted in their baptism are assured of their freedom from malevolent powers, which He overcame in death. Burial, in this context, can mean only the completeness and reality of Christ's death as a surrender to God's will in an ultimate obedience (as in Phil 2:8). This is preferable to an alternative understanding which sees the submission to be to evil powers, for 2:15 says plainly that He overcame them on the cross, i.e. before His burial. Paul must be stressing the burial because he has the baptismal actions in mind, and recalling how the believer is submerged in the rite with his body buried momentarily under the water. This is symbolic of the death of his old nature, which is left in the grave as his new nature is raised to newness of life (Rom. 6:4). The application of this summons comes in 2:20: You died to the spirits which tried to enslave Christ (cf. 3:3, 9), and in 3:10: You have put on the new nature, alive unto God.

(c) Resurrection

The third member of the triad of metaphors is resurrection (v. 12b). It is not clear whether Paul's relative clause, beginning with the Greek words *en ho* should be taken to refer back to "baptism" or to a more distant antecedent in the name of "Christ." The alternative renderings are: "in baptism you were also raised with him through faith" and "in Christ (i.e. in union with Him) you were also raised with him through faith." Many expositors (see Dunn, pp. 154f.) prefer the second inter-pretation in spite of the awkwardness of the translation "*in whom* you were also raised *with him*"; they do so on the ground that Paul is thinking of the Christian's share in Christ as the risen one. Christ is the principal theme throughout, and Paul is not contemplating a picture of believers emerging from the baptismal water under the figure of a resurrection.

But the case against this view (stated by G. R. Beasley-Murray, *Baptism in the New Testament*, pp. 153f.) is compelling, and we should incline to the belief that Paul does directly associate the believer's experience of a spiritual resurrection to new life with the imagery of an emergence from baptism. To be sure, the extra parallelism of "raised with Him" = newness of life, does mark an advance on the (pre-Pauline) teaching of Romans 6, and we should suspect a reason for it. W. L. Knox (*St. Paul and the Church of the Gentiles* [1939], p. 149) thought that the heretical teachers gave baptism only a negative value as a cleansing of past sins and insisted that for further progress their prescriptions were needed. Paul rebuts this suggestion by his affirmation of the adequacy of apostolic baptism, "which was not only a 'death' (to past sin) but also a 'rising again' (to a new life). Thus the Colossian asceticism was mistaken: no rite other than baptism was necessary" (W. F. Flemington, *The New Testament Doctrine of Baptism* [1948], p. 62).

There is one further point to be observed. Paul safeguards himself from misunderstanding by the inserting of the phrase "through faith in the working of God who raised him from the dead." To have written simply, "in your baptism you were also raised with him (Christ)" or even "through baptism" (as he does in Rom. 6:4) might well have suggested the idea of a magical transformation effected simply by the submission to the rite, just as it could be erroneously imagined that circumcision *per se* worked automatically to ensure a place of salvation within Israel's community. Paul knew, however, that the true Israelite needed to make good his circumcision by a life of obedience and devotion to God and His law (Rom. 2:25–29; 1 Cor. 7:19; Gal. 6:15). So Christian baptism which answers to the spiritual circumcision which Christ's redemption achieved requires personal acknowledgment and acceptance on the part of those who are baptized. This means the indispensability of faith directed not to the rite itself but to the God who works in the "sacrament," applies the saving efficacy of the death and resurrection of Christ in which believers died and were raised, and places them in that sphere of divine life in which sin is conquered (Rom. 6:7,9–11). Henceforth, the Christians at Colossae are called to become in their moral conduct what they already are "in Christ" (1:2,13), and this can be realized only by their continuing faith-union with God in Him. The teaching here picks up the earlier strains in the letter that reconciliation and redemption are accomplished by personal activity (on God's part no less than on man's), not by a non-moral, automatic fiat, as in much gnostic thought (see earlier, pp. 49, 57).

VIII

DEFENCE OF CHRISTIAN LIBERTY

2:16—3:4 *Therefore let no one pass judgement on you in questions of food and drink or with regard to a festival or a new moon or a sabbath.* [17]*These are only a shadow of what is to come: but the substance belongs to Christ.*

[18]*Let no one disqualify you, insisting on self-abasement and worship of angels, taking his stand on visions, puffed up without reason by his sensuous mind,* [19]*and not holding fast to the Head, from whom the whole body, nourished and knit together through its joints and ligaments, grows with a growth that is from God.*

[20]*If with Christ you died to the elemental spirits of the universe, why do you live as if you still belonged to the world? Why do you submit to regulations,* [21]"*Do not handle, Do not taste, Do not touch*" [22](*referring to things which all perish as they are used), according to human precepts and doctrines?* [23]*These have indeed an appearance of wisdom in promoting rigor of devotion and self-abasement and severity to the body, but they are of no value in checking the indulgence of the flesh.*

3. *If then you have been raised with Christ, seek the things that are above, where Christ is, seated at the right hand of God.* [2]*Set your minds on things that are above, not on things that are on earth.* [3]*For you have died, and your life is hid with Christ in God.* [4]*When Christ who is our life appears, then you also will appear with him in glory.*

THIS LENGTHY AND INVOLVED SECTION FALLS INTO TWO PARTS answering to a statement of what was being introduced as heresy at Colossae (2:16–23) and a clarion call (begun at 2:20) by the apostle which summons his readers to act upon the teaching they have received from his representatives, notably Epaphras (3:1–4). Our knowledge of the "Colossian heresy" (as Lightfoot termed it), at the most fragmentary and indirect, is derived from this passage, and our curiosity is aroused by a desire to know wherein its spell and appeal lay. But we are hindered by the cryptic nature of this part of the letter. Some verses are so tightly constructed (notably vv. 18,21,23) that their clear sense is not possible to the modern interpreter. One further complication is that, on occasion, Paul seems to be citing the actual wording of the heretical slogans (clearly in v. 21; and probably in vv. 18,23) before giving a judgement on their pernicious character. Ancient writers did not use quotation-marks or footnotes, so there is no certainty in this regard, and our knowledge of the actual language of the propaganda is at best inferential.

The whole passage is best described as a "Defence of Christian liberty" (so Masson). This writer aptly remarks on the close connexion between doctrine and practice. False notions about the person and work of Christ (denounced in 2:8-15) have their inevitable corollary in strange aberrations on the practical level. Paul then proceeds to show the folly of any course of *action* based on wrong theological premises. He has pointed out in clear terms the real nature of the specious doctrine which is being taught at Colossae: it is nothing less than "philosophy, empty deceit" (2:8). It is man-devised and caught in bondage to "elemental spirits" which stand in diametrical opposition to Christ. Indeed, these evil powers were defeated and publicly disgraced by Christ. How foolish, then, of the Colossians to accept a way of life based on such wrong-headed notions!

In the course of his practical discussion, Paul will have an even more damaging criticism to level against these self-appointed sophists who are "bursting with the futile conceit of worldly minds" (v. 18, NEB). They do not hold fast to the Head (v. 19), that is, Christ. Thus wilfully departing from the church's Lord and the universe's ruler, they are branded as self-condemned heretics whose teaching is to be utterly refused. And if their doctrine is thus in error, their ethical admonitions are clearly shown to be misguided as merely "human precepts and doctrines" (v. 22) and as emanating from "self-made religion" (v. 23). Paul gives a "blow-by-blow rebuttal of their pretentious claim" (Lohse).

2:16-19 "Therefore" links the present section to the foregoing with its demonstration of Christ's victory over evil powers. With His victory standing to the credit of His people, they can ill-afford to give attention to mistaken criticisms which the false teachers would pass on them. The points at issue are detailed: "food and drink" are prescriptions belonging to an ascetic way of life. Several groups in the New Testament church and in the ancient world accepted these scruples and avoided certain foods on religious grounds: Romans 14: 1ff.; 1 Timothy 4:2,3; Titus 1:14f.; Hebrews 9:10; 13:9. Many of these prohibitions are forced into the mould of religious taboos; and as such they betray an immature stage of spiritual development.

The holy days, whether annual, monthly or weekly, were also the subject of controversy at Colossae. Again the root principle needs to be noted. Paul is not condemning the use of sacred days and seasons. The evidence of Acts shows his own interest in observing them (Acts 20:16; 27:9). What moves him here is the wrong motive involved when the observance of holy festivals is made a badge of separation and an attempted means of securing salvation out of fear and superstitition. It is bad religion that Paul attacks.[1]

2:17 The reason for his attack is now supplied. Immaturity in religious observance betrays a misunderstanding of God's purpose in bringing men into the perfect light of His revelation in Christ. It means being content to live in the shadow-side of religion where fears lurk and inhibitions abound. The "shadow" presages what is to come; and the time of the "substance" has arrived, thus antiquating all that pointed forward to it. That "substance" is Christ. His new age delivers men from the bondage of fear and superstitious dread. He sets them free from false notions and insubstantial hopes, and gives them a taste of reality in religion as they come to know in Him true communion with the living God. This reality is what Paul means in his earlier references to the "hope of the gospel" (1:5,23) which his readers are not to abandon.

"Substance" is in fact one rendering of the Greek term (sōma) for "body." This has suggested to some interpreters (Lohmeyer, Masson, Moule) but not all (E. Best, One Body in Christ [1955],

---

[1] It is a moot question whether the main influences on this Colossian theosophy were Jewish or pagan. The allusions to dietary restrictions and to sacred days and festivals seem, at first glance, to settle the issue in favour of a Judaizing tendency. J. B. Lightfoot, in 1875, pointed to the example of the Essenes who practised a type of asceticism and separatism. Since then, the literature of an Essene-like sect at Qumran has given more understanding of their discipline and ethos, notably in the observance of a heterodox calendar with diverse feast-days from those of Palestinian Judaism. Moreover, certain verbal correspondences between the Dead Sea scrolls and this epistle have been explored by W. D. Davies, "Paul and the Dead Sea Scrolls: Flesh and Spirit," The Scrolls and the New Testament, ed. K. Stendahl, 1958, pp. 166–169; and P. Benoit, "Qumran and the New Testament," Paul and Qumran, ed. J. Murphy-O'Connor, 1968, p. 17. The latter concludes: "A return to the Mosaic Law by circumcision, rigid observance concerning diet and the calendar, speculations about angelic powers: all this is part and parcel of the doctrines of Qumran." This may be so, but the singular absence of any debate over the Mosaic law at Colossae and even the absence of the word for law (nomos) should make us pause before accepting too close an identity, as E. Lohse reminds us, op. cit. pp. 171,188f. and "Christologie und Ethik im Kolosserbrief," Apophoreta, 1964, pp. 157f. This consideration militates against W. Foerster's thesis ("Die Irrlehrer des Kolosserbriefes," in Studia Biblica et Semitica, 1966, pp. 71–80, that the heresy was a sort of successor to the Qumran teaching. For a more balanced assessment of the evidence of the scrolls see E. Yamauchi, "Qumran and Colosse," Bibliotheca Sacra 121, 1964, pp. 141–52.

pp. 121f.) that Paul has the church as Christ's body in view. In fellowship with Christ and His people "all the great 'realities' were found—pardon, sanctification, communion with God, etc.— of which ritual, whether Jewish or non-Jewish, was only a shadow" (Moule). This reference to a corporate expression of faith, found in Christ, seems required by the train of thought which follows. There Paul will continue the contrast between false religion and the true faith of the body, of which Christ is the head (v. 19).

2:18-19 These verses abound with difficulties, both linguistic and conceptual. Mercifully the drift of Paul's thought is clear. It is couched as a warning lest his readers should allow themselves to be cheated out of their prize (see Phil. 3:14 for "prize," *brabeion*, which lies at the heart of Paul's verb *katabrabeuein* here) by heeding the false teachers who offered as a substitute for his gospel a system of religion which was the product of their own minds. Paul obviously has a low opinion of these sophists. He bluntly calls these men the victims of a sensual outlook because they refuse to submit their thinking to divine revelation, and boast in their native wisdom and pride (see Rom. 1:21,22; 1 Cor. 2:14f.; Phil. 3:19 for similar judgements on men who despise God's way of life and devise their own religious customs and ceremonials). They stand under the most tragic of all condemnations: they are willing to be detached from Christ the Head of the church. So they put themselves out of touch with the source of all true life, just as a limb loses its life once it is severed from the human torso.

The human body provides the analogy for Paul's description in verse 19. As an anatomical structure, it is supplied with and bonded together by joints and ligaments and so grows in strength and size as God purposes its growth (so Moule). The application is pointed. Human limbs are meant to be an integral part of the human frame. Once they become detached, they lose that vital contact with the source of life and nourishment. Paul is saying: the false teacher who ceases to depend on the Head, ceases to belong to the body. He who cuts himself off from Christ cuts himself free from the church (Masson). So closely are Christ and His body joined: and so important is it for His people to remain in living union with Him who is their Head. False teachers have proved themselves self-excluded from the church by reason of their forsaking Christ as true God and man; let the Colossians not be enticed into the same trap (2:8).

Obviously Paul does not mince his words. The danger facing the Colossians is a serious one, full of momentous consequences. Can we know more precisely what it was?

The key-terms are found in the phrase: "insisting on self-abasement and worship of angels, taking his stand on visions, puffed up without reason by his sensuous mind." Recent study of this verse, notably by F. O. Francis,[1] has identified certain conclusions, as follows: (a) "insisting on" (Greek *thelōn en*) indicates the desire on the part of the errorists to impose their views on the Colossian church. Francis renders "bent on" to show the strength of this determination and its attractiveness (other translators give "delighting in" from a Septuagintal model of the verb, e.g. 1 Samuel 18:22: Saul had delight in David).

(b) "self-abasement" is literally "humility" (Greek *tapeinophrosunē*). Often used in a good sense of a Christian virtue (as in 3:12), the word here must carry a nuance of mortification or self-denial. Specifically it may well mean "fasting" as in second and third century Christian authors (Hermas, Tertullian). Francis draws attention to an important strain of Jewish pietistic literature which offered the reward to ascetic practice of entering into the heavenly realm and catching a vision of the divine. This has an important bearing on the next terms.

(c) "worship of angels." The difficulty here is to know how to interpret the phrase: is it "worshipping of angels" or "worship conducted or practised by angels" which is reprobated? Francis argues for the latter (loc. cit. pp. 126–130) with great ingenuity and so relieves his interpretation of the difficulty (on the first view) that there is little evidence that within orthodox Judaism the Jews worshipped angels.[2] There is, however, a fatal objection (voiced by Lohse) to the second interpretation, viz. this reading "breaks down on the statement in verse 23 where the worship is explained as a cult performed by men." In some way veneration must have been paid to the angels as part of the cultic apparatus of this theosophical religion.

(d) "*taking his stand* on visions" is clearly a paraphrase of the single Greek verb *embateuōn*. Its primary meaning is "to enter," whether

[1] Article, "Humility and Angelic Worship in Col. 2:18," *Studia Theologica*, xvi, 1961, pp. 109–134. His position is accepted and extended by A. J. Bandstra, *The Law and the Elements of the World. An Exegetical Study in Aspects of Paul's Teaching*, pp. 160ff.

[2] See A. Lukyn Williams, "The cult of Angels at Colossae," *Journal of Theological Studies*, x, 1909, pp. 413–438.

in a neutral sense ("set foot on") or an aggressive sense ("invade"). Sometimes the meaning is figurative, as in the English idiom: "to enter in" = investigate with a view to gaining control of a subject (see 2 Macc. 2:30, NEB, "It is the province of the original author . . . to take possession of the field").

Some commentators, both ancient (Chrysostom, Athanasius) and modern (H. Preisker, *TDNT*, ii, pp. 535f.) argue for this last-named sense. Preisker insists that Paul is refuting an insatiable thirst for knowledge which characterized the gnostic-Jewish philosophy at Colossae and elsewhere (2 Tim. 3:7; 2 John 9). All the fulness of divine knowledge is in Christ. "To keep to Him and thus to participate in divine growth (2:19), there is no need of syncretistic methods of producing visions and therefore knowledge. If we go the way of the false teachers, we shall always have to wait for such moments of ecstatic vision, and we shall then have to enter (*embateuein*) by painful investigation into what has been seen in ecstasy."

This view certainly would seem cogent, were it not for the further evidence of another meaning which makes the verb something of a technical expression in the mystery religions. It refers to the initiates entering the sanctuary on completion of the rite. Dibelius-Greeven make a lot of the inscriptional data from the sanctuary of Apollo at Claros (2nd century A.D.?).[1] On this reconstruction, Paul is referring to a familiar rite—the initiate enters the oracle grotto at the completion of his mystical experience —and the claim of the Colossian teachers is that they too have penetrated the secrets of the universe and received a climactic vision. There is no need to argue that these words in our text are consciously borrowed from the mystery cultic practice—clearly the two situations are not parallel, as critics of Dibelius have remarked;[2]

[1] The use of this inscription to understand Colossians 2:18 was made earlier than Dibelius by William M. Ramsay, *The Teaching of Paul in Terms of the Present Day*, 1914, pp. 286ff. One inscription runs: two enquirers "having been initiated, entered" (the sacred enclosure). Another reads of an enquirer: "having received the mysteries, he entered." The verb in both cases is *embateuein*, i.e. they entered on a new life, and intended to continue therein (op. cit., p. 290). Used in the context of the Colossian strange teaching "it is a sarcastic reference to a solemn act, by which once on a time the leader of the movement had symbolically expressed his deliberate choice (*thelōn*) of a 'New Life'" (op. cit., p. 299).

[2] Francis, loc. cit., pp. 120f.; A. D. Nock, "The Vocabulary of the New Testament", *Journal of Biblical Literature* 52, 1933, pp. 132f.; similarly S. Lyonnet, "Col 2,18 et les mystères d'Apollon Clarien" *Biblica* 43, 1962, pp. 417-435 surveys the evidence afresh and concludes that Paul borrows the term *embateuon* from the Claros mysteries to enforce his point at Colossae. But in order to do this he need not give to the term the technical and cultic sense of "crossing the threshold" to enter the sacred enclosure, which does not very well fit in with the context. He could just as well give the term the metaphorical sense of "investigate" (*scruter*) (p. 435).

but there are two observations to be registered in favour of some interpretation akin to that of Ramsay, Dibelius, and W. L. Knox who follows them (see below). First, the Claros inscription does contain the word used by Paul and in a semi-cultic context which Paul's writing seems to require. This point would give the interpretation the edge over Francis' view which maintains that the entry is into heaven as part of the general theory of the journey of the soul from earth to the heavenly regions. Secondly, E. Lohse states an important fact when he stresses that Paul in verse 18 is not arguing against the Colossian heresy *explicitly* but simply citing the heretical watchwords. There is no need (he proceeds) to submit that the text must be altered to produce a rendering which would be a judgemental polemic against the cult and its pretensions.[1] Our understanding of the Colossian menace is assisted if we regard all the terms, "humility," "veneration of angels" and "penetrating into visions he has seen" as slogans of the false teachers and as all of a piece. They formed the cultic procedure by which devotees could gain a knowledge of the "elemental spirits of the universe" (2:8) and could lay claim to some esoteric experience which unlocked the mysteries of life and destiny. The conclusion that a pride in special knowledge (*gnōsis*) lay at the root of the Colossian error seems certain in view of Paul's next phrase, which *does* pass judgement on the claim.[2] Those who were making this proud boast were "vainly inflated by reason of their worldly way of thinking." Elsewhere Paul commented that an inordinate aspiration to knowledge of divine mysteries serves only to fill the claimant with conceit (1 Cor. 8:1; cf. 1 Cor. 4:18).

Is it possible to fit these terms of verse 18 into a pattern? And to relate it to the warning against a wrong-headed observation of fasts in verses 16,17? W. L. Knox's[3] explanation has the merit of producing such a coherent pattern and commends itself on that score. He writes:

[1] J. R. Harris, *Side-lights on New Testament Research*, 1909, pp. 198ff. discusses the history of the text from the AV's inserting a negative: "intruding into those things which he hath not seen," the RV's rendering which omits the negative (correctly): "dwelling in the things which he hath seen" to textual emendations, e.g. "talking windily of what he has seen," "walking, as it were, on the wind." The story of textual experiments is continued by J. Rendel Harris in his contribution "St. Paul and Aristophanes," *ExpT* 34, 1922/23, pp. 151–56. F. F. Bruce, p. 249, has a full note on these variant translations.

[2] Unless we run together the two parts of Paul's sentence as suggested by N. Turner (*A Grammar of New Testament Greek*, Vol. III, 1963, p. 246) and translate "upon what he vainly imagined in the vision of his initiation."

[3] *St. Paul and the Church of the Gentiles*, 1939, pp. 170f.

"The Colossians must not allow themselves to be impressed by the assumed superiority of those who sought to impose on them a system of ordinances, of rules as to eating and drinking and the observance of special days as sacred . . . Nor must they let themselves be impressed by those who sought to impose on them higher standards of special fasts, enjoined as a means of propitiating the angels, whose appearance to them in vision would mark the stages of their progress to higher things . . . Access to the heavens was only to be obtained by union with Christ, who, as head of the Church and the cosmos, provided to everything in it that life which enabled it to grow with a divine increase."

2:20–23 One final proof that verse 18 refers to the heretics' fear of the astral gods which could only be appeased (they believed) by a regimen of asceticism, abstinences and angel-veneration is given in verse 20. Paul recalls what happened when the Colossian Christians passed in their baptismal experience from paganism to fellowship with Christ. By their faith-union with Him in His death and resurrection (2:12-15; Rom. 6:4f.) they passed from under the control of these cosmic powers and were "transferred . . . to the kingdom of his beloved Son" (1:13). No longer held captive in the domain of darkness, they rejoiced to take their place in the heritage of God's people (1:12) and confessed a new allegiance and lordship (2:6). The vividness of Paul's writing brings out the dramatic sense of this transition from bondage to liberty in Christ. J. A. T. Robinson's translation[1] succeeds in capturing the unusual construction: "Ye died with Christ out from under the elements of the world," suggesting a death to an old order which liberates the sufferer from all the claims that order had on him (as in Paul's argument of Rom. 7:1-4).

The application is made in the form of a rhetorical question. If this decisive change in your loyalty happened to you in your baptism, and you henceforth determined to live under Christ's sole command, why do you intend to go back to living as though Christ had never set you free? In particular, why do you listen to spurious teaching which would bring you into bondage to a legal code and impose on you a series of taboos and negative rules?

The prohibitions of verse 21 are given by Paul as part of what the

[1] *The Body. A Study in Pauline Theology*, 1952, p. 43.

propagandists were teaching. It is they, not he, who are laying down the regulations: Don't take, don't taste, don't touch. In this list, the first and last verbs are almost synonyms and the line of distinction between them is hard to draw. It looks as though all three verbs are warnings against the consumption of food and drink, though possibly there was a disdain of marriage too. See earlier, p. 16. "Take" (RSV "handle") carries the former sense in both the Greek and English idioms (see Arndt-Gingrich, under *haptesthai* for illustration). If this interpretation is correct, it would reinforce Paul's earlier teaching against being side-tracked by a false scrupulosity which is "paralysed by an uncertainty of what precautions to take in order to safeguard a purity which is always threatened" (Masson). The rule-of-thumb in this legalistic religion is then applied: avoid *all* possible sources of moral defilement, and practise by your abstemiousness a rigorous discipline for fear of losing your "spirituality."

Paul's teaching, on the contrary, is a charter of freedom. But his reasoning is meant to provide some rationale for his opposition to a false ascetic piety. We may set down some of the principles on which his counter-claim rests:

(a) "Why do you submit to regulations?" (v. 20) disguises (for the sake of intelligible English, we may add) a Greek verb (*dogmatizesthe*) which recalls verse 14. There Paul has described the work of Christ on the cross as one which wipes out the debt we owe because of our sins. That condemnation is expressed in terms of the "legal demands" (Greek *dogmata*) which were ranged against us as law-breaking sinners. But Christ's death did more than wipe the slate clean and give us a fresh start. Not only are the legal accusations of a broken law blotted out; the reign of law as a way of acceptance with God is brought to an end (so G. Kittel, *TDNT*, ii, p. 231). This fact lies at the heart of Paul's question in verse 20: "Why do you allow yourselves to be dictated to by regulations which have no authority?" In effect, why do the Colossians wish to re-impose a legalistic religion on themselves when Christ's cross has forever set men free from this type of legality?

(b) Matters of food and drink are of no consequence in the practice of Christian piety (Rom. 14:17)—when a test-issue is made of abstinence or enjoyment. Over-indulgence leading to gluttony and drunkenness is not in question; Paul never fails to point out the dangers of excess (1 Cor. 5:9; Eph. 5:18). Nor is he here concerned with food offered to idols, as in 1 Corinthians 8. The reason why items of food and drink cannot affect a Christian's relationship to God is given in verse 22, which picks up the same thought as is used in the gospel teaching (Mark 7:6,7 = Matt. 15:8,9). Both passages go back to a common Old Testament source for authority: Isaiah 29:13, LXX which reads: "But in vain they worship me, teaching the commandments and teachings of men." The Pauline use of the text drives home a single point. The Colossians have no reason to pay heed to false ascetic rules, for what these teachers recommend are simply human ordinances, born out of man-made fears and frailties (cf. 2:5; Tit. 1:14 for a similar indictment). And food is quickly forgotten as it passes through the mouth into the digestive system and so "perishes."

(c) Rules and regulations to order human bodily functions and appetites have a semblance of appeal. They *appear* to offer a life of self-discipline and spiritual mastery of the instincts. They give the impression of being for human good and of leading to self-conquest. But while Paul elsewhere values the need for self-mastery (1 Cor. 9:24–27), in this context he speaks only in a critical voice of this kind of asceticism.

His chief complaint lies in the word translated "rigour of devotion" (Greek *ethelothrēskia*), which is a composite term meaning "self-made religion" or "would-be religion." The latter rendering suggesting the thought "pretended" or "quasi" worship (proposed by B. Reicke[1] and F. O. Francis) is not as acceptable as the former, which seems to be the necessary sense needed in Paul's argument. The gravamen of his charge is that the errorists have imported on to the scene at Colossae a manner of worship which is essentially their own innovation. It is branded by Paul "self-made" i.e. bogus, and so for that very reason invalid and not to be entertained by his readers. The Colossian sophists may express their pleasure (note the same Greek verb in verse 18 as in the prefix: *ethelo-*) in their religiosity and ascetic piety. It may give them inward satisfaction in keeping their body under iron discipline. But "it entirely fails in its chief aim" (Lightfoot).

Or rather, perhaps it succeeded only too well by inducing a state of trance-like ecstasy which in turn led to a visionary experience. The term in verse 23 may well be "a sarcastic borrowing from his opponents' language" (so W. L. Knox, op. cit., p. 171, note 1)

---

[1] Article, "Zum sprachlichen Verständnis von Kol. 2:23," *Studia Theologica* vi, 1952, p. 46.

like a similar quotation from their terms in verse 18. Or, more likely it is his deliberate *parodying* of their claim in verse 18 by his coined term expressing his ridicule at what claims to be ultimate truth.

Paul grants that asceticism may produce visions but his condemnation falls on the motive and the result. The motive is a lust for spiritual experience which by-passes Christ and seeks gratification in a sensuous elation. The end result is a sense of spiritual pride and this Paul terms a capitulation to the "flesh," i.e. man's unrenewed nature, as in Galatians 5:20.

This way of looking at "self-made religion" would explain Paul's negative attitude to what seem to be wholesome practices (fasting, self-denial and keeping the appetites on tight rein). "Paul is handicapped by the difficulty of admitting any value in external practices without appearing to justify the claims of his opponents" (Knox, *ibid.*).

The first words of the verse are problematic.[1] One would expect a continuance of Paul's criticism in pointing out the inherent weakness of a legalistic ritualism. Therefore an ancient interpretation, shared by both Greek and Latin church fathers, that Paul's charge against asceticism is that it does not "satisfy the reasonable wants of the body" can hardly be correct. The apostle is not timidly remarking that ritualism fails by "not holding *the body* in any honour." On the contrary, his word is one for "flesh", not body; and the Greek word for the former, *sarx*, must carry Paul's more usual sense = "lower nature," "sensual indulgence" (so E. Lohse, p. 186, note 4). The obvious weakness in this type of religious endeavour is that it provides no check for man's lower nature which, though using his bodily instincts and appetites to hold him prey, is really different from them. His "flesh" (*sarx*)[2] gains control of the entire person and rules it as "the mind that is set on the flesh," but no amount of bodily restraint or self-denial will hold this sin-principle in check. It requires a higher "law"—"the law of the

---

[1] See the lucid discussion of the various possibilities in Moule, pp. 108–110, prefaced by a cautionary dictum: "This verse is by common consent regarded as hopelessly obscure—either owing to corruption or because we have lost the clue." On the former possibility, a proposed emendation may be mentioned. B. G. Hall, "Colossians II. 23," *ExpT* 36, 1924/25, p. 285 changes the word for indulgence (*plesmone*) into *epilesmosune* thus reading: asceticism "is of no value to the *forgetting* of the flesh." But altering the text at will is an ultimate confession of the commentator's despair.

[2] This word may well represent Paul's version of the Rabbinic term "evil impulse" (*yeser ha-ra'*) which according to Jewish anthropology held men in bondage and goaded them into sin. See W. D. Davies, *Paul and Rabbinic Judaism*[2], 1955, pp. 17–35.

Spirit of life in Christ Jesus" (Rom. 8:2), the power of the Spirit (Gal. 5:16–25) and a "true" mortification (3:5) which presupposes a new nature (3:10)—to give a man the victory. He must be renewed in the spirit of his mind (Eph. 4:23) before he can hope to gain the mastery over his sensual mind (2:18) and appetite (2:23).

Besides, religious ascetic piety, as evidently practised and advocated at Colossae, was liable to abuse. It set out ostensibly to promote the devotee's highest spiritual interest, but did so in a way which served only to make him a proud man. It exploited his love of secret knowledge; it professed to offer him the key to the riddle of God and the universe; it invited him to explore the secrets of destiny by placating the "elemental spirits" and venerating angelic hosts; it promised a reward to a regimen of discipline, fasting and self-mortification in the granting of visions of heavenly things, true "realities" beyond the world of matter and sense-perception; it gave him a sense of self-mastery which set him apart from other men who toiled with their temptations and vices.

All of this, Paul flatly objects, is so much "beguiling speech" (2:4). In so far as it succeeds in its declared and pretended aims, it fails to keep the "flesh" in check. Rather it promotes a selfish and senseless spirit which claims a private experience open only to a select few. It is unlike his gospel which is for all men (1:23,28). The heresy laid claim to being a progressive religion, instinct with life and power. Paul's rejoinder is that it is his gospel which truly grows (1:6) throughout the world (1:23), because it is a divine growth (2:19). In detail, it stands under judgement in the following ways:[1]

---

[1] What follows in the text is purposely restricted to an attempted exposition of Paul's handling of the situation at Colossae. But some modern parallels to the strange practices and bizarre claims of the Colossian theosophists will come to mind. In particular we think of the intended purpose underlying the modern cult of "transcendental meditation" either with or without the use of psychedelic or hallucigenic drugs like LSD. The quest of experience beyond sense-perception (offered as the climax of a "trip") has been labelled "neomystical" by Harvey Cox (*The Feast of Fools* [1969], chapter 7) who is partly sympathetic and partly critical. He correctly notes, however, that the issue behind the modern drug scene is primarily theological and not (as many think) social or even medical. And Timothy Leary's slogan, "The only Hope is Dope" (in his book *The Politics of Ecstasy*, [1970]) would confirm this assessment. Drug users seek escape into a world of visionary experience where all is "love," "peace," and "light." But this escape is a flight from reality which in the Jewish and Christian tradition is rooted in events of history. The Christian church celebrates its festivity by re-living the dramas of God's past acts in history and so making them present. But a lust for non-personal, non-eventful absorption into a state of euphoria is sheer flight from responsibility—whether at Colossae or a marijuana party or a "rock" festival under the dazzling strobe lights.

(a) The Colossian heresy derogates Christ from His eminence. It is a system "not according to Christ" (2:8), for it refuses to accord Him His true stature as the centre and locus of divine revelation, the source, sustainer and goal of the universe (1:15–20) and the embodiment of deity (2:9) in His historical life (2:9).[1] The divine fulness is not scattered throughout the manifold spiritual beings which make up the *pleroma;* it is concentrated in the God-man Jesus. (b) It professes to bring its followers to perfection—Dibelius thinks that "fulness of life" (2:10) is a claim first made by Paul's enemies at Colossae—and to put them in touch with reality. In fact, it belongs to the shadows (2:17) cast by the light of Christ and His coming to earth. (c) It clings to dark superstitions and trades on unwholesome fears in its insistence on paying honour to the "elemental spirits" (2:8,20) and on reverencing angels (2:18). Christians who listen to this mumbo-jumbo are heedless of what the death and victory of Christ achieved (2:11–15) and what benefits accrued to them in that event, which was made personal to them in their baptism (2:20). (d) So this false reliance on asceticism, legalism and ritualism stands under the judgement of verse 23: it is a man-thought-out cult, with doctrines and practices devised by some theosophical thinker whose seductive appeal must be refused. He professes to be offering an improved version of Christianity; in fact, he has lost his hold on Christ (2:19) and is an apostate, anti-christ figure.

On the other hand, Paul's gospel brings genuine life and liberty as the "gospel of truth" (1:5). It centres on the person of Jesus Christ, true God and real man (2:9). By His death on the cross He accomplished a dual work of divine grace, spelled out in terms of a cosmic victory and a moral salvation.

He overcame the enslaving powers of malign spirit-forces which were ranged against Him (2:15) and now has obtained the rank of "head of all principality and power" (2:10), i.e. those very forces which sought to destroy Him. Moreover, in His victory His people have a share; and in their baptism they do symbolically what He did in reality—they put off the authority of these cosmic powers and pass from their control to the domain of Christ the Lord

---

[1] Commenting on "bodily," Knox says: "It seems to be a summary reply to the argument that Jesus could not have been divine, for He had a real body and was really crucified, which is impossible for a divine being" (op. cit., p. 168 n. 3). Less likely is F. H. Borsch's suggestion (see ref. on p. 41) that the adverb recalls Luke 3:22 and refers to the bestowal of divinity on Jesus, as the later gnostics supposed.

(2:20). Dead and buried with Christ, they answer a resounding No to every claim these spiritual powers make on them. In particular, they forsake the dark world of superstition, appeasement and religious uncertainty, and enter into an experience of God's personal favour and care which banishes all dread and devitalizes all negative religion.

On the level of personal experience, the Colossians tasted the joys of forgiveness by Christ's dramatic act (2:13,14), and this certainty, confirmed in baptism (2:12) ought to have left its indelible impress upon them. It qualified them to enter their inheritance as God's own people and set them free from striving to find acceptance with God by their own effort. In particular, living by God's forgiveness and grace brought a system of taboos and unreal inhibitions to an end (2:16,17,20–22); it declares that God's creation is good and that He as both creator and redeemer takes delight in giving His children all that makes for a full life (1 Tim. 4:1–5; 6:17) so they have come to fulness of life in Jesus Christ (2:10).

3:1–4 Clearly the opening of verse 1 matches the reminder given in 2:20, and complements it. The Colossian believers are bidden to reflect on what their new life in Christ meant to them. It was a death to the old order of servitude and fear. By a faith-union with Christ in His death they died—to the evil powers which held them in bondage to superstition and a false way of life. But they also rose with the risen Lord (2:13), and now new horizons should fill their vision. "Were you not raised to life in Christ?" (NEB). Paul's use of a simple past tense is intentional; it is meant to recall the specific occasion of Christian baptism when his readers entered upon their new life. The RSV translates literally, "if then . . ." and so needs the additional thought that when the apostle says "if" in these contexts, he really means, "if—as is the case," "since."

The summons is to aspire to interests and ambitions which are "above." The contrast is made with 2:20. Living as if they still belonged to the world, with a limited outlook and still captivated by human precepts and doctrines should now be a thing of the past. Let the Colossians allow God's new order to control their mind-set and attitude of life. *Seek* (Greek *zēteite*) and "set your minds" (*phroneite*) are important words in Paul's ethical vocabulary. They mean a chosen orientation—as the needle of a compass "seeks" the pole (H. C. G. Moule)—whether in a worthwhile or other (Rom. 10:3; 1 Cor. 1:22) direction, followed by a clear resolve to follow that chosen path.

The second term whose range and depth of meaning can be seen by referring to Philippians 1:7; 2:2 (twice), 5; 3:15 (twice), 16 (in Received text), 19; 4:2,10 (twice) is the more important and frequent of the two. It means much more than a mental exercise, and signifies rather "sympathetic interest and concern, expressing as it does the action of the heart as well as the intellect" (J. H. Michael on Phil. 1:7). It is the outworking of thought as thought determines motives, and through motives the conduct of the person involved. A word like "concern" catches something of the spirit of the verb. Letting your thoughts dwell on the higher realm (NEB) is a necessary preliminary for future action, as our attachment to God's kingdom of which the Colossians (1:13) like the Philippians (3:20) were members prepares us to express that allegiance in positive endeavour and enterprise.

The Christian who is risen with Christ has a new focal point. His spring of motivation is set in the world of God to which he looks upward. Paul's call is a resounding *sursum corda:* up with your hearts! No longer is the believer earth-bound and circumscribed in his outlook and attitudes like the "man that could look no way but downwards, with a muck-rake in his hand," whom Interpreter showed to Christiana. Yet that heavenly frame of reference will make him a better citizen of society and give him new impetus to serve God and the world in His name.

The heavenly realm is the place of Christ's triumph (as in Eph. 1:20). He not only became victorious in death (2:15) and was raised in power to become victor and head over all alien powers (2:10). He is now installed in the seat of honour, "seated at the right hand of God." This is an allusion to Psalm 110:1 which stands first in the list of Old Testament verses laid under tribute by the New Testament writers to express the exaltation and dominion of the regnant Christ (see Mark 12:36; 14:62; Acts 2:34; 1 Cor. 15:25; Rom. 8:34; Eph. 1:20; Heb. 1:3,13; 8:1; 10:12f.; 12:2; 1 Pet. 3:22). Moreover, session at God's right hand carries a special overtone: :t denotes (as in Phil. 2:9) co-regency, i.e. the receiving and enjoyment of a dignity equal with God (W. Foerster, *TDNT* ii, p. 1089). The thought, therefore, includes the promise given to the church that, having been raised with Christ above the control of the "elemental spirits" and cosmic powers, Christians share with Him His life of freedom in God. The enthroned Christ "assumes the place of the *heimarmene* (fate). As the Exalted One he becomes the One who holds fate, the whole course of the world, in his hands, because no power of fate can match him" (E. Schweizer).[1]

Paul can go on to describe the new life as "hidden with Christ in God" (v. 3, NEB). His readers "died" (as in 2:20) and in that act of faith-exemplified-in-baptism they passed beyond the range of the spirits' control. They became sharers in a new life, such as Christ the fulness of God (2:3) enjoys in His Father's presence (Rev. 3:21, a pledge addressed to nearby Laodicea) and were joined with Christ their life (v. 4; actually Paul writes "our life," if the harder reading is preferred. The latter phrase is unique in Paul who does, however, speak of "my life," Phil. 1:20, Gal. 2:20). But Paul is careful to insist that there is no mystic absorption which blurs the distinction between the Redeemer and the redeemed. That error was made in gnostic religion, and the apostle's language in verse 3, while naturally suggesting the believers' security in Christ, equally asserts that "our union with Christ is of a historical, not a mythic-mystical, kind. It is established on the basis of the historical act of Christ's death" (H. Conzelmann, on 2:12) and His resurrection, which in turn is an anticipation of the Christian's resurrection-life to come (1 Cor. 15:12ff.,20,23).

A even more pointed inference is to be drawn from this verse if 2:18 is taken to mean that the Colossian errorists were advocating a cultic discipline which gave them a trance-like entrance into the heavenly world. Paul's rejoinder is forthright. Christians already have attained that goal, with their life hidden in Christ with God, and their access to the unseen world above—the *summum bonum* of every true gnostic—is already part of assured experience!

The reality of this experience is partly past (as Paul harks back to the Colossians' response to the gospel when the church was founded, 1:6–8) and partly present. The new life is already being received and appreciated at Colossae; and Paul's teaching is a veiled warning lest it should be lost by acts of apostasy and abandonment of his gospel in favour of the heretics' propaganda (1:23; 2:8). He is concerned to give reasons for refusing both the theoretical and practical effects of the Colossian heterodoxy. Christ has set the people free from such strange notions as in 2:18 and from such restrictive practices as in 2:20,21. This emphasis may well explain Paul's teaching which elsewhere is not so insistent on the present aspect of being already risen with Christ. Some commentators

[1] *Lordship and Discipleship*, 1960, p. 105.

find in this "realized eschatology" a sign of a post-Pauline writer.[1] But verse 4 hardly warrants this conclusion.

The apostolic thought moves into the future with this reminder of a prospective epiphany. It is scarcely adequate to treat the words "when Christ appears" as an erratic reminiscence taken from early Christian eschatology (as Lohse does), supposing that Paul's disciples ventured to include this. Verse 4 is a necessary complement to verse 3 which speaks of the (present) hidden life of the church. What is veiled now, in the eyes of the world, viz. their quality of life in a pagan society and their devotion to Christ which refuses all gnosticizing "improvements" of theosophical doctrine and mystic asceticism, will one day be revealed. And when it is revealed at the *parousia* of Christ, they will be vindicated as His true followers. The note of "eschatological reserve" is here sounded. The admonition is in line with 1 Corinthians 4:5; and both texts point to a future dénouement and serve as justification for Paul's apostolic ministry.

With this recall of the church's life in Christ—now latent, then to be revealed—Paul has concluded his task set out in 2:6,7. He has expounded what it means to the Colossians to "live in him" in a situation where the temptation to be moved away from the hope of the gospel (1:23) was strong. He has dealt faithfully with the Colossian danger, exposing its pernicious wrong-headedness in both belief and behaviour. In contrast to false ideas he has shown the true calling of the Christian to a life of liberty and to an unhindered awareness of fellowship with God in Christ based on forgiveness and confidence.

But the pendulum often swings in the opposite direction. We have the painful example of Romans 3:8,31; 6:1,2 to remind us that Paul's gospel of free grace and full forgiveness by the cross of Christ apart from law-keeping can easily be misunderstood and travestied into licence. His call to Christian liberty can quickly be heard as an invitation to irresponsible libertinism and moral indifference, as at Galatia (Gal. 5:13-15). The danger of false asceticism, condemned in 2:21-23, may well give rise to the equally dangerous ideas that the Christian is exempt from all moral restraints and can indulge his physical appetites and emotional

[1] See the discussion leading to this position in R. C. Tannehill, *Dying and Rising with Christ. A study in Pauline Theology*, 1967, pp. 47-54.

"hang-ups" at will. The danger-signal of antinomianism, that is, a supposed freedom from all law on the ground that the believer lives a charmed life untouched by evil or that he has already begun a celestial life on earth,[1] may have seemed to Paul very clearly visible. Hence he moves on in his epistle to counter this erroneous deduction by teaching a true self-denial and authentic mortification (3:5,8) in the framework of a future hope (3:4) and judgement (3:6,24).

Other reasons may be suggested for Paul's continued exhortation. First, he has already hinted at the believer's experience of following his Lord's example in baptism (2:11,12,20; 3:1,3). He has already depicted the nature of the conflict in which Christ set the pattern by divesting Himself of His flesh, attacked by evil powers (1:22; 2:11,15) and overcoming His cosmic enemies in a dramatic way (2:20). Now Paul must apply this teaching. He must show how the once-for-all victory of Christ on the cross has a personal and existential relevance to the Colossians. He must summon them to strip off the old nature (3:8,9) by submitting to a death-like renunciation of the claims of their lower selves (3:5); and then beckon them to rise with the living Christ to a newness of life in which their "new nature" (3:10), put on in baptism, is given full expression in a life of shining virtues (3:12ff.).

Our insight into the state of the Colossian congregation is only partial; indeed what comes to view is refracted through the prism of Paul's letter, and we have no independent, factual source either of the strange teaching or of the Colossian reaction to it. We cannot tell whether the heresy was "home-grown" and produced within the ranks of the members, finding its leadership in some forceful,

---

[1] Like the Corinthian "spiritualists" (1 Cor. 4:8; 15:12) and the false teachers of 2 Timothy 2:18 who declare that "the resurrection has already taken place" and that Christians in their baptism and experience of new life are already embarked on a heavenly life while still alive on earth. The upshot of this inference—roundly condemned in 2 Timothy—is to claim a perfectionist state *now* by an assertion of a spiritualized eschatology which cuts itself loose from any future hope and ignores the eschatological tension which Paul insists on between "already risen with Christ" and the final resurrection at the *parousia*. The perfectionist teaching, by placing a false interpretation on the sacrament of baptism as effecting a physical change and by undercutting the future hope (expressed in Rom. 6:4; 5–8), leads inevitably to a slackening of the moral fibre. "Glory begun below" can easily be perverted into a false sentiment which cuts the nerve of moral progress, overlooks the conflict and fears with which the Christian must wrestle in this age, and forgets that the final glorification of the church awaits a future fulfilment (as in 1 Cor. 15:22–28, 49–54). So Paul adds the pointer to a prospect not yet achieved in verse 4. See, for fuller discussion, based on the assumption of a post-Pauline modification of the Romans 6 teaching, E. Grässer, "Kol 3,1–4 als Beispiel einer Interpretation secundum homines recipientes," *Zeitschrift für Theologie und Kirche*, 64, 1967, pp. 139–168, especially pp. 149ff.

free-thinking member who sought to draw away others after him, or if it was an importation from outside the church to which the members gave ready hospitality.[1]

W. Foerster bases his conclusion that the latter is the case on the exegetical ground of 2:19 and 2:20. The former verse: "and not holding fast to the head" is usually taken (he says) to mean that the fault lay in the heretics' abandoning the church's Head, Christ. But the verb *kratein* can also mean "to seize," "to restrain," (as in Matt. 28:9) and the action condemned may be a hostile attempt to restrain or hold back the growth of the church, which attempt Paul insists they cannot succeed in achieving. This would then clearly be an action from outside the church, appropriate to the description in verse 18c. But the evidence of texts where *kratein* means "to restrain" (see *TDNT*, iii, pp. 911f.) shows that the contexts are of physical action; when the verb is used metaphorically, the sense of "to retain" (as in Heb. 4:14) is more prominent. Paul's warning is more naturally directed to a Christian whose teaching is of such a nature that it leads to apostatizing, i.e. by forsaking Christ.

The other verse, 2:20: "why do you submit to regulations?" (Greek *dogmatizesthe*) matches 2:4 where the Colossians are in danger of being deluded, though Paul is confident (2:5) that they will not succumb. Foerster argues that this is much more likely to reflect an outside disturbance caused by Essene-like Jews who had stirred up the Colossians by their pretended superiority (p. 80) in matters of ritual and legalistic observance. But this is to beg the whole question of the nature of the Colossian heresy which Paul labels "philosophy" (2:8), a term hardly suitable for a Judaizing aberration (cf. Galatians).

But it is a safe assumption that the church was divided over the question, else Paul would not have given such a detailed exposition of the danger and its antidote. The danger of a community rent by dissension and debate, with tempers frayed and uncharitable dispositions displayed, was one which the pastoral concern of Paul could not ignore. The section which follows is replete, then, with reminders of how Christians should live and act within the body of Christ, and how their profession should affect their tempers (3:5),

---

[1] See Dibelius-Greeven, op. cit., p. 38; Lohmeyer thinks that the question is unanswerable; more recently W. Foerster, "Die Irrlehrer des Kolosserbriefes," *Studia Biblica et Semitica* Festschrift T. C. Vriezen, 1966, p. 72, has argued for an outside influence which encroached on the church.

speech (3:8,9), obligation to seek true unity (3:11) in compassionate attitude to one another (3:12), in a forgiving spirit (3:13) and with love to crown their mutual relationships (3:14). At Christian corporate worship, here as at Corinth, certain flash-points of strife were predictable; so Paul sets down a model to be followed (3:15–17).

For this reason, we find it difficult to take seriously Masson's submission that 3:5–11 is non-Pauline because (on his view) it is unlike the other sections of Pauline exhortation (e.g., 1 Thess. 4:1–12; Phil. 3:17–4:9; Gal. 6:1–10) which are inspired by the concrete situation of the churches Paul writes to. The Colossians' passage, he avers, "on the contrary remains with generalities and addresses itself to the church as in Ephesians, without being aimed at a particular community." The purpose and destination of Ephesians are really separate matters[1] and the paraenetic sections in Ephesians 4–6 are not quite comparable with these verses in Colossians where, though some verbal echoes are found, the application to a local scene is more direct and the personal bond between Paul and his readers, who are greeted *by name* and invited to recognize his assistants *by name*, in 4:7–17, is clearly to be seen.

A more forceful argument against the authenticity of the verses as reflecting a pastoral involvement would be that of E. Lohse. He maintains (p. 199) that the catalogue of vices (in 3:5) is not occasioned by the situation of a church finding itself so addressed but by the use of traditional material. This may be shown by the parallels drawn from other New Testament passages of ethical lists. But it is significant that the closest parallel is with Galatians 5:19–21[2] in which Paul retails the "works of the flesh." May it be that Paul's use of a similar list of vices was dictated by his desire to show how true mortification *does* serve to check "*the indulgence of the flesh*" (2:23)? And he will thereby offer his readers an effective reply to a false teacher who is "inanely inflated by the *mind of the flesh*" (2:18).

[1] For some consideration of these issues, I may refer to an article, "An Epistle in search of a life-setting," *ExpT*, 79, 1968, pp. 296–302.

[2] See the study by P. Joüon, "Note sur Colossiens III. 5–11," *Recherches de Science Religieuse*, 26, 1936, pp. 185–189.

IX

TRUE SELF-DENIAL WITHIN THE CHURCH'S LIFE

3:5–11 Put to death therefore what is earthly in you: immorality, impurity, passion, evil desire, and covetousness, which is idolatry. ⁶On account of these the wrath of God is coming. ⁷In these you once walked, when you lived in them. ⁸But now put them all away: anger, wrath, malice, slander, and foul talk from your mouth. ⁹Do not lie to one another, seeing that you have put off the old nature with its practices ¹⁰and have put on the new nature, which is being renewed in knowledge after the image of its creator. ¹¹Here there cannot be Greek and Jew, circumcised and uncircumcised, barbarian, Scythian, slave, free man, but Christ is all, and in all.

THE SUBJECT-MATTER HERE IS "WHAT IS EARTHLY," A PHRASE carried over in Paul's thinking from verse 2. The statement of verse 3: "you have died" to a former way of life was couched in the indicative as Paul recalled the past experience of conversion and baptism which signalized a dramatic renunciation on the part of the Christians at Colossae. But some enforcement of a past fact is needed. So he slips into an imperative mood with this call. "Let the old self which is already dead in baptism remain dead" is the tenor of his admonition, as in Romans 6:11,12,13: "so you also must consider yourselves dead to sin . . . let not sin therefore reign in your mortal bodies . . . do not yield your members to sin as instruments of wickedness." This text from Romans clarifies our understanding in one further particular. It specifies that Paul is directing his attention to the Christian's "members," i.e. his limbs or bodily life "which constitute active and concrete corporeality under sin" (J. Horst, *TDNT*, iv, p. 565), as in Romans 8:13 which speaks of "the deeds of the body" to be put to death by deliberate self-denial.

Clearly Paul is not advocating a self-mortification which does away with temptation by self-injury (for instance, as by voluntary castration which the church father Origen suffered); nor does he wish to have all healthy instincts bottled up in an unnatural and unwholesome repression. His teaching is not a tom-tom call to self-immolation which robs life of its true joys and fullest expression. Yet his summons could be wrongly understood, as Jesus' stringent words in Matthew 5:29,30 have sometimes been.[1]

To safeguard himself from misunderstanding, Paul therefore spells out the exact sort of thing he has in mind. The human body can become an instrument of evil because man's fallen nature so chooses. Some of the bad fruit which grow on a diseased tree (Matt. 7:17-19) are listed: immorality (or sexual irresponsibility as in 1 Thess. 4:3; 1 Cor. 5:10f.; 6:9f.; 2 Cor. 12:21; Eph. 5:3;1 Tim. 1:9f. as well as Matt. 5:32; 19:9, where it means "marriage within prohibited degrees of kinship" [Lev. 18]) heads the roster, as in Galatians 5:19 in Paul's other list of "works of the flesh."

"Impurity" (Greek *akatharsia* = moral uncleanness) joins its partner in Galatians 5:19, and means very much the same thing. "Passion" which in English can be used in several senses, both good and bad, here seems to describe "sexual perversion, and it thus denotes erotic passion" (W. Michaelis, *TDNT.*, v, p. 928).

"Evil desire" is found also in Galatians 5:16 under the phrase "the desires of the flesh," which are to be resisted by a practised walking in the Spirit. They are to be treated as registering an invalid claim, since believers "have crucified the flesh with its passions and desires" (Gal. 5:24) and are not slaves to lust, like the pagans (1 Thess. 4:5).

The final vice in the list of five—the number is significant (vv. 8,12 also have five moral terms apiece)—is "covetousness" (Greek *pleonexia*). In other contexts the term means grasping greed, possessiveness (Luke 12:15), an insatiable longing to lay hands on another's property—even his wife (Ex. 20:17). The sexual overtone of the word is possibly found in 1 Thessalonians 4:6 where "wrong his brother" may have this vice in view. But this is not certain since the noun from this verb (*pleonektein*) occurs in 1 Corinthians 6:10 and means there "greedy." "Covetousness" breaks the sequence in the present list by switching the readers' thought from sexual vices to the sin of avarice. It "shows how important was the battle against sins of possession in the primitive Christian community (1 Tim. 6:10; 2 Tim. 3:2; Heb. 13:5) . . . [and was] a special threat to the new life of the Christian. It brings him under an ungodly

[1] Masson therefore seeks an easement of the Pauline teaching by wishing to take the reference to "members" (not translated in RSV) as a vocative "you members (of Christ's body)" addressed to the Colossians. But this ingenious solution would only be feasible in a context which speaks of Head-body-members (as 1 Cor. 12:12-27), as Dibelius-Greeven note.

and demonic spell which completely separates him from God through serving an alien power" (G. Delling, *TDNT*, vi, p. 271). To that extent it is no better than a spirit of idolatry, the worship of Mammon (an Aramaic word for wealth which the rabbis personified as a demon, Matt. 6:24). Idolatry stands under the judgement of Galatians 5:20 as another trait of a life dominated by the unregenerate self, the flesh.

3:6,7 The presence of a covetous spirit disqualifies a man from entrance into the divine kingdom (Eph. 5:5). On the contrary, a person who resigns himself to a life of wanton ways has only the prospect of divine judgement before him. The "wrath of God" is not fitful emotion or vindictive outburst on God's part; it is rather His judicial reaction to evil and evil-doers. It "is coming" in the eschatological sense that moral evil will be exposed and judgement meted out at the final Day. The process of retribution has already begun (Rom. 1:18—present tense); now Paul anticipates its future and final exhibition (as in Rom. 2:3-11,16; 1 Cor. 4:5; 2 Cor. 6:10). His eschatology is clearly flexible enough to hold together both time-aspects, just as he can move from the statement of the Christian's security of being risen with Christ to the ethical rigorism of a life of self-denial.

The contrast between the old life patterned on coarse ways and the new existence of the man in Christ is a frontispiece (in verse 7) to Paul's next section. The "once" of verse 7 prepares the ground for his triumphant announcement: "But now" (as in Eph. 2:11,13, though the terms of reference are different). Earlier in our epistle Paul has alluded to the Colossians' way of living before their conversion (2:13). He marks the turning-point at this juncture.

Paul's appeal to the decisive change which Christian conversion has brought about is the characteristic feature of his moral teaching. In its content and form, listing vices to be shunned and virtues to be cultivated, this ethical instruction is closely parallel with specimens found both in Greek-speaking Judaism and in hellenistic popular philosophy associated with the Stoics. But the distinctive character of Paul's moral code is the basis he lays in the death and resurrection of Christ which the believer shares in his baptism and consequent new life. A second distinctive element is mentioned by H. Conzelmann (commentary on 3:5ff., p. 151). This is the setting of Pauline ethics in the context of the church over against current ethical appeals which were addressed to men as individuals.

The apostle's tacit understanding of Christians living together within the family of God plays a decisive rôle in his inculcating the highest moral ideals. His ethics are always related to the common life in the body of Christ.

3:8–11 The operative verbs which carry the chief weight of moral activity are: "put away" (Greek *apothesthe*) and "put off" (Greek *apekdusamenoi*). The first word is common property in the New Testament vocabulary of catechetical instruction, especially applicable to recent converts who were being educated for their new way of life[1] (Rom. 13:12; Eph. 4:22; 1 Pet. 2:1). The second verb belongs to the act of baptism where the new disciple was instructed to regard his taking off his garments for the ordinance as a pictorial renunciation of an old life-style (Gal. 3:27; Rom. 6:4ff. and earlier in our letter, 2:11,12). It was the "old nature" derived from fallen humanity which was divested and old habits, desires and goals jettisoned, to be replaced by a new life-style, which was put on like a new set of clothes. The Christian turned his back on a former pattern of living, and henceforth entered upon a vivid experience as a member of the new humanity. That this experience, inalienably personal and life-changing, was equally corporate and social is clear from two parts of Paul's description.[2]

First, the vices in verse 8 and the generalizing reference in verse 9 ("the old nature *with its practices*") are all anti-social, laden with harm to other people. In the change-over to a new way of behaviour, the effect will be seen in the Christian's new social and inter-personal attitudes. His speech affecting others will be the index of a renewed character (3:13,16,17).

Then, it is in the new segment of humanity fashioned by God in Christ as a fresh order of creation (2 Cor. 4:6; 5:17) that racial, religious, social and cultural distinctions are done away (v. 11). The little connecting word "here" at the head of this verse has an importance not to be minimized. It is in the church of Christ that verse 11 comes to life; and the individual believer puts on the new nature as he enters the fellowship of that society by confessing his faith in Christ in baptism.

3:8,9a The sins to be disowned are all related to a person's speech:

---

[1] See P. Carrington, *The Primitive Christian Catechism. A Study in the Epistles*, 1940.

[2] Commenting on the terms "old nature," "new nature," C. F. D. Moule observes: "These phrases do not merely mean 'one's old, bad character,' and 'the new, Christian character' respectively, as an *individual's* condition: they carry deeper, wider, and more *corporate* associations, inasmuch as they are part of the presentation of the Gospel in terms of the two 'Adams', the two creations" (p. 119).

first, anger, of the kind reprobated in the Sermon on the Mount
(Matt. 5:21,22), which so quickly poisons human relationships by
an impetuous name-calling or calculated insult. "Wrath" is a close
member of a common unhappy brood, hardly to be distinguished
from anger in an undistinguished company of human faults. "There
is no material difference between them" (F. Büchsel, *TDNT* iii,
p. 168); and "wrath" is found in the ethical list of Galatians 5:20.
"Malice" represents a general term for moral evil (Greek *kakia*) and
is used in passages which depict the havoc to human society caused
by evil-speaking (1 Pet. 2:1; James 1:21; Eph. 4:31). One form of
such malice is "slander" (literally "blasphemy"), a spoken word of
cursing directed to God or of defamation directed to man. Indeed the
latter abuse includes the former in the light of James 3:9. An insult
levelled at a person is a shaft aimed at the image of God which
he represents, and so is a derogatory attack upon God Himself.
"Foul talk" clearly shows that while the human tongue can be a
source of encouragement and uplift to others (Eph. 4:29) it may
also be a cruel weapon of the speaker's hatred and spite. Or else it
may simply be an unthinking indulgence in crude talk for its own
sake or a recourse to expletive when tempers are frayed. One
further sin of speech is held up to condemnation. "Lying" is
universally branded as destructive of mutual trust between parties.
The same admonition recurs in Ephesians 4:25 with special reasons
given. Lying is condemned in the Old Testament (Zech. 8:16), and
failure to honour one's word leads to a breach of Christian fellowship because it breeds suspicion and distrust, and so destroys the
common life in the body of Christ (Rom. 12:5) by which "we are
members one of another."

Two parts of the New Testament bear upon the importance of a
Christian's speech: Matthew 12:33-37 and James 3:1-12, and both
should be our frequent reading. "For the mouth speaks what the
heart is full of" (Matt. 12:34, TEV) is a profound insight, anticipating
the discovery of man's true nature as *homo loquens*, who gives
expression to his real self by his verbal communication.[1]

[1] Recent commentators draw attention to the close parallels between Col. 3:5,8 and 1QS
iv. 10,11 in the Dead Sea scrolls:
"But the ways of the spirit of falsehood are these: greed, and slackness in the search for
righteousness, wickedness and lies, haughtiness and pride, falseness and deceit, cruelty and
abundant evil, ill-temper and much folly and brazen insolence, abominable deeds
(committed) in a spirit of lust, and ways of lewdness in the service of uncleanness, a
blaspheming tongue, blindness of eye and dullness of ear, stiffness of neck and heaviness of
heart, so that man walks in all the ways of darkness and guile". (Vermes' translation, pp.
76,77).

3:9b,10 The twin actions of "putting off," "putting on" are expressed in the Greek aorist tense, which points back to an experience in the life of the readers of which Paul is now reminding them. At first glance, this might be taken to refer to their original faith-union with Christ in conversion, without which indeed their Christian life could not have begun. But further consideration of this and parallel passages suggests an emphatic association with their baptismal experience, in which they signified their desire to have done with the old life and their dedication to walk in newness of life (Rom. 6:4).[1] The link with the reminder of having divested oneself of the old nature is clear in 2:11,12, just as the summons to live in the light of a new investiture matches Paul's teaching elsewhere (Rom. 13:12,14; Eph. 4:24, though other texts are more general in scope: 1 Thess. 5:8; Eph. 6:11,14). But the most emphatic statement of the link connecting the experience of "putting on" the new nature with Paul's teaching on baptism is Galatians 3:27: "As many of you as were baptized into Christ have put on Christ."

An objection to this view which sees Paul's teaching in a baptismal setting will occur to those who wish to press the exact force of the Greek participles. Ever since the influential study of D. Daube on the use of Greek participles as imperatives,[2] it has been customary to apply his conclusion to a text like Colossians 3:9. On this basis, we are inclined to answer Lightfoot's question, Are these participles part of the command, continued from the preceding, Don't lie, or do they assign the reason for the command? by accepting his recommendation, "The former seems the more probable interpretation."

More recent commentators have abandoned this interpretation in favour of a return to Lightfoot's alternative. So the text reads: "seeing that you did (at baptism) put off the old nature . . . and (again at baptism) put on the new." The aorist participles express what has already taken place (so C. Maurer, *TDNT*, vi, p. 644).

---

[1] This is the premise on which E. Larsson, *Christus als Vorbid. Eine Untersuchung zu den paulinischen Taufe- und Eikontexte*, 1962, 197f. bases his detailed discussion of Colossians 3:10–14 (pp. 188–223). J. Jervell, *Imago Dei. Gen. 1, 26f. im Spätjudentum, in der Gnosis und in den paulinischen Briefen*, 1960, gives an equally full survey of the verses under the headings: "The image of God concept as a motive for exhortation (paraenesis); The old and the new Man; The exemplar (*Vorbild*); The new life of Man as the image of God." The teaching of Genesis 1:26f. plays a decisive rôle in Jervell's understanding of this ethical instruction, especially verse 10.

[2] D. Daube, "Participle and Imperative in 1 Peter," in E. G. Selwyn, *The First Epistle of St. Peter*,[2] 1947, pp. 467–488. His thesis is that the participles are used for commands in the ethical injunctions of certain rabbinic writings.

This view seems to be in every way in line with Paul's thought throughout the chapter. He is harking back to past events in the lives of His readers and making these the foundation for his present ethical appeal (so Jervell, p. 236).

The grammatical point we have discussed is of some consequence. Its elucidation has an influence on how we are to enter Paul's mind here. The choice is before us in the following alternative: is he calling upon the Colossians to take action in following through on his previous counsels—to give up their old habits and then to strip off their old nature with all its evil deeds, replacing this with a new life of God-likeness? Or, is he recalling them to what has already taken place in the once-for-all commitment to Christ they have made in baptism, and encouraging them to act upon that past event *by being true to it?* Jettison your evil habits of speech, for these are unworthy of the new life you have already embarked upon as members within the body of Christ. Through your baptismal confession and dedication you publicly professed membership in that community: now make good your profession and live up to it![1]

The possibility of interpreting the call of 3:5ff. as a summons to act out the decisive change already begun in baptism is not considered by J. D. G. Dunn, *Baptism in the Holy Spirit*, 1970, p. 158. His view that Paul "can urge them to repeat what they did once at the beginning of their Christian lives" leads him to conclude that Paul does not have baptism in mind at all. We may agree with him that Paul "is certainly not asking them to repeat their baptism," but his failure to take into consideration the above possibility leads him to an incomplete exegesis.

Expressed in this way, the antithesis seems clear; and we should not hesitate to follow the second line of explanation as being in keeping with earlier parts of the letter which describe the Colossians' decisive entry into God's realm (1:13), their baptismal experience (2:12,13,20) and present life in Christ (3:1,3).

The same understanding clarifies the puzzling terms: "old nature" (literally "old man"), and "new nature." These are not primarily terms of individuality but are corporate associations. Paul is calling

---

[1] G. Bornkamm handles the tension in the apostle's teaching between the indicative ("you have died with Christ in baptism") and the imperative ("put to death . . . put off the old nature") in his essay, "Baptism and New Life in Paul," *Early Christian Experience*, 1969, pp. 71–86, and concludes provocatively: "The obedience of believers cannot penetrate further than to what has happened to us at the beginning. It takes place in the constant 'crawling-under-baptism' (Luther) . . . Baptism is the dedication of the new life, and the new life is the appropriation of baptism" (p. 84).

upon his readers to sever their allegiance to an old order of life which has already been condemned, crucified and done away (Rom. 6:6). He is inviting them to live as those who have entered a new world, as members of the new humanity alive unto God. And in making these clear distinctions in this corporate way Paul's mind is open to new modes of expression never previously explored (so Jervell, p. 240); and Paul uses these powerful figures of speech to drive home the single point that Christians at Colossae have something better to guide their ethical decisions than man-made rules and a species of fake-religion (2:16–23). His alternative is a reminder of a new lordship under which they have passed at the time of their conversion and spiritual renewal (2:13). They have forsaken the old way of irresponsible and selfish pursuits which belong to the old Adam. They have enlisted in a new society which draws its life from the new Adam. The decisive transition and change of lordship has been made. They must now act upon it. All this teaching is new with Paul.

But there are in the Old Testament certain anticipations, especially in the presentation of the first man who came from the hands of his maker as a bearer of the divine image (Gen. 1:26f.). That image was defaced by man's fall into sin, and only dimly reflects the glory of God (1 Cor. 11:7). Man as a sinful creature has lost that ideal for which he was created (Rom. 3:23), even though it hangs over him as a haunting reminder of what he once was—and may still become.

A new start in humanity's long story is made with Christ's coming, and it is fundamental to Paul's whole theology and expression of the Christian faith to exploit the deepest meanings of Christ as the new Man, the ultimate Adam (Rom. 5:12–21; 1 Cor. 15:20–2,45–50).[1]

What makes the present passage unusual and important is the full description Paul gives of the renewal process both in its pattern and content. Believers are endowed with the new nature which is being renewed (a) after the image of its creator, and (b) in knowledge.

But who is "its creator"? First impressions would recall the Genesis account of man's creation by God (Gen. 1:26,27) and reply that it is God who provides the prototype for humanity's renewal.

---

[2] I have essayed a treatment of this part of Paul's christology in *Carmen Christi: Philippians ii. –11*, 1967, pp. 102–120 in a discussion of Christ as the image of God.

But Paul's thought is christological here. His teaching is that Jesus Christ fulfilled the rôle of the last Adam as the perfect Man in whom the image of true manhood is to be seen. So He is designated the "last Adam" (1 Cor. 15:45), the "second man" (1 Cor. 15:47) of whom Adam was a "type" (Rom. 5:14) and here—on this view—"the new man" whose image is renewed in His people, in a process elsewhere spoken of in 2 Corinthians 3:18; 4:16; 1 Corinthians 15:45, and Romans 8:29.

This equation of "the new man" (RSV, new nature) and Jesus Christ is made clearly in Ignatius, *Ephesians* 20:1: "I will show you concerning the dispensation of the new man, Jesus Christ." But it is sometimes denied in reference to our verse. Lightfoot insists that the term refers not to Christ Himself but to "the regenerate man formed after Christ". This denial is resisted by most modern commentators, of whom Lohmeyer is representative. His counter-argument for identifying the new man with Christ is based on the way in which the apostle can speak elsewhere of the Christian as putting on Christ (Gal. 3:27; Rom. 13:14), and the declaration of Colossians 3:11 that Christ is both everything (Greek *panta*) and "in all" (Greek *in pasin*). He interprets the second phrase to indicate that Christ indwells all the members of the church (Col. 1:27) as they have received Him (2:6) and been endowed with Him. "So our passage can hardly be interpreted otherwise than that Christ is the new man" (Lohmeyer).

The alternatives posed by Lightfoot, Christ or the regenerate man are, to be sure, not the only possibilities. S. Hanson[1] takes the expression to refer to the new race of men incarnated in Christ as the second Adam (based on Eph. 2:15; cf. Eph. 4:22ff.). He makes the phrase "new man" relate to "Christ incorporating saved humanity." The attractiveness of this view is that it aptly prepares for verse 11 which describes the new quality of life available in the new humanity where Christ is both its pattern and inspiration.

The "new man" is undergoing renovation in knowledge. This content is best understood in the light of 1:9. The "knowledge" (Greek *epignōsis*) is directly related to God's will and purpose and so is a practical and ethical term. Jewish interpreters of Genesis 1:26 made the possession of the divine image by man an ethical incentive

---

[1] *The Unity of the Church in the New Testament. Colossians and Ephesians*, 1946, pp. 144f. See also C. K. Barrett, *From First Adam to Last*, 1962, pp. 97–99, for the view that "new man" refers to the new community in Christ.

so that man showed his unique relationship to God by obeying His voice and following His ways. Paul picks up this same teaching in a Christian context, which tacitly rebukes the heretics' claim to "knowledge" conveyed in mystical experience.

3:11 In the society of Christians a new type of humanity is being formed. Christ's life flows out to His people and is reproduced in their midst. One single proof of this new life was seen in the cancelling of restrictions and inhibitions which made the ancient world so socially stratified and class-conscious. Paul had earlier shown how in the church barriers of race, social distinction, and sex were being broken down (Gal. 3:28) as Christians acted upon their baptismal profession of initiation into one body (1 Cor. 12:13). The present verse represents the full flowering of his thought.

The divisions of humanity are set out according to a classification of nationality (Greek, Jew), religious affiliations (circumcized and uncircumcized) and social rank (slave , free man). In the church of Christ these distinctions have now come to an end because Christ is the creator of a new humanity embracing both Jews and Gentiles (1 Cor. 10:32) and forming a third race of men, the new Israel (Gal. 6:16). He has abolished the former privileges of the circumcised Jew (Rom. 2:25-29; 1 Cor. 7:19; Gal. 6:15) by introducing the "true circumcision" (Phil. 3:3) in which Gentiles by race can have a share and so are in no way disadvantaged. Social inequalities count for nothing in a society where service is the keynote of corporate living and the materially rich stretch out their hands to those who are economically under-privileged as slaves (1 Cor. 11:33), though the selfish abuses of the communion meal at Corinth indicate that Christians were slow to recognize their social responsibilities in these matters (1 Cor. 11:20ff.). Paul's teaching in 1 Corinthians 7:17-24 puts a new face on the existence of slaves and free men in Graeco-Roman society. His counsel seems to be (the interpretation of verse 21 is disputed): slaves should treat their place in society as a matter of indifference and use even their servitude to good effect (Col. 3:22f.) as free in the Lord, while the free man must recognize his voluntary subjection as a slave of Christ. Only on this view can we make sense of Paul's logical conclusion in 1 Corinthians 7:17,24: "each must order his life according to . . . his condition when God called him . . . each one . . . is to remain before God in the condition in which he received his call" (NEB).

In the list of verse 11 "barbarian," "Scythian" stand out. They are not opposites, as we might have expected, but complementary terms for non-Jewish groups who stood outside the circle of Greek culture. The sense of this former is "uncivilized" (as in Acts 28:2,4) because their language seemed to cultured Greeks "barbaric" and gibberish (1 Cor. 14:11). The Maltese of Acts 28 spoke Punic. Paul's commitment to proclaim the gospel to Graeco-Roman society included a mission to these peoples on the fringes of the Roman empire (Rom. 1:14). H. Windisch (*TDNT*, i, p. 552) suggestively remarks that Paul may have Spanish people in mind as he proposes to use Rome as a launching-pad for his mission to the western Mediterranean area (Rom. 15:24).

In our verse he may have intended a comprehensive coverage of all the ethnic groups of his missionary travels. Then "barbarians" would aptly describe the Celts of Galatia (Gal. 3:1) and/or the Lycaonians of Acts 14:11. "Scythian" represents "the lowest type of barbarian" (Lightfoot) and as such the title became almost a synonym for the slave-class since slaves were taken from the lower strata of society, especially from tribes around the Black Sea, who were known by the name of Scythians. Quite probably the Colossians were familiar with such a title in their region whose social structure was based on the division of masters and slaves (3:22–4:1).

Paul's final statement nobly expresses the new reality which entered the world of men with the advent of Christ's church (so Lohse). The visible demonstration of Christ's exaltation and lordship is seen in His people's communal lives which form a new society. This is nothing less than a new beginning to humanity in which all the old divisions, hatreds and stratifications have lost their bitterness and meaning. Christian believers are enrolled in "one body" (1 Cor. 12:13) to form "one man" in Christ (Gal. 3:28) which "dispossessed and obliterated all distinctions of religious prerogative and intellectual preeminence and social caste" (Lightfoot). The new humanity of Christ-in-His-church is "one new man" (Eph. 2:15), a new order of society which is asserting its presence in the world and so witnessing to Christ's transforming power in modern society—in Wolverhampton, England; Atlanta, Georgia; and Johannesburg, South Africa, no less than in ancient Colossae.

X

THE DISTINCTIVE CHARACTER OF CHRISTIAN LIVING

3:12–17 *Put on then, as God's chosen ones, holy and beloved, compassion, kindness, lowliness, meekness, and patience,* [13]*forbearing one another and, if one has a complaint against another, forgiving each other; as the Lord has forgiven you, so you also must forgive.* [14]*And above all these put on love, which binds everything together in perfect harmony.* [15]*And let the peace of Christ rule in your hearts, to which indeed you were called in one body. And be thankful.* [16]*Let the word of Christ dwell in you richly, as you teach and admonish one another in all wisdom, and as you sing psalms and hymns and spiritual songs with thankfulness in your hearts to God.* [17]*And whatever you do, in word or deed, do everything in the name of the Lord Jesus, giving thanks to God the Father through him.*

THE CALL TO "PUT ON" THE NEW NATURE MAY WELL HAVE sounded too idealistic and ethereal for Paul's first readers. The apostle therefore proceeds to make his appeal more specific and practical as well as more positive. He moves from a list of affirmative virtues to be cultivated (v. 12) through a statement of how the believer will react to certain human situations when his equilibrium is disturbed (v. 13) to a reminder that his distinctive badge is one of love (v. 14). Christ's peace will act as an arbiter when choices have to be made (v. 15). The church's worship will serve a dual purpose of aiding his growth in Christian knowledge and fellowship with his brethren, and of giving him an outlet for praise (v. 16). Indeed, the whole of life is to be brought under the aegis of his discipleship as he performs his tasks in the spirit of devotion to Jesus Christ (v. 17).

3:12 In a previous section Paul has accented the negative requirements of the gospel's moral call (3:5–9). "Put to death," "put away," "put off"—these injunctions are couched in the deadly serious tone of self-discipline and ethical rigorism. Now it is time to turn to depict the manner of living which belongs to God's "chosen ones," His elect. That term (Greek *eklektoi*) belongs to Paul's favourite way of expressing the truth that men do not become Christians simply by choice and decision on their part (Rom. 8:33; 16:13). Underlying human response is the free grace of God who takes the initiative and so moves the human will that it finds its true freedom in willingly surrendering to the divine call (1 Thess. 1:4; 2 Thess. 2:13,14). In a clear statement (in Eph. 1:4f.) Paul acknowledges how God's pre-mundane choice ensures that men and women who hear the gospel through the apostolic witness and preaching will respond in faith (Eph. 1:13). Here we confront the mystery of divine election which runs through much of the New Testament. Some guidelines of interpretation may be helpful.

The New Testament writers proclaim God's electing mercy not as a conundrum to tease our minds but as a wonder to evoke our praise. They offer this teaching not as an element in God's character to be minimized but as an assurance that our lives are in His powerful hands rather than in the grip of capricious fate, which was a fear first-century man knew well. And the same dread of life's meaninglessness still lurks in the mind of modern sophisticated man. The doctrine of election is never stated as an excuse for carelessness in spiritual matters, but always as a reminder that Christians have a moral responsibility "to confirm [their] call and election" (2 Pet. 1:10) by following the highest ethical standards. We are chosen "that we should be holy and blameless" (Eph. 1:4); the elect are equally to be "holy and beloved."

In this powerful reminder of the Christians' standing before God, Paul, in fact, is accomplishing two objectives. As Lightfoot has shown, the three descriptive terms—chosen, holy, beloved—are borrowed from the Old Testament and transferred from Israel after the flesh to Israel after the Spirit. Paul had a deep sense of the continuity of God's purpose which ran through both Testaments. And his eye may again have been set on some false teaching at Colossae which laid claim to being the true fulfilment of the Old Testament (see note on 2:11–13; 20–23).

His more obvious purpose was to remind the Colossians that their lives should measure up to their profession. Let them become in practice what they already were by divine calling and design.

Five moral qualities are listed. "Compassion" is literally "a heart of pity," an expression formed from two separate words which are found side-by-side in Philippians 2:1, "affection and sympathy." The Greek word often rendered "heart" is literally "internal organs" (*splanchna*). In ancient thought the viscera were regarded as the seat of emotional life (of God, Is. 63:15, as well as of man, Jer. 4:19; Phil. 1:8). The second word (Greek *oiktirmos*) signifies the outward expression of deep feeling in compassionate yearning and action. So the composite term conveys the sense of a deeply-felt compassion which goes out to those around us with ready aid.

"Kindness" and "lowliness" are a pair, matching the Christian's relation to others and to himself. Again, he will show a genial regard to other people and do his best to help any in need, though strictly *chrēstotēs* is "a kindly disposition toward one's neighbour not necessarily taking a practical form" (Lightfoot, on Gal. 5:22). The impact of a kindly spirit is well exemplified by Augustine's tribute to Ambrose's influence upon him. Though he had little interest in Ambrose's preaching, the latter's kindness to him moved Augustine beyond words: "And I began to love him, not at first as a teacher of the truth, which I despaired of finding in Thy church, but as a fellow-creature who was kind to me" (*Confessions*, Book V, Ch. 13).

L. H. Marshall[1] who quotes from Augustine makes the valid point that the person who receives kindness from a Christian is open to interpret this concern for him as a manifestation of the love of God. The Pauline writings continually remark on the kindness of God shown to needy men and women (Rom. 2:4; 11:22; Eph. 2:7; Tit. 3:4) who in turn will want to reflect the same generous regard and interest in their dealings with other people.

"Lowliness" is the same word as is normally translated "humility;" earlier (2:18,23) it had been used in a bad sense of false humility. Now Paul includes it in an obviously different way, to denote the Christian's appropriate attitude of self-regard, exactly as in Romans 12:3, in neither becoming haughty nor self-depreciating. True humility is, as Masson aptly says, "the sovereign antidote to self-love which poisons relations between (Christian) brothers."

"Meekness" and "patience" are partners also, denoting the exercise of the Christian temper in its outward bearing towards others. So Lightfoot comments, and he proceeds to define the terms by their opposites. "Meekness" is best seen by contrasting it with "rudeness," "harshness;" while the opposite of "patience" is "resentment," "revenge," "wrath." More fully, we may say that "meekness" (Greek *prautēs*) has two elements in it:[2]

---

[1] *The Challenge of New Testament Ethics*, 1946, p. 297.
[2] Cf. L. H. Marshall, op. cit. p. 300.

(*i*) consideration for others; (*ii*) willingness to waive an undoubted right (as in 1 Cor. 9:12ff.). Considerateness is seen in Paul's teaching elsewhere (See Gal. 6:1; 1 Cor. 11:33; 12:14, 15; Phil. 2:4) and also in his own character and behaviour (1 Cor. 4:6; Gal. 2:18).[1]

"Patience" is a picture-word suggesting "long-temperedness"; it "refers to the endurance of wrong and exasperating conduct on the part of others without flying into a rage or passionately desiring vengeance" (Marshall, op. cit., p. 294). Only our cultivation of this last disposition will make possible our tolerance and the forgiving spirit, spoken of in verse 13.

Two comments on these Christian graces may be made. "All five terms are indicative of the way the Christian should treat his fellowman" (Lohse), primarily within the church's fellowship, as verse 13 shows. Then, in each instance, Paul's choice of terms seems dictated by the qualities which in the first place are appropriate to God's attitudes and actions. God in Christ is merciful, kind, humble, meek and long-suffering (Rom. 12:1; 2:4; Phil. 2:5ff.; 2 Cor. 10:1; Ps. 103:8). Nothing could be clearer than Paul's intention to hold up the divine character as a sublime model and to encourage his Colossian friends to catch the divine spirit. God's dealings with sinful men are the amazing proof of His love—and He calls His people to be like Him in their mutual relations and conduct (Eph. 5:1).

3:13 The twin dispositions of forbearance and a forgiving spirit continue in the same vein. The occasion of the latter is given in the words "if one has a complaint against another." It is hardly likely that Paul has in mind a concrete situation in the Colossian church. The reference is more general, though his choice of a rare Greek word rendered "complaint" (or "reproach") is unusual. Perhaps, as Masson suggests, we should understand: "if anyone has a grievance or grudge against another person." Then, there is room for the exercise of these peace-making attitudes as we seek to curb our impatience with that person and to show a charitable and forgiving spirit. The reason and justification for this conciliatory mood are of the highest, "the Lord has forgiven you." With this Pauline rationale we are back in the world of the Lord's prayer with its plea for

[1] "He develops a singular sensitiveness to what the other man is thinking and a singular courtesy in dealing with his fellow men. The sensitiveness shows itself in several passages . . . the courtesy in Galatians ii. 18, where he allows his meaning to be obscured by substituting himself for Peter as the person open to criticism (cp. I Cor. i. 13)." C. A. A. Scott, *Saint Paul, The Man and the Teacher*, 1936, p. 14.

forgiveness "as we also have forgiven our debtors" (Matt. 6:12). The Lord is Christ Himself (a variant reading in the text) who mediates to us God's forgiveness (2:13). It is characteristic of Paul to recall the self-sacrifice of Christ in His act of salvation to provide the motive-power for Christians to turn their bitterness into forgiving love. This is part of what has been called his "conformity"-teaching, in which Christ's human life is not simply a model to be imitated by following in His earthly footsteps. On the contrary, Paul emphasizes the total impact of Christ's incarnation and especially His self-offering on the cross as providing a paradigm of a life-style to which the believer henceforth conforms (Rom. 15:7f.; Eph. 5:2, 25,29: cf. 4:32; Col. 3:13 are the texts given by N. A. Dahl).[1]

3:14 The excellence of love as the Christian's distinctive dress is given special place as we may have anticipated from the writer of 1 Corinthians 13 and Galatians 5:6. "Above all" may carry the thought of "on top of all the other 'articles of clothing'" to be put on (v. 12) (so Moule). Love is the uniting force which holds all other virtues in place, gives them motive and meaning, and so produces the fulness of Christian living. Love gives cohesion to the perfect life by producing "the perfect fellowship that ought to exist among Christian men. Love is the bond that unites them in a common service."[2]

Paul's thought is never narrowly individual and pietistic as though his chief design was to write a manual for the interior life of saint-hood. His concern is ever with the Christians' corporate life, and the perfection he sets before his readers is attained only in the fellowship of believers whose attitudes and living together reflect something of the graces of verse 12 and the spirit of verse 13. How we get along with other people is quite often the decisive test of the quality of our Christian living, and a truer index of our character than our pious feelings or private devotions.

3:15 The need to have a Christian community living together in unison and tolerance is further stressed. What happens when strife and friction enter as disturbing elements? The umpire in any dispute is Christ's peace—both the peace He embodies and which He alone can give—which is the desired prize in all Christian relationships (John 14:27). He is our peace (Eph. 2:14) in the special

---

[1] "Formgeschichtliche Beobachtungen zur Christusverkündigung in der Gemeindepredigt' in *Neutestamentliche Studien für Rudolf Bultmann*, ed. W. Eltester, 1957, pp. 3–9 (p. 7).
[2] R. Newton Flew, *The Idea of Perfection in Christian Theology*, 1934, p. 70.

sense of uniting Jews and Gentiles in the church as both groups are reconciled to God. The call here is to allow no alien spirit to creep into church members' relations with their fellow-believers, which would destroy that "peace." Probably the Old Testament idea of "wholeness," "integrity," "soundness" (implicit in the Hebrew term *shalom* = peace) is in the background.

The harmony of the church is God's will for His people. To that goal they are called as the one body of Christ who is the appointed Head (1:18,24). As He rules in His house and settles every faction ("rule" means "arbitrate," "give a verdict" in either a legal case or an athletic contest), so His peace is realized in the church's becoming in fact what it is intended to be by God's design. It is nothing less than the coming into visible reality of that new man of verse 10; a new society is born and grows and is distinguished by a corporate life of "wholeness" affecting every dimension of the church's existence in the world. W. Foerster can therefore correctly designate the peace of Christ as "a kingdom in which the believer is protected" (*TDNT*, ii, p. 414) as long as he seeks the will of the King and is obedient to the Head of the body. And he shows that response by the measure of his acceptance of a life-style patterned on the spiritual qualities of verse 12 and a forgiving disposition which reaches out to any who bear him malice (v. 13).

The manifestation of this new society is a cause for thanksgiving to God. In that segment of human life where God's will is honoured and obeyed and in which the new life of His Son is at work and in which a new humanity is taking shape, the appropriate response must be one of gratitude. As Paul has sounded this note in 1:12 to preface the recital of God's mighty deeds in redemption, so now he concludes fittingly with the same thought. In the sphere of the church, Christ's body and His new people who reflect His image (3:10), the hymn of praise takes on fresh significance.

3:16,17 Some recent study of New Testament hymnody draws attention to the importance of these verses (with the parallel in Eph. 5:19f.).[1] One assumption is made which would throw light on the arrangement of the verses. This is that the call, "be thankful" (v. 15b) is not an appendix to what has gone before, but a sort of rubric or heading indicating the next topic of catechetical instruction.

[1] J. M. Robinson, "Die Hodajot-Formel in Gebet und Hymnus des Frühchristentums," in *Apophoreta*. Festschrift E. Haenchen, 1964, pp. 194–235. See R. P. Martin, *Worship in the Early Church*, 1964, pp. 135–138; and J. T. Sanders, *The New Testament Christological Hymns* 1971.

This is to be linked with 1 Thessalonians 5:16: "Rejoice always" as a call to hymnic praise at the head of a list of seven admonitions (1 Thess. 5:16–22). What is notable is that the free rein which is given at Thessalonica, with the warning inserted: "Don't quench the Spirit" is restricted at Corinth in the injunction that the spirits of the prophets should be subject to the prophets (1 Cor. 14:32), and at Colossae a decisive shift is made away from ecstatic and spontaneous hymnic speech in the direction of a more stereotyped and didactic form of church worship. In Paul's latest description the emphasis falls more obviously on the instruction given by the word of Christ (i.e. the missionary message which centres in Christ, 1:5; 4:3); believers are encouraged to teach and admonish one another by the use of the gift of wisdom (1 Cor. 12:8) and so to share in the apostolic task (1:28); and 'while singing is mentioned as a feature of corporate praise and thankfulness, a restrictive ban on freely created and ecstatic songs (sung in *glossolalia* = by the use of a tongue?) may be seen in the way in which such hymnody is subordinated to the ministry of teaching and exhortation. And it is "in the heart" and "to God" that the most meaningful hymns are offered—not by the use of a tongue, and expressed publicly in the full congregation which is assembled for worship.[1]

The oldest allusion to early Christian hymns is found in 1 Corinthians 14. There is evidence to show that the "psalm" (Greek *psalmos*) in verse 26 was in the nature of an ecstatically-inspired hymn of thanksgiving to God, as the worshipper was caught up in an emotion of ecstasy and poured forth his praise in blessing God. Nothing, however, is known of the content or form of such spontaneous creations.

We may assume that "psalms" in our present verse carries the same notion, though older commentators (Lightfoot, Lock[2]) thought that probably the Psalms of David would be included under this caption. "Hymns" are sometimes taken to be expressions of praise to God or Christ (so Lock). "Spiritual songs" is a phrase

---

[1] This distinction between the practice of *glossolalia* in congregational worship (1 Cor. 14:19, 23,26,28) and its use as a private exercise of Christian devotion seems to be an important key to an understanding of 1 Corinthians 14. Paul senses the inherent dangers in the former practice, while reserving his measured approval (based on his own experience, 1 Cor. 14:18) for the latter, which may be the same as the type of prayer-speech referred to in Romans 8:26,27.

[2] W. Lock, "Hymn," Hasting's *Dictionary of the Bible*, ii, 1899, pp. 440f. Further bibliography will be found in my essay, "Aspects of Worship in the New Testament Church," *Vox Evangelica*, ii, 1963.

which uses a general term for a musical composition (Greek *ōdē*) with its special meaning decided by the adjective "spiritual," i.e. inspired by the Holy Spirit. There are characteristic references in the Book of Revelation to the songs of the heavenly worshippers (Rev. 5:9; 14:3; 15:3).

It is very doubtful if these firm distinctions can be drawn, and no exact arrangement of New Testament hymns seems possible on the basis of the different words. The adjective "spiritual" may be taken to extend to all the terms, leading to the conclusion that it is the Spirit who stirs the worshipper and directs his thought and emotion in lyrical praise, whatever be the precise musical form.

Another general conclusion is that the common motif running through the variety of liturgical expressions is thanksgiving to God (Col. 3:16,17; Eph. 5:20; 1 Cor. 14:16; 1 Thess. 5:18) whose mercy in Christ, His person and work no doubt formed the chief theme of Christian canticles, to judge from Colossians 1:15–20 (cf. 1:12); Ephesians 5:14; Philippians 2:6–11; Hebrews 1:1–4; 1 Timothy 3:16; John 1:1–14 (to mention the outstanding specimens of New Testament hymns). These hymns set forth the cosmological rôle of the church's Lord in the double sense of that adjective. First, His pre-existence and pre-temporal activity are made the starting-point of the hymns; then, at the conclusion of His earthly life He takes His place in God's presence, receiving the universal homage and acclamation of the cosmic spirit-powers which confess His lordship. His saving work is seen as that of bringing together the two orders of existence (the heavenly and the earthly), and His reconciliation is described in a cosmic setting.

The hymns are essentially soteriological in their purpose, displaying the saving deeds of the pre-existent Christ who came from God to restore the universe to God and has now returned to the divine presence. As we observed in the case of Colossians 1:15–20 (see p. 55) the person of Christ is seen in relation to His work and the christology is functional, not speculative. But inasmuch as He accomplished what God alone can do—the pacification of the hostile powers of the universe, in particular—and has taken His place on His Father's throne (Phil. 2:9–11; 1 Tim. 3:16; Heb. 1:3,4; Rev. 3:21, 5:1–14) as the divinely appointed world-ruler and Judge of all history, it was a short step for the early Christians to take to set Him "in the place of God" in their cultic worship. Within a few decades they were singing hymns "to Christ as to God" (in the description of Christian worship in Bithynia, AD 111–112, according to Pliny).

Already the ground was being prepared for this acknowledgement of Christ as divine Lord in such a passage as 3:17. The hymns to God (v. 16) which centre on Christ's mission and accomplishment and exalted place lead on to the call to do everything "in the name of the Lord Jesus." Singing gratefully (v. 16) matches "giving thanks" to God *through Him*. He is seen as mediator and advocate; by His redeeming work and intercessory ministry He makes our worship possible and stands in the divine presence to gather up the church's oblation of praise and present it to the Father (Heb. 7:25; 12:24; 13:15; 1 Pet. 2:5). The theme is one of praise to God through Christ rather than petition and supplication (so A. Oepke, *TDNT*, ii, pp. 68f.).

Further, Paul's pastoral concern may have developed in a more positive direction by the time he came to write verse 17 of our passage. If the two passages (1 Thess. 5:16–22 and our present section) are parallel, his earlier warning, "Keep clear of every appearance of evil" is couched in severely negative terms. Now he rephrases this prohibition to offer a total stance towards life in positive tones. "Do everything in the name of the Lord Jesus, giving thanks . . ." The name of the Lord Jesus is not a magical formula to be thoughtlessly appended to our enterprises; nor is it anything to do with mystical fellowship. Rather, "the whole life of the Christian stands under the name of Jesus" (H. Bietenhard, *TDNT*, v, p. 274). The new convert was baptized "in the name of the Lord Jesus" in the Pauline churches (1 Cor. 6:11) and made his baptismal profession by invoking that name (Rom. 10:9,10). The meaning of the "name" in these contexts is seen in the way that the new Christian on his profession and admittance to the church passed under the authority of Christ and became thenceforth His "property". In his new way of life he is simply making good his baptismal allegiance by placing the totality of his life under Christ's lordship.

Whether this change of emphasis is correct or not, there is no mistaking the ringing, life-affirming tenor of verse 17. The reference should not be confined simply to acts of worship performed in a church service but embraces the whole of life. However, there is a sense in which every phase of life is an act of worship and all our activities even the most mundane and routine can be offered up as part of the "living sacrifice" we are called upon to make. This is our "spiritual worship" (Rom. 12:1), says Paul in a sentence which stands as the frontispiece to a most down-to-earth discussion of the Christian's responsibility in the church and in the world. Those who take seriously their calling in this way "make the everyday round of so-called secular life into an arena of the unlimited and unceasing glorification of the divine will."[1]

[1] E. Käsemann, "Worship and Everyday Life. A Note on Romans 12," *New Testament Questions of Today*, 1969, p. 191.

XI

FAMILY DUTIES

3:18—4:1 *Wives, be subject to your husbands, as is fitting in the Lord.*
19Husbands, love your wives, and do not be harsh with them. *20Children,*
obey your parents in everything, for this pleases the Lord. *21Fathers, do not*
provoke your children, lest they become discouraged. *22Slaves, obey in*
everything those who are your earthly masters, not with eye-service, as
menpleasers, but in singleness of heart, fearing the Lord. *23Whatever your*
task, work heartily, as serving the Lord and not men, *24knowing that from*
the Lord you will receive the inheritance as your reward; you are serving
the Lord Christ. *25For the wrong-doer will be paid back for the wrong he has*
done, and there is no partiality.
   4. Masters, treat your slaves justly and fairly, knowing that you also have
a Master in heaven.

"WITHOUT APPARENT TRANSITION PAUL NOW ADDRESSES THE
members of the Christian family." But we may query
whether this remark of Masson's is correct. Is there in fact
no logical connexion between the two paragraphs? At first sight
there seems to be none. But we should recall how in his earlier
discussion of church worship (1 Cor. 14) Paul found it needful to
include an injunction to spell out the general rubric: "all things
should be done decently and in order." In particular, women
members of the Corinthian congregation are counselled against
speaking in public worship (14:33f.) and are summoned to be
"subordinate" (Greek *hypotassesthōsan*). It is "disgraceful" (v. 35)
for their voices to be heard. Clearly, Paul cannot be issuing an
anti-feminist tirade nor can he be complaining about women's
chatter in the church! Something more serious is in view, namely,
that Corinthian women, exploiting their freedom in society and
their rôle in the church to pray aloud (1 Cor. 11:5–16), had gone
to excess and were exercising and abusing a spiritual gift of tongues.
Paul calls them to be subject to their husbands and to restrain their
desire for knowledge by refusing to fathom deep mysteries (v. 35,
cf. 14:2). Rather, let them consult their husbands in private. In a
similar context, 1 Timothy 2:11 uses the same Greek term rendered

"submissiveness" (*hypotagē*) to caution women would-be teachers to keep silence in the church.

The inference is, then, that Paul's directory of public worship at Colossae is rounded off with a similar call. He has encouraged the church to be attentive to the exercise of spiritual gifts, expressing thanks to God in song and profiting from a ministry of mutual exhortation and teaching. Now he will enter a cautionary reminder that order and decorum should mark out the conduct of women members. They should be subject (Greek *hypotassesthe*) to their husbands in congregational assembly.

3:18 The restriction is, however, of wider application. Church service is only part of life. In domestic relationships with their husbands and family Christian spouses are summoned to accept their place in the divine ordering of family life (1 Cor. 11:3-9).[1] A reason is supplied: it is "fitting," i.e. socially acceptable. Ephesians 5:4 gives the opposite: what is socially reprehensible, not "proper." Paul is using here a Stoic maxim which appealed to a way of conduct which was "the right thing to do." He christianizes it, however, with the phrase "in the Lord." It is a wife's duty to take her appropriate place in society; indeed, Paul goes on, it is her Christian duty (NEB).

Husbands are reminded of their responsibility: to love their wives. The splendid passage in Ephesians 5:25ff. which takes its starting-point from this statement is not reproduced here; and in a sense what follows is a kind of anti-climax. But the warning "do not be harsh with them" is a salutary reminder that Christian love is to be exercised in a realistic fashion and should have a controlling influence on character and everyday living. Our life with those closest to us in the family circle is subjected to strains and stresses which we can easily brush off in less personal relationships in the outside world. How we act in the intimacy of the home and marriage circle is a true indication of the quality of our love as Christians. In a strange quirk of human behaviour we can often injure thoughtlessly those we love the most; so Paul's caution is well taken: Husbands, do not be embittered (Arndt-Gingrich) against your wives by nursing resentment and harsh feelings (see W. Michaelis, *TDNT*, vi, p. 125).

3:20,21 Paul's practical realism is again to the fore in his message

---

[1] On this section see now W. J. Martin, "1 Corinthians 11:2-16: an Interpretation." In *Apostolic History and the Gospel*, F. F. Bruce *Festschrift*, 1970, pp. 231-246.

to both children and fathers. The "generation gap" is needlessly widened by unthinking attitudes on both sides. Children in the Christian household are called to act in a way which, above all, is acceptable and pleasing to the Lord. This is no exceptional case, for Paul uses the same word (Greek *euarestos*, rendered elsewhere "well-pleasing") of the Christian's goal and motive in the entire range of his life (Rom. 12:1f.; 14:18; Eph. 5:10; 2 Cor. 5:9). Indeed, this is his life's ambition (see commentary on Col. 1:10, p. 31). The filial obedience of children is thus part and parcel of the total response which believers of all ages and position make to the will of God which is "noble, well-pleasing and ideal" (Rom. 12:2).

Fathers are bidden to do nothing which would alienate their children. Paul's word suggests a desire to irritate which may begin in a playful way but can often take a spiteful and dictatorial turn. Or else, it could be by nagging at them—or, more seriously still, by deriding their efforts and wounding their self-respect (Paul's verb keeps company with other hurtful associations in Epictetus). The net result will be the unfortunate outcome that children become exasperated and "give up" on their parents in despair of ever understanding their mentality. While it would be a liberty to suggest that Paul is speaking to a modern situation, his insights are pertinent and helpful. Nor should we overlook how revolutionary these counsels were in the ancient world. "The sensitive understanding of children, with the realization that they might become discouraged and lose heart, is a striking feature of this new chapter in social history" (Moule).

3:22 The "household code" embracing wives, husbands, children and fathers has so far been expressed in short, lapidary statements, with a minimum of comment or justification for the commands given. Now Paul turns his attention to another familiar feature in contemporary society: the slaves. His teaching (like that in 1 Pet. 2:18-25) follows the line set in 1 Corinthians 7:21-24 (cf. Eph. 6:5-8) and is addressed to *Christian* slaves. Paul is not making a social comment on a prevailing custom. He is addressing himself to Christian readers.

The church was born into a society in which human slavery was an accepted institution sanctioned by law and part of the fabric of Graeco-Roman civilisation. The problem was not one of an acceptance of the institution *per se* or how to react to a demand for its abolition (which not even the epistle to Philemon hints at), but the way slaves were to accept their status, and the treatment Christian slave-owners were to give to slaves in their control. Modern readers of these verses (3:2—4:1) need to recall the historical circumstances of the first century world and to be on their guard lest they ask questions of the New Testament which do not come within the purview of the latter. Otherwise we shall be amazed that the Pauline call is one to obedience and not to revolt. This latter course would have been suicidal as W. Bousset has perceptively noted:[1]

> Christianity would have sunk beyond hope of recovery along with such revolutionary attempts; it might have brought on a new slave-rising and been crushed along with it. The time was not ripe for the solution of such difficult questions.

With this in mind we shall not be surprised to hear the summons, "Slaves, obey in everything your earthly masters". It follows the line of the New Testament generally, which is a call to acquiescence and not protest. Instead, the sting is partly drawn from this inhuman practice by the slaves' attitude as Christians, as well as by the apostle's earlier statement (3:11) that in the church all such social distinctions of "slave" and "free man" are cancelled out. Paul's characteristic stress falls in verse 24b: "you are serving the Lord Christ." This is a consciously attempted play on words: "Slaves . . . you are slaves of your true Master, Christ."

What it means to be a slave of Christ (the precise title given in Eph. 6:6) is spelled out with some pointed application. It entails serving the slave-owner with "singleness of heart." This is best taken in conjunction with the preceding negative: "not merely with an outward show of service, to curry favour with men". The ethic Paul insists on is therefore one of true motivation. The slave should be diligent in his tasks even if no one is there to observe him and then to reward him for his hard work. The work should be done in a disinterested manner, with no desire to impress and so gain favour with the boss. But Paul is sufficiently pragmatic to know that some motivation is needed. "Work for work's sake" is not his way of putting the case. "Fearing the Lord" is a gentle reminder that even when no human supervisor is checking on us, the great Taskmaster's eye sees all, especially the true motive and the hollowness of "work outwardly correct but without the heart put in it" (Masson).

[1] W. Bousset, *Die Schriften des Neuen Testaments*, ii. 1929, p. 101.

3:23 The same call to do one's work faithfully and well is repeated, and an extra motive is given, with further motives added in later verses. The menial occupation of the slave is given a new dimension of dignity if it is seen as "serving the Lord and not men." The same idea is popularly read into Matthew 25:31ff., namely, that service to others in the name of Christ puts a new face on what we do as we serve other people for His sake.

In this context the meaning is more limited. The purpose implicit in the words "work heartily" is to lift the slave's tasks above the realm of compulsive necessity (in any case he had no choice: either he must work or be punished for disobedience or idleness) and give it a new freedom. Some of the ennui and distaste would be taken out of his forced labour if he could offer even his servitude to the Lord as part of the cost of discipleship. "As if you were doing it for the Lord" (NEB) transforms even our routine chores and dull hack-work into something which has meaning, and so is invested with an aura not to be missed.

3:24 Paul's ethical instructions do not disdain the thought of reward. For the slave's earthly commendation is not to weigh (v. 22). What should be sought is the praise of his Master, whose slave he is. Perhaps Paul is attempting a second pun in his use of "reward" (Greek *antapodosis*). A similar term (Greek *antapodoma*) is found in the Greek Old Testament and in Romans 11:9 in the sense of "punishment," "retribution," and this type of treatment is what the slave normally associates with the master's attitude to him. The Christian slave's heavenly Master is different. He takes note of his servant's fidelity and will not allow it to pass without acknowledgement. He can be trusted to pay His "reward" at the end of the day—not in rebuff or fault-finding, but in the granting of a share of His possession, eternal life (Masson). Paul would be familiar with the rabbinic teaching which praised God's fairness in rewarding His faithful ones: "Faithful is thy taskmaster who shall pay thee the reward of thy labour. And know that the recompense of the reward of the righteous is for the time to come" (*Aboth*, 2:16). This promise and prospect should be a sufficient incentive to a hard-pressed slave that his servitude to Christ has a worthwhile end in view.

3:25 The prospect of future reward needs to be complemented by the sober realization that evil slave-owners who treat their slaves as chattels and think only in terms of punishment and penalties will themselves be judged at Christ's tribunal. Only this interpretation, we believe, gives a meaning to Paul's connecting "for . . ." and adequately accounts for Paul's verb in the phrase "the wrong-doer" (lit. he who does unjustly). The question is, how could a slave with no legal standing "act unjustly" against his master? A. Schlatter (cited by Masson) believes that the slave may have imagined that his wicked action had no importance in God's sight because he was a slave. But this view hardly explains Paul's verb. NEB suggests that it was by dishonesty, as Onesimus proved dishonest (the same language is used in Philemon 18: "and if he has done you any wrong") in his master's affairs and apparently ran off with some of Philemon's money or property. But G. Schrenk (*TDNT*, i, p. 160, note 11) shows the difficulty with this view. Further, the continuation of Paul's instruction (4:1) that slave-owners are to give their slaves what is just and fair suggests that the earlier use has in mind slavemasters who were defrauding their slaves and are threatened with the sobering reminder that all injustice will be answerable at the divine court, and God the supreme Judge has no favourites. Inhuman masters will not be able to bribe their way out of a full exposure of their misdeeds. Moreover, this is the sense of the parallel counsel in Ephesians 6:9 (so Conzelmann).

4:1 The remedy is clear, and is in the hands of the slave-owners themselves. While Paul does not advocate a wholesale abandonment of the system, he clearly points to an amelioration of the slaves' lot. The masters should treat their slaves in as human and humane a way as possible. This requirement would include fairness in treatment and an honest remuneration (perhaps implied in the verb rendered "treat," literally "grant"), with the possibility that there should be no unduly harsh measures of repression or victimization of those in a helpless position.

Again, Paul lifts the slave-masters' gaze above the social structure. He reminds them that, as earthly masters (Greek *kyrioi*) they too have a heavenly Master (*kyrios*), the same Lord Christ whose slaves are in their control. And their common Master dispenses justice to all irrespective of social status and worldly influence. He does not turn a favourable glance in the direction of the rich and important people—strict impartiality is a part of His character (Rom. 2:11; James 2:1; Acts 10:34)—and will call these slave-owners to render account at the final day.

XII

PRAYER AND CONDUCT

4:2–6 Continue steadfastly in prayer, being watchful in it with thanksgiving, ³and pray for us also, that God may open to us a door for the word, to declare the mystery of Christ, on account of which I am in prison, ⁴that I may make it clear, as I ought to speak.

⁵Conduct yourselves wisely toward outsiders, making the most of the time.
⁶Let your speech always be gracious, seasoned with salt, so that you may know how you ought to answer everyone.

THE FOCUS OF PAUL'S INTEREST CHANGES TO TAKE IN A WIDER angle of vision. From the various members of the household and of society he moves on to consider duties which belong to the entire family of faith. This small paragraph handles the themes of the Christian life, irrespective of marital, family or social qualification. The call to prayer and to positive witness in the world is addressed to all the believers. But there are some special emphases. First, prayer in general is encouraged; then the specific occasion (4:3) is given.

4:2 The verb "to continue" (Greek *proskarterein*) is one which belongs prominently to the New Testament vocabulary of the church's devotional and "liturgical" life (Acts 1:14; 2:42,46; 6:4; Rom. 12:12; 13:6). It suggests a certain persistence and determination in prayer, with the resolution not to give up (Luke 11:5–13) or grow weary (Luke 18:1–8). The noun from the verb is rendered "perseverance" in Ephesians 6:18.

Two accompaniments of "persevering prayer" are also aids. We shall best heed the importance of resolution in the practice of prayer if we keep an eye on cultivating the wakeful spirit and the thankful heart. "Watch and pray" was Jesus' advice to the disciples both in the Garden (Mark 14:38) and in His eschatological admonitions (Luke 21:34–36; Mark 13:32–37). These two references offer a choice in our interpretation of Paul's call to be watchful. Is he reminding the Colossians of the need to overcome the tendency to drowsiness when the mind at prayer concentrates in a spiritual exercise? Or, can it be that his thought takes in an eschatological

dimension as he bids his readers be on the alert in expectation of the
coming Lord (so Conzelmann)? If the second possibility is preferred,
this gives a more pointed nuance to the encouragement to prayer.
Paul will be saying: Don't give up in your prayers for the coming
of God's kingdom and in your anticipation that the cry *Maranatha*
(1 Cor. 16:22) will be heard. "Our Lord, come" is to be your
eager longing, and never let this hope (3:4) grow dim, when you
are in danger of being enticed away from the hope (1:23) of the
gospel which my colleagues brought to you (1:5). Rather, remain
firm and thankful that this gospel is your inalienable possession.
Thankfulness of spirit will then mark out the Christian prayer, as
we have in review the mercies and mighty acts of God in Christ,
past, present and to come.

4:3,4 The specific request is that this church will take to its heart
the needs of the Pauline mission and accept some responsibility in
intercession for Paul and his fellow-preachers. Paul writes as a
prisoner (4:18) under close surveillance and so restricted in so far as
an active ministry of public preaching is concerned. He is "bound"
in chains (as his Greek verb *dedemai* makes clear) and is not simply
"in prison." The gist of his request is that, by the Colossians'
prayer on his behalf, the door of active service, now closed by his
confinement, may be opened once more, so that he may "tell the
secret of Christ" (NEB) in a plain, uninhibited way.

There are many allusions in this short section which are worth a
second glance, and taken together they help us to form some picture
of what life was like for him in his prison. Whether they speak
decisively to the vexed problem of the place of his imprisonment
is not clear. We discuss this matter in the Appendix (pp. 154–60).

One thing stands out. Paul was no social or political prisoner,
paying the penalty for a crime. His imprisonment was "on account
of" his message as a Christian preacher. That message is described
here as earlier (1:26; 2:2) as "the mystery of Christ," that is, the
unimagined news of God's saving purpose in Christ, which no
human mind could have discovered unaided, one which no human
ingenuity could have invented. That "secret" is now being disclosed
by the apostolic preaching, "but because it is a divine secret it
remains mystery and does not become transparent to men".[1]

[1] G. S. Hendry, art. "Mystery", *A Theological Wordbook of the Bible*, ed. A. Richardson,
1950, p. 156. "The sense it (the term "mystery") bears is rather different from that of 'mystery'
in modern English. In modern usage a mystery may be defined as a secret or riddle to which no
answer has been found. Then a crime is a mystery so long as the author of it has not been

To the neutral observer of the first-century scene the Christian preacher was no better than any other purveyor of a religious message (Acts 17:18) and the church just another conventicle of odd people. But to the eye of enlightened faith, this "word" was God's power to salvation and new life as "good news" (Rom. 1:16), destined for all men (1:23,28) and offering the very reality which the ancient world most needed: hope for the future and freedom from evil powers. These are the twin components of Paul's gospel in this epistle, and match the pressing needs of the society in which this infant Colossian church was set.

Again, the congregation at Colossae looked undistinguished and ordinary. But God's miracle and mystery are there to be experienced from within. Christ lives in the midst of His people (1:27); and because of this, barriers which disfigured family, social and cosmopolitan life in the ancient world are crumbling under the pressure of a new humanity already appearing on the scene (3:10,11), and a new way of life is already being known (3:12-17) both in the home (3:18-21) and in society (3:22-4:1).

It is small wonder that Paul chafes under the strain of seeing the "door" of missionary opportunity closed. He uses this expression of a "door" in 1 Corinthians 16:9 and 2 Corinthians 2:12 (cf. Rev. 3:8) to indicate the scope of his evangelistic and pastoral labours (the metaphor, taken to mean an opportunity presented for someone to exploit, is found in the Jewish rabbinic writings), and it is part of his life's work to use all available means to enter into strategic missionary territory (Rom. 15:17-29). His present captivity is a limiting factor, which he longs to see removed. Then, with his freedom regained, he can display the wonder of God's mystery in Christ, which he knows to be his bounden obligation (1 Cor. 9:16-18) to do (v. 4).

4:5,6 Formerly in days before their conversion (1:6) and entrance into the divine realm (1:13) the Colossian readers lived in a way no different from the pagan society around them (3:7). Now they have come "inside" the family of God, but not to be recluses cut off from the world in which they still have to live. They have a responsibility for their former associates, those "outside" (a term for the uninitiated, non-disciple which is found in Mark 4:11, as well as 1 Thess. 4:12; 1 Cor. 5:12f.).

---

discovered, but when he is discovered, it is no longer a mystery." But God's mystery still remains "hidden," accessible only to faith.

The Christians' behaviour is to be marked by wisdom, such as they have themselves come to know in the gospel (1:9f.; 1:28; 2:3; 3:16). A similar recommendation is found in Ephesians 5:15 as part of the general advice for believers to conduct themselves in a becoming manner. The best way to practise this "applied wisdom" in our dealings with those outside the church is, as E. Lohse comments, to live such a self-scrutinized life that no cause for stumbling or misrepresentation will be placed in another person's way (1 Cor. 10:32). But the life that attracts others to Christ is not negative.

Every moment is a precious gift to be exploited and capitalized to the full. The verb in Paul's Greek phrase (as in Eph. 5:16) is drawn directly from the commercial language of the market place (Greek *agora*). The Greek is *exagorazomenoi* where the prefix *ex* denotes an intensive activity, a snapping up of all the opportunities (Greek *kairos*, a moment of truth and destiny) which are available at the present moment. That "time of salvation" will not be extended indefinitely (1 Cor. 7:29) and Paul was realistic enough in his appraisal of the present age to want to use every available occasion for service and witness which he could (Gal. 6:10). The Christian's stewardship of time as God's priceless commodity is the teaching here, with a call to invest our energies in occupations which will be a positive and attractive witness to those outside the church's fellowship.

Nor is the winsome life which draws other people insipid and dull. Our conversation is the index here, especially when it comes to our advocacy of the good news in personal talking and dialogue (your "speech" [Greek *logos*] seems to be a deliberate recall of Paul's preaching of the "word" in verse 3). We owe it to the message itself to present it in an attractive dress, since its clearest profile is one which has the grace of God much in evidence. "Grace" (Greek *charis*) and "gracious" are so intimately related that it is difficult to separate them. Jesus' sermon at Nazareth was given in words which His hearers instinctively remarked on as "words of grace" (Luke 4:22). They not only spoke of the divine grace; they were performative in conveying that grace to His hearers, whether they would receive it or not. Our glad task is to speak with like attractiveness, avoiding any manner of speaking in public discourse or private conversation which would leave the impression that the gospel message is dull and flat and uninteresting. "Never insipid"

(NEB) captures the sense of the more prosaic "seasoned with salt."

Salt was used in seasoning food and in preserving it from corruption. Either way, Paul's use of this metaphor is suggestive. Conversation should be as entertaining and enjoyable as food is made palatable and tasty by herbs and spices and salt (Job 6:6: "can that which is tasteless be eaten without salt?"). The use of salt as a preservative is in the background of such verses as Matthew 5:13; Mark 9:49,50; Luke 14:34, and may be Paul's intention here. We may compare Ephesians 5:4 with its rebuke of all corruptive forms of speech. This is the positive side. Let your speaking act as a purifying, wholesome influence, rescuing the art of conversation from all that debases and perverts. Or, possibly Paul borrows from the rabbinic idiom which uses salt as a metaphor for instruction in wisdom.[1] The virtue of this view would be that it helps to explain Paul's following remark. Our vocal witnessing is to be gracious and to concentrate on God's offer in Christ the wisdom of God (1 Cor. 1:24,30; 2:6), so that those who hear our words may sense that we are speaking to their need and matching their questionings with God's provision in the message of His love and wisdom in Christ's cross, as in 1 Peter 3:15.

---

[1] See W. Nauck, "Salt as a metaphor in instructions for discipleship." *Studia Theologica*, vi, 1952, pp. 165–178. "The Torah is like salt" is a common comparison (Strack-Billerbeck, i, pp. 232–6; ii, pp. 21–23; iii, p. 631).

XIII

PLANS AND PERSONALIA

4:7–17 Tychicus will tell you all about my affairs; he is a beloved brother and faithful minister and fellow servant in the Lord. ⁸I have sent him to you for this very purpose, that you may know how we are and that he may encourage your hearts, ⁹and with him Onesimus, the faithful and beloved brother, who is one of yourselves. They will tell you of everything that has taken place here.

¹⁰Aristarchus my fellow prisoner greets you, and Mark the cousin of Barnabas (concerning whom you have received instructions—if he comes to you, receive him), ¹¹and Jesus who is called Justus. These are the only men of the circumcision among my fellow workers for the kingdom of God, and they have been a comfort to me. ¹²Epaphras, who is one of yourselves, a servant of Christ Jesus, greets you, always remembering you earnestly in his prayers, that you may stand mature and fully assured in all the will of God. ¹³For I bear him witness that he has worked hard for you and for those in Laodicea and in Hierapolis. ¹⁴Luke the beloved physician and Demas greet you. ¹⁵Give my greetings to the brethren at Laodicea, and to Nympha and the church in her house. ¹⁶And when this letter has been read among you, have it read also in the church of the Laodiceans; and see that you read also the letter from Laodicea. ¹⁷And say to Archippus, "See that you fulfil the ministry which you have received in the Lord."

PAUL NOW TURNS HIS ATTENTION TO THE COLOSSIAN CHURCH'S desire to know about his own situation. In anticipation of the sending of the letter he announces that this will be entrusted to Tychicus. Onesimus also will be a bearer of news as he accompanies Tychicus on his journey. Then follows a list of personal names as Paul looks around him in his imprisonment and sends various greetings to Colossae in the name of the men who are close at hand. The nearest equivalent to this list is Romans 16, which also picks out a list of names for personal greetings. Paul had a genius for friendship; and the evidence of his many friends, colleagues and helpers is seen in these two chapters. "We cannot but infer from the tale of his friendships that Paul the Christian Apostle had a magnetic personality".[1]

---

[1] C. A. A. Scott, *Saint Paul, The Man and the Teacher*, 1936, p. 19. E. Lohse, "Die Mitarbeiter des Apostels Paulus im Kolosserbrief" in *Verborum Veritas*. Festschrift Gustav Stählin, 1970,

4:7-9 The Colossians would be naturally deeply interested to learn how the apostle was faring in prison. Tychicus will be his messenger.

According to Acts 20:4, Tychicus was a representative of the churches of Asia who had accompanied Paul on his visit to Jerusalem. His name is a common one in inscriptions which have been found in Asia Minor. Later he was sent to Ephesus (2 Tim. 4:12) in his native region, and there is another proposal to send him or Artemus to Crete mentioned in Titus 3:12. It seems that his presence with Paul continued throughout the latter's ministry—up to the end.

Three parts of a commendation follow. Tychicus is warmly described as a "beloved brother" (a normal Christian practice to emphasize the way Christians thought of themselves as part of God's family). "Faithful minister" picks up the Greek term *diakonos* to describe his personal service to Paul. From this word we get our title "deacon," but at this stage of development, the word denotes "not the holder of a fixed office, but anyone who performs a specific service" (Lohse). In particular, Tychicus was Paul's right-hand man and ai-de-de-camp. Does "fellow-servant" (Greek *syndoulos*) mean that Tychicus was actually in prison with Paul? Perhaps not, since the same description is given to Epaphras in 1:7, but the case of Aristarchus (v. 10) and Epaphras (in Philemon 23) raises the possibility.

"I have sent him" means that Tychicus will be the letter-carrier, and this is a special way in Greek of attaching a ccvering note to a letter in which the bearer is mentioned. He will be able to supplement the contents of the epistle with verbal messages to reassure the readers that Paul is in good heart. So they will be encouraged.

A second messenger will add his news too. But Onesimus is returning to Colossae for a different purpose. He was the runaway slave whose conversion and restoration to Philemon his owner form the subject-matter of the epistle to Philemon. To be sure, there is no compelling reason why we should identify the Onesimus of our text with the man of this same name in Philemon 10 since

---

pp. 189-194 also draws attention to the parallel list in Rom. 16. But he uses Col. 4:10-17 to argue that the purpose served by these references is not to convey simple greetings but to witness to a situation after Paul's death when the Pauline mission needed confirmation in the eyes of the churches that it was true to the authentic apostolic gospel. These men's names are the guarantee of the post-Pauline mission which the churches should recognize. This conclusion however drawn by Lohse is by no means obvious nor compelling.

this was a common name, especially of slaves. It means "useful" and would often no doubt be a convenient way of identifying a nameless slave in the hope that he would justify his adoptive name by his hard work! But the customary inference that it is one and the same person is reasonable in view of the close verbal connexions and name-links between the two epistles as well as the parallels with Ephesians 6:21f. The way Onesimus is commended suggests that his Christian profession is now assured by Paul and he is to be welcomed back to his native townsmen with every confidence and given a warm reception into the church fellowship.

4:10 The description "my fellow prisoner" used of Aristarchus presents a nice problem. If Paul's captivity at the time of writing is that at Rome, we may trace Aristarchus' presence there to his joining the party in Acts 27:2. Perhaps we are to imagine he was actually in prison with Paul—a conclusion argued for by Lohse on the score that no qualifying term (e.g., prisoner *in the Lord*, or *of Christ*, as Eph. 3:1; 4:1) is added. NEB gratuitously adds this extension in its phrase "Christ's captive like myself." On the other hand, Paul's use may be simply dictated by his fondness for military terms ("prisoner" is really "prisoner of war," so recalling 2 Cor. 2:14; 10:3-5) both here and in Philemon 23 where it is Epaphras who is Paul's fellow prisoner (however, with an accompanying phrase "in Christ Jesus") and in the following verse Aristarchus is named without description. This name belongs to a man of Thessalonica (Acts 20:4) whose Christian origins would then go back to Paul's mission in that area (Acts 17:1-9). He had visited proconsular Asia previously (reported in Acts 19:29; 20:4) and would be known to the Colossians to whom his salutations are sent.

Greetings also came in the name of Mark. He is evidently not too widely known at this time; hence he is commended as Barnabas' cousin. Paul's link with Mark went back to their first encounter on the missionary journey to Cyprus (Acts 13:5) and beyond (Acts 13:13). Over this defection at Perga and Mark's decision to turn back to Jerusalem, Paul and Barnabas fell out (Acts 15:36-41), and Mark found his future service in the company of his cousin. It is pleasing to note that Paul and Mark are again on friendly terms, while an even more moving display of reconciliation comes in 2 Timothy 4:11 where Mark is unhesitatingly commended as a faithful Christian worker. At this stage, Mark is perhaps only slowly winning back his reputation in the Pauline churches and needs the special plea of Paul: "receive him," i.e. without censure or doubt

4:11 A third member of the trio is otherwise quite unknown to us. But he was a man of sufficient importance for Paul to identify him by his double name. "Jesus" was his Jewish name, and "Justus" was probably added to distinguish him from other Jewish Christians who bore the name "Jesus", itself a common name among the Jews (Acts 13:6) until the time of the second century AD when "Jesus" disappears as a proper name on account of the conflict between the synagogue and the church (see W. Foerster, *TDNT*, iii, p. 286). The practice of a double nomenclature is well illustrated in the case of Paul himself (Acts 13:9).

These men are further identified as Jewish Christians, "men of the circumcision"[1] who are praised for their support of Paul's work "for the kingdom of God," i.e. his concern to bring the gospel to Israel and to point to the hope of the Jewish people in their Messiah (Rom. 1:16; 9:1–5; 10:1). Paul, known as "an apostle to the Gentiles" (Rom. 11:13), never lost his interest in this side of the gospel's appeal, temporarily frustrated because of Israel's disbelief (Rom. 11:25), though his special vocation to the Gentile world alienated him from his fellow Jews. It is not surprising that the three men mentioned are so few in number that they can be named, and their faithful presence was especially gratifying to Paul. They have been a "comfort" (Greek *parēgoria*—a touching word, found on grave inscriptions and used of consolation in the face of death's reality; see Moulton-Milligan, *Vocabulary s.v.*) to him.

4:12,13 Now in place of some names which are only remotely familiar to the Colossians, Paul calls upon Epaphras to voice a greeting. He is the one who has represented Paul at Colossae (1:7) and has returned to the apostle with news of the church's good order (2:5) in the face of stern conflict with false teaching (2:8ff.). Epaphras was a native Colossian and, like Paul, a slave of Christ in His service. Only in Philippians 1:1 does this title appear again, in reference to Paul's colleague, Timothy.

---

[1] Perhaps they were Jewish Christians of a particular stamp who took a non-proselytizing attitude to the law and co-operated with Paul in evangelizing the Jews on the basis of that law. See E. E. Ellis, "'Those of the Circumcision' and the early Christian mission," *Studia Evangelica* iv, 1968, pp. 390–399, who describes the apostolic tribute to these Jewish Christian preachers as an acknowledgement of "a venture in ecumenical Christianity" (p. 396) as "Paul and certain Hebrews were pursuing their distinctive missions in a co-operative fashion." But this description of a concordat sounds a little *too* modern.

During his absence from the city, Epaphras' ministry had been a limited yet valued one of prayerful intercession. Nor was this ministry taken lightly. He had "laboured" (Greek *agōnizomenos*) in his supplication, says Paul, using a term at the heart of which is the word for conflict and struggle (*agōn*). We are perhaps meant to take this term in a specific way. It is possible that Epaphras has come to seek Paul with news of the Colossian church and, finding him imprisoned, had himself been arrested and so had become the apostle's "fellow-prisoner" (Philemon 23). This detention from his pastoral responsibility at home filled him with painful anxiety, and his "agony" is a heartfelt condition.

Paul knew this exertion in his own ministry (see 1:29 where "striving" translates the same Greek participle *agōnizomenos*). Nor should we overlook the description of Jesus' Gethsemane prayers, in Luke's version: "And being in an agony (Greek *agōn*) he prayed more earnestly" (Luke 22:44: cf. Acts 12:5; Rom. 15:30). These verses illustrate the cost of intercession, as Christians enter into the trials and sorrows of others, and take some of the burden upon themselves. Prayer is the Christian's delight and joyful exercise of spirit. But there is another side of the coin from which we learn, and experience confirms it, that prayer is difficult and arduous, taxing our strength of will and demanding our utmost effort of concentration, energy and application. "To work is to pray" runs the Benedictine rule; the opposite is equally true.

The theme of Epaphras' petition for his congregation is set in true pastoral style. It is that they should attain to a maturity and conviction which will be a token to him that they clearly understand what God's will for them is. For He designs that they should be mature and assured in their Christian standing. This is clearly more than a pious wish or vague generality. Both terms, rendered "mature" and "fully assured", are set against the background of the Colossian situation.

The key lies in the second verb (Greek *peplērophorēmenoi*). We have met several related forms of this participle earlier in our epistle (1:9,19; 2:9,10) and we may recall the teaching on "fulness" (Greek *plērōma*) which runs through both the heresy and Paul's antidote. Paul has shown that the divine essence resides totally and without remainder in Christ, and that in Him believers have come to fulness of life. Paul's prayer is that these Colossians may be filled with the knowledge of God's will in all wisdom and perception taught by the Spirit. And it is a further endorsement of the same thrust that Epaphras prays that they may attain perfection (Greek *teleioi*, evidently chosen to counteract the gnostic aspiration to "perfection" by their regimen and cult) and full persuasion, which will anchor them in God's truth and not permit them to be drawn away to erroneous ideas. The pastor's prayer, like the apostle's teaching, is aimed at offering a counterblast to the pernicious "philosophy" (2:8) lurking at the threshold of the church door.[1]

Just exactly how Epaphras had "worked hard" for his people is not clear. Perhaps Paul is continuing the idea of his labours in prayer, which included in their scope all the churches of the Lycus valley. Or, possibly, it is that Epaphras had done his best to answer the claims of heresy before he left his "parish" to seek the counsel of Paul as to how best to answer the heretical propaganda (so Lohmeyer). There is no suggestion that Epaphras had deserted his post and needed to have his actions justified by Paul in spite of his "short-lived defection" (Masson). Paul's testimonial is rather that he has done his best in a difficult situation and cannot be blamed if the answer to the false teaching needed a more thorough treatment than he was competent to supply.

This tribute to Epaphras forms an important part of W. Marxsen's thesis (in his *Introduction to the New Testament* [ET 1968], pp. 177ff.) in regard to the origin and purpose of this letter. He sees that one of the chief reasons for the letter is to supply an apostolic authorization of Epaphras whose teaching is claimed to represent the mind of Paul. He argues that Epaphras is thought to stand in an apostolic succession, now that the apostle Paul is no longer alive (p. 180). Hence, the letter derives from a post-Pauline period and reflects a developed ecclesiastical situation, characteristic of the "early catholicism" of the sub-apostolic age.

To read this type of rôle for Epaphras out of these two verses is really a *tour de force* and to argue that "Epaphras is recognized by Paul as a fellow-servant who works in the church 'in the place of' the apostle" (from 1:7) is to confuse the ministry of Epaphras the "deacon" with that of Paul himself as apostle to the Gentiles. There is no suggestion of apostolic succession anywhere in this epistle, where even Paul's apostolic claims are never explicitly thrust to the fore. Paul calls himself a "deacon" (1:24) and looks

[1] For the close correspondence in language between Epaphras' pastoral concern and that of Paul's missionary *agōn*, see V. C. Pfitzner, *Paul and the Agon Motif*, 1967, pp. 125f.

upon Epaphras as a fellow-servant of Christ, along with Tychicus
(4:7). (See the Appendixes for the dating and authorship of the
epistle.)

4:14 The names of Luke and Demas recur together in 2 Timothy
4:10,11 but with some obvious differences. Here Luke is called
"the dear doctor"—a description which has given the impetus to
somewhat fanciful ideas about his presence with Paul in his captivity
as the apostle's attending physician (so Lohmeyer and Thompson).
There is nothing to support this, and Philemon 24 calls him simply
one of "my fellow-workers." Luke evidently joined Paul's party
at the outset of the voyage to Rome (Acts 27:1, which marks the
commencement of a so-called "we-section" in Acts). His profession
as a doctor is so unusual that Paul comments on it and this became
an accepted part of church tradition. The anti-Marcionite prologue
to Luke (*c.* AD 170) calls him "a physician by profession" and places
his origin in Antioch. Jerome says the same: "Lucas medicus
Antiochensis." It is more doubtful, however, if we should conclude
from this verse which separates him from Jewish Christians (in
vv. 10,11) that he was a Gentile Christian, as is popularly thought,
mainly on the basis of this verse. There is considerable evidence to
argue the case that he was a hellenistic Jew.[1] If this is possible, it
becomes equally feasible that he is to be identified with the Lucius
of Romans 16:21.

Demas is passed over with a bare mention; a consequence of this
man's failure under trial is given in 2 Timothy 4:10 when Luke is
singled out for a special remark which stands in vivid contrast with
Demas' default (4:11). The fellow-worker of Philemon 24 had
deserted Paul at the time of his great need and returned to
Thessalonica (his home?).

4:15–17 This short section stands out for a variety of reasons.
For one thing, Paul now switches from conveying greetings to the
Colossians on behalf of other people to a mention of his own
greetings. In particular, he salutes the church at Laodicea and picks
out the household of Nympha. The Greek name underlying the
masculine Nymphas is Nymphodorus and the abbreviated form is
uncertain. There is a textual uncertainty in the phrase "in her
house," some authorities reading the masculine pronoun (Greek
autou in place of *autēs*). This would make the name a man's name,

---

[1] See E. E. Ellis, *The Gospel of Luke* (Century Bible), 1966, pp. 52f., drawing upon the
pioneering work of E. C. Selwyn, *St. Luke the Prophet*, 1901 and in *Expositor*, 7, 1909, pp. 547ff.

which many commentators accept. Modern translations (RSV, NEB, Jerusalem Bible) opt for a feminine Nympha and render "the church in her house." Lightfoot admits that, on face value, this is correct, but "a woman's name . . . hardly can be so" because "a Doric form of the Greek name here seems in the highest degree improbable." This denial has been countered by J. H. Moulton who sees the alpha-ending in Nympha to be a true feminine form (*Exp T* 5, [1893–4], pp. 66f.; *A Grammar of New Testament Greek*, i, [1908], p. 48). Lightfoot suggests that the original reading was *autōn* (for which there is some manuscript evidence; see his commentary, p. 254) and that the original text read "Nymphas and his friends." Subsequent copyists altered this, not perceiving the classical constructions, some in the direction of Nymphas and others of Nympha. Perhaps the two names represent those of a married couple whose house was a meeting-place for Christian worship.

The use of the home for Christian assembly is well-attested in the New Testament period. In addition to the house of Nympha in Laodicea we know that in nearby Colossae Philemon's house was similarly used as a meeting-place (Philemon 2). At Philippi there was Lydia's home to which Paul resorted (Acts 16:15,40) and at Corinth Gaius is spoken of as "host . . . to the whole church" (Rom. 16:23). Aquila and Priscilla seem to have made their dwelling-places available for Christian purposes both in Ephesus and Rome (1 Cor. 16:19; Rom. 16:5).

About these "house churches" we know little. Christians were driven to meet in private homes out of necessity. Not until about the middle of the third century did the church begin to own property for the purposes of worship. O. Cullmann[1] rightly emphasizes the importance of the fact that the whole community should gather in *one* place; and this pattern would most probably be derived from the setting of the church's birthday at Pentecost when the believers were assembled in one place (Acts 2:1). This place may well have been the house of John Mark's mother (Acts 12:12) in which perhaps Jesus had taken the last meal with the disciples before the cross. When the church gained in strength after Pentecost, believers met in houses, according to Acts 2:46, 5:42. And so the pattern of house-congregations was established.

The custom of early Christians to meet as house-congregations has more than a historical or academic interest. Recently it has been

[1] *Early Christian Worship*, 1953, p. 10.

maintained (by the liturgical scholar J.-P. Audet) that when
Christians abandoned the house church as a model they accepted a
new pattern of worship in which the basilica replaced the house and
family instruction gave way to a preaching oratory. "If you invite
a small number of relatives and friends to your house, you will ask
them to sit down at your table and you will yourself serve them . . .
If fifty people came you would alter the time of the occasion and
arrange for refreshments . . . If two hundred people are invited you
would put the matter in the hands of professional caterers and you
would greet personally only some of your guests and make a little
speech . . . What I want to underline is that numbers necessarily
change the form and content of human relationships." The wise
comment (quoted in the *Soldier's Armoury*, August 11, 1970) on
this is *apropos*. It was not pure gain when the church began to
gather in large congregations. Happily these is a return to house-
fellowship as Christian cells of worship and witness are formed.

It is an unsolved problem of Paul's letters to the churches why he
should single out these members of the Laodicean church for
greeting when, on the usual view, he was writing separately to
that church (v. 16). Perhaps, with Dibelius-Greeven, we should
say that he wished to cement relations between the two churches
in this way.

4:16 We have little definite information about the structure and
content of early Christian worship. In this area of study every
scrap of data is precious; and it is this fact which gives special
importance to our verse. We learn that Paul expected that his
letter would be read out to the assembled church, presumably at
worship; and then he advised that it should be passed on to the
Laodicean congregation for similar treatment there. Also there
would be an exchange of letters by which his "letter to the
Laodiceans" would find its place as a document to be read out to
the Colossians. To this practice, which involves both the distribution
and public reading of Paul's letter (further attested by 1 Thess.
5:27 and Philemon 2) we may trace the rise of canonical authority
which came to be attached to these pieces of pastoral correspondence.[1]
The reference in 1 Thessalonians is important since it shows that
the practice of reading aloud the Pauline letters during worship
was established early. Thus Marxsen's further argument (op. cit.

[1] See R. P. Martin, *Worship in the Early Church*, 1964, pp. 71ff. for further evidence drawn
from 1 Corinthians 16:20–24 and 2 Peter 3:15,16.

p. 185)—that the public reading of Paul's epistolary correspondence is a mark of sub-apostolic Christianity—in favour of a later post-Pauline dating of the epistle falls down.

Not all these "epistles of circumstance" (to use W. Goossens's term) have survived. A case in point is the document here called "the letter from Laodicea." Obviously it is a Pauline composition sent in the first place to the church at Laodicea. The meaning of the preposition "from" (Greek *ek*) in the phrase "from Laodicea" is "the letter that is at Laodicea" (Blass-Debrunner-Funk, *A Greek Grammar of the New Testament* [1961], section 437) and is to be sent on from there to Colossae. It cannot mean, as some church fathers supposed, a letter from the Laodiceans to Paul. Paul wishes that it should be circulated among the churches, or at least that it should be communicated to the Colossian assembly. He evidently thought that its contents were worth preserving and were appropriate for the Colossians to read. But did the church either at Laodicea or Colossae think the same? Were they willing to allow this document to drop into oblivion and perish? And to permit this *not* to happen in the case of what appears a much more ephemeral document, the note to Philemon?

Reluctance to draw this inference that the letter has been lost has motivated some interesting proposals. One view is that the letter so described is really our epistle to the Ephesians (as in the canon of Marcion, which gave the title "To the Laodiceans" to Ephesians in its list); another view sees in the epistle to Philemon the presence of this letter, but it is rather the case that Philemon lived at Colossae (see Col. 4:9 for Onesimus as a slave of Philemon at Colossae), not Laodicea. No extant Pauline composition seems adequately to fit the description, and we are left with the inevitable conclusion that the letter to the Laodiceans has not survived. Perhaps it perished accidentally, being destroyed during the earthquake in the Lycus valley in AD 60–61 (so P. N. Harrison). Perhaps the letter was meant for a splinter group of the Laodicean church which resided in Colossae (so W. Schmauch), and was destroyed once the church at Laodicea was united. But can we go further, and submit that it did not survive because it was deliberately suppressed, perhaps because its contents were critical (like an earlier letter from Paul to the Corinthians, written "out of much affliction . . . and with many tears," 2 Cor. 2:4?) or because the Laodicean church, at the time when Paul's letters began to be

assembled into a corpus, had come under the judgement of
Revelation 3:14–22 and had lost its Christian character? We
cannot tell.[1]

4:17 Archippus was a member of Philemon's household (Philemon
2), possibly his son (as Goguel thought likely). He is personally
addressed at the close of the letter with a strong admonition to
make good the service to which he has been appointed by the Lord.
As with Tychicus' designation as a trustworthy "deacon" (Greek
diakonos) in verse 7, so here we should interpret Archippus'
"diaconate" (Greek *diakonia*) not as a regular ecclesiastical office but
as a specific task committed to his hands. He is encouraged by
Paul's words to fulfil his responsibility in the "discharge of certain
obligations in the [Christian] community" (H. W. Beyer, *TDNT*,
ii, p. 88). We have no means of knowing for sure what this task
was. Possibly it had to do with the collection for the Jerusalem
church. Paul often dignifies this responsibility as a service (*diakonia*):
2 Corinthians 8:1–6; 9:1,12f. cf. Acts 11:29f.; 12:25.

John Knox,[2] however, has made this verse something of a
lynch-pin for his theory that Archippus played a decisive rôle in the
release of Onesimus. On his view Archippus was the slave-owner
and the main body of the epistle is addressed to him. Paul's
recommendation to Archippus in that letter is pithily summed up
in the Colossian verse: the "ministry" he has received is a roundabout way of reminding him of his duty imposed as a Christian
obligation ("in the Lord") to allow Onesimus to return as a free
man to Paul. It cannot be said that this reading of the text is
convincing. It is "surely too ingenious. It is difficult to see why such
a request should be called a 'ministry' (*diaconia*). Moreover, what
need was there for so cryptic and yet so public a reminder? How
could anyone have refused Paul in the mood of this letter [to

[1] A full discussion of all the possibilities provoked by this verse, including a treatment of the
apocryphal epistle which goes under the name of the epistle to the Laodiceans, is given by
Lightfoot, pp. 272–298. More recently, C. P. Anderson, "Who Wrote 'the Epistle from
Laodicea'?" *Journal of Biblical Literature* 85, 1966, pp. 436–440, has sought to solve the set of
conundrums posed by the existence of a letter which will be relevant to the Colossians as
much as to the Laodiceans but which is distinguished from the Colossian epistle; by the
disappearance of the second letter and its consignment to oblivion; and by the fact that we are
unable to discover a sufficient motive for Paul's writing the second letter. He submits that
there is only one circumstance which can account for all these facts, viz. that it was Epaphras
who wrote the epistle to the Laodiceans in view of his inability to accompany Tychicus on the
return to the Lycus River valley (Philemon 23). The main hesitation we have with this theory
is the need to explain why Paul does not say explicitly that it is not his epistle in question,
but Epaphras'.
[2] *Philemon among the Letters of Paul,*[2] 1959.

Philemon]?" (Johnston). For further discussion and critique of Knox, see Moule, pp. 14–18.

We may only guess that Paul's personal encouragement to Archippus had to do with the local situation at Colossae. If Paul was still apprehensive about the threat to the church from heretical teaching and had some reserve about Epaphras' ability to deal with the matter on his return, then this is an appeal to the man on the spot to bend his efforts and do what is needful (his "ministry") to defend the gospel against this propagandizing movement. This is then a call for Archippus to accept as his bailiwick the pastoral responsibility formerly held by Epaphras.

XIV

FINAL WORDS

4:18 I, Paul, write this greeting with my own hand. Remember my fetters. Grace be with you.

PAUL'S LETTERS WERE NORMALLY WRITTEN BY THE HAND OF A scribe (Rom. 16:22 names Tertius as one such amanuensis) at the dictation of the apostle. At this point in his letter-writing, however, he himself takes over to append a personal message and final greeting, as he apparently does at Galatians 6:11 and 1 Corinthians 16:21. It may be that this was to be seen as a mark of affection and personal interest, especially if the church at Colossae felt in some way disgruntled because Paul had not been able to visit them in person. See on 1:24; 2:1.

But a more sinister reason for this apostolic autograph may be sought. We learn from 2 Thessalonians 2:2 that Paul had to reckon with letters forged in his name which were being sent out to his congregations. One way in which he answers these forgeries was to append his own signature to the genuine letter as a token of authenticity (2 Thess. 3:17: "this is the mark in every letter of mine; it is the way I write"). It becomes just possible that there was this need at Colossae—and especially when letters from Paul would be circulating among the congregations of the Lycus valley— to safeguard Christians against the risk of giving heed to spurious documents, purporting to represent Paul's mind. So he adds a personal word "with my own hand", exactly as he had done in 2 Thessalonians 3:17.

The call to "remember my fetters" matches this situation. "The reference to 'bonds' is not chiefly a matter of pathos but of authority" (Moule), and Paul is not morosely inviting his readers to spare a tender thought for him in his distress. Rather, he is summoning them to respect his authority (as in Philemon 9) as a prisoner for the gospel's sake and on behalf of the Gentiles whose interests he has at stake in his apostolic sufferings (1:23–25). He lies in prison on account of his vocation and because he will not surrender his commission to be an apostle and teacher of the Gentiles. The appeal to his fetters is therefore a powerful incentive which he calls into play that the Colossians should give heed to his teaching and not yield to the heretical doctrine which encroaches upon them. "Remembrance" does not mean in this context primarily an invitation to pray for the apostle; it is more an obligation to heed his apostolic instruction and to honour him by remaining firmly committed to it in the face of those who would lead them astray from his gospel (2:4,8).

"Grace be with you" is his closing note. With extreme brevity and economy of words he expresses the confidence that God's grace will sustain and defend His church. With this confidence he began in his salutation (1:2). The same encouragement on account of the Colossians' good order and firm solidity (2:5,7) has run through the letter. He is assured that they will repel the heretical intruders and stay close to his apostolic counsel, both in doctrine and practice. Epaphras, their minister, joins him in the same heart-felt wish (4:12). God's keeping power will see to it that, if they are faithful and fixed (1:23), the church will continue to enjoy the benefits of that gospel he has brought them in the person of his delegates. But human fidelity and perseverance are not enough. As Photius remarked in his ninth century commentary, quoted by Lohse, "They need grace to be saved; for what could a man do apart from grace?"

APPENDIXES

A. The Place of Paul's Imprisonment

The epistle to the Colossians belongs to a group of Pauline letters known as the Imprisonment Epistles. The reason for this name is simply the fact that four of his letters give evidence that he was "in bonds" when he wrote: Ephesians 3:1; 4:1; 6:20; Colossians 4:3,10,18; Philippians 1:7,13,14; Philemon 1,9.

Of this collection of four, three letters stand together. Colossians 4:7f. and Ephesians 6:12f. speak of Tychicus as a bearer of the two epistles, and there are indications of "the most extensive verbal contact" between the two letters at this point (so Dibelius-Greeven, on Eph. 6:21,22). Moreover, Tychicus had as his companion on the journey to the Lycus valley Onesimus who is mentioned in the note to Philemon as returning at what is presumably the same time (Philemon 12). So this "covering letter" is brought into the same orbit as Colossians-Ephesians. The place of Archippus adds a confirming feature. He is addressed in Colossians 4:17 and also in the list of recipients (in Philemon 2). On the other hand, there is nothing in Philippians which suggests a dating at the time of these epistles, if we are to judge from the memoranda of proper names and travel plans.

A further observation is of some importance. Paul's future, as reflected in Philippians, was full of uncertainty and anxious foreboding. His life was in the balance (1:20ff., 30; 2:17) and he had no way of predicting which way the decision would go, though he hoped for a release on pastoral (1:24–26) and theological grounds (2:24) rather than trusting to any favourable turn in his legal position as a prisoner. Indeed, on the latter score, he can contemplate his fate as a martyr for Christ (1:21; 2:17).

The other three prison epistles show none of this apprehensiveness and alarm for the future. The tone of Colossians is calm and even; there is nothing to compare with the perturbation of spirit suggested in Philippians. If these two letters belong to the same captivity, we are forced to imagine that Paul's situation worsened considerably in the interval between the two letters,[1] requiring that, if the imprisonment is identified with the one recorded in Acts 28:30, Colossians (but not Philippians) may well belong to the earlier phase of the two-year detention at Rome. This is the traditional view.

I

The basis for this identification appears to be laid as early as the time of Eusebius' *Church History*. He records (II. 22.1) that Paul was brought to Rome and that "Archippus was with him, whom also somewhere in his epistles he suitably calls a fellow-prisoner." That elusive reference is to Colossians 4:10. This mention of Archippus matches the reference in Acts 27:2 where this companion of Paul is specifically singled out. Other pointers indicative of a placing of Colossians in the Roman imprisonment are:

(*a*) Paul's sojourn in Rome and his confinement "without restraint" (Eusebius' term, borrowed from Acts 28:30) suggests a freedom and easement of conditions which would make both letter-writing (requiring the presence of a scribe: see commentary on 4:18) and the companionship of friends (in 4:7-17) possible.

(*b*) These names link up with similar lists in Philemon (23,24) and bring into the picture the case of Onesimus. He was a fugitive slave who had sought asylum in Paul's presence. It is argued that a runaway slave, fearful of being caught and punished, would seek the anonymity of the imperial city in whose shadows he could safely disappear from public notice.

(*c*) No other imprisonment recorded in Acts seems a viable alternative. At Philippi (Acts 16:23-40) he was in the gaol for one night only. At Caesarea (Acts 23:33—26:32) he was held for two years (Acts 24:27) but had no prospect of an early release, suggested by the request of Philemon 22, and no easy-going conditions which would make it possible for friends to visit him and stay by his side. Nor is the setting at Caesarea at all likely to have provided an outlet for evangelistic opportunity, such as he refers to in Colossians 4:3,4. Finally, Caesarea is not a likely refuge for a slave on the run and seeking an inconspicuous hiding-place.

---

[1] See the discussion in my commentary on Philippians (Tyndale New Testament Commentaries, 1959) pp. 20f.

II

The case for a Caesarean imprisonment has never been strong, although its advocates in recent years have included some weighty names: E. Lohmeyer, W. G. Kümmel and B. Reicke.[1] The main track of supportive evidence is the presence of several Greek-speaking Christians at Paul's side in Caesarea (which matches the data in Philemon 23f.; Col. 1:7; 4:7–14). This is the inference Reicke draws from Acts 20:4,16, and the likelihood is that Onesimus would seek Paul's protection in such congenial company. Reicke further suggests that Paul intended to visit Colossae on his way as a prisoner to Rome, once he had uttered the fate-laden words, "I appeal to Caesar" (Acts 25:11), thus quashing all local proceedings against him. Other pieces of data appealed are more tenuous, viz. that Philemon 9b: "*now* also a prisoner" indicates that Paul had been arrested only shortly before and so considers his imprisonment to be a new situation. In fact, he had been arrested in Jerusalem and later transferred to Caesarea where he spent two years (AD 58–60).

Almost certainly decisive against this position is that such a small city as Caesarea could hardly have been the home of active missionary work requiring the presence of a number of Paul's helpers of Gentile origin (Col. 4:11), as Kümmel grants;[2] and in this concession he is now joined by E. Lohse for whom the question is really an academic one, since he finds the epistle to reflect a post-Pauline situation and so Paul's captivity is described in idealized terms. Nor is there any hint in the record of Acts that Paul contemplated an early release once he had asked for his case to be remitted to Rome.

III

Is the case for a Roman imprisonment cogent? A number of doubts make an affirmative answer open to question.

(a) The distance between Colossae and the place of Paul's

---

[1] E. Lohmeyer, *Meyer Kommentar* ix/2[13] 1964, pp. 14f.; W. G. Kümmel, *Introduction to the New Testament*, ET 1966, p. 245; M. Dibelius-W. G. Kümmel, *Paul*, ET 1953, p. 138; B. Reicke, "Caesarea, Rome, and the Captivity Epistles," *Apostolic History and the Gospel*; F. F. Bruce Festschrift, edd. W. W. Gasque and R. P. Martin, 1970, pp. 277–286. See too L. Johnson, "The Pauline letters from Caesarea," *ExpT* 68, 1956–57, pp. 24ff. And for a critique of the last-mentioned, see D. Guthrie, *New Testament Introduction: The Pauline Epistles*, 1961, p. 98 n. 2.

[2] Cf. J. Moffatt, *Introduction to the Literature of the New Testament*[3], 1918, p. 169. Caesarea "cannot be said to have been the centre of vigorous Christian propaganda" as in Col. 4:3,4.

imprisonment is a factor since certain journeys have been made prior to the letter (Epaphras and Onemimus have come to Paul) and others are contemplated (Tychicus and Onesimus will return). The question is one of feasibility, whether it is likely that these journeys across land and sea, some 1,200 miles one way, are intended by the evidence.

(b) Would Onesimus have risked his safety and been able to evade the watchful eye of the *fugitivarii* throughout such a long voyage in order to bury himself in Rome?

(c) If Epaphras (Philemon 23) has been arrested and is a prisoner in Paul's cell at Rome, on what ground was action taken against him in this pre-Neronian period? And the same goes for Aristarchus (Col. 4:10) who even more clearly is called "my fellow prisoner."

(d) If Paul's hopes of a release from prison are granted, he is expecting to visit Colossae (Philemon 22). But this prospect entails a going-back on his earlier resolution to turn his face westwards to Spain (Rom. 15:28) in the conviction that his missionary and pastoral work in the eastern Mediterranean sector is completed (Rom. 15:23f.). While there is no reason to charge Paul with inconsistency here and we must allow room for a change of plans, it needs to be noted that if Colossians comes out of Rome, a shift of missionary strategy and perspective is required.

Furthermore, Paul's hopes of *early* release (which seems implied in the wording of Philemon 22) were to be followed by a journey to Colossae; but this is a strange request—"prepare a guest room for me"—when he knows he has to face a mammoth sea and land trip before he can reach Philemon's home.

This last point raises the issue of a third possibility, and opens the question of Paul's so-called Ephesian imprisonment.[1]

IV

The detention of Paul at or near Ephesus is an inference to be drawn from a series of connected and cumulative facts. They are:

(a) The portrayal of 1 Corinthians 15:32 which speaks of Paul's

---

[1] I may refer to *Philippians* in the Tyndale Commentary series for discussion of this theory, pp. 26ff., and to a treatment in Guthrie, op. cit. pp. 92–98,171–174. Fullest accounts are given by A. Deissmann, W. Michaelis, and G. S. Duncan, *St. Paul's Ephesian Ministry*, 1929. But the evidence has never been more forcefully presented than by C. R. Bowen, "Are Paul's prison letters from Ephesus?", *The American Journal of Theology*, 24, 1920, pp. 112-135, 277–287.

enduring a life-and-death struggle at Ephesus. 2 Corinthians 1:8–10 is thought to relate to the same harrowing experience. Romans 16:3f. speak of Paul's exposure to peril and his rescue by Prisca and Aquila.

(b) There is the extra-biblical witness. A local tradition mentions a watch-tower in Ephesus which is known as Paul's prison. In the Marcionite prologue to Colossians, there is an ascription: "The apostle in bonds writes to them from Ephesus." There is also the aprocryphal story of Paul and the lion in the Ephesian arena. But the value of these traditions is very limited.

(c) Evidence of imprisonments other than those recorded in Acts is forthcoming in 2 Corinthians 11:23; and Clement of Rome (AD 96) mentions seven imprisonments.

If we grant the possibility of such a captivity, it becomes a reasonable exercise to test whether we can place Colossians more satisfactorily in this period of Paul's life, viz. in the third missionary tour, AD 53–54.

(a) The proximity of Ephesus to Colossae is a decided point in favour of this hypothesis. Onesimus is just as likely to have sought refuge in metropolitan Ephesus as in far-away Rome. "He would make for the nearest town . . . He would want to go far, but Ephesus, of which he must have known and heard not a little, would surely be his limit. He could go the whole distance by foot. He would not need to be at the expense or risk the exposure of embarking on board a ship. He would have been more or less familiar by hearsay with Ephesus, the greatest city of Asia, while none of his fellows are likely ever to have been in Rome."[1]

(b) The request made in Philemon 22 now becomes more realizable, since Paul's captivity while short and sharp had none of the legal indictments of his arrests in Jerusalem, Caesarea or Rome. He can therefore await with confidence his release once his Roman citizenship is known (cf. his experience at Philippi). His visit to Colossae will be en route to his westward destination once the collection-mission to Jerusalem has been attended to.

(c) The personnel surrounding Paul in his confinement are satisfactorily accounted for on this theory. As C. R. Bowen remarks (loc. cit. p. 132): "Of the ten companions of Paul named in these letters, four (Timothy [Acts 19:22], Aristarchus [Acts

---

[1] B. W. Robinson, "An Ephesian Imprisonment of Paul," *Journal of Biblical Literature*, 29, 1910, p. 184.

19:29], Tychicus [Acts 20:4], Luke [Acts 19–20 = a "we-section"])
seem quite certainly to have been in Ephesus with Paul, three
(Epaphroditus, Epaphras, Onesimus) could have been there much
easier than in Rome, the other three could have been there as
easily as in Rome, while for no one of the ten is there *any evidence*
(save inference from these letters) *that he was in Rome*, at least in
Paul's time" (italics in the author's quotation).

(*d*) The same writer, as we have already observed (see p. 3),
has offered as an independent support the impression he has received
from the text that Colossae had only recently been evangelized
when Paul wrote to the church there. If there is substance in this
claim that the congregation was newly formed, this would be an
extra argument for locating the letter in the period between Acts
19:10 and Paul's subsequent imprisonment in the region around
Ephesus.

(*e*) Counter-arguments from the development of Paul's theological
themes are not conclusive, and we cannot categorically say that
his christological and ecclesiological thinking was possible only at
what happened to be the end of his life. Enforced disengagement
from missionary activity (at whatever place) and the catalyst of the
church's threatened danger from false teaching would be enough
to set his mind to work; and his "prison christology" in Colossians
is a plausible extension of his earlier thought in 1 Corinthians.[1]

We may compare the creative thought and writing of Dietrich
Bonhoeffer in his Tegel prison during 1943–44. See E. Bethge's
section, "The Cell at Tegel", *Dietrich Bonhoeffer*, 1970, pp. 732ff.

(*f*) A. F. J. Klijn (*An Introduction to the New Testament* [1967],
p. 116) has recently indicated his view that the only argument
against an earlier dating of our epistle is the fact that the letter
states in 1:6,23 that the gospel has been preached in the whole
world. But clearly this is a polemical statement of the apostle,
intended to show the universality of his proclamation over against
the restrictive exclusivity of the heretics' esoteric message. And he
probably has more than just his personal ministry in mind; this is
a statement which attests the genuineness of the apostolic preaching
in general. Moreover, there is another objection. If these verses
were not true in AD 53–54, how could they be validated only six
or seven years later on a Roman imprisonment dating? The logical

[1] See F. F. Bruce, "St. Paul in Rome 3. The Epistle to the Colossians," *Bulletin of the John Rylands Library*, 48. 2, Spring 1966, p. 280.

conclusion is that the epistle emanates from a period well after Paul's death and represents the apology of his disciples in his name and urged on by a love for their master (*amore Pauli*, in the later phrase). While this understanding of a Pauline composition is defensible in respect of an encyclical, impersonal epistle of catholic proportions like Ephesians,[1] it is hardly justified on exegetical grounds for Colossians, an epistle addressed to a specific congregation with closely defined needs.

V

Our conclusion stands that this apostolic letter belongs to that tumultuous period of Paul's life, represented in Acts 19–20 when for a brief space his missionary labours were interrupted by an enforced spell as a *détenu* near Ephesus. Epaphras came to bring him news of troubles on the horizon at Colossae; and our epistle is the reply, as Paul brings the mind of Christ to bear upon a pressing theological and religious issue.

His answer, couched in epistolary form, met a species of false teaching which increasingly in future years was to afflict the church. The Pauline gospel and Greek thought (in a hellenistic-Jewish dress) were engaged in struggle; and the letter to the Colossians "thus represents the first confrontation of Christianity with a trend against which it was to be forced to defend itself for centuries to come" (Klijn).

B. THE AUTHORSHIP QUESTION

So far we have assumed that the epistle is a genuine composition of Paul, written at his dictation and sent out in his name. This view, of course, does not exclude the possibility that Paul incorporated other material into his letter and there is considerable evidence to show that 1:15–20 had an independent existence as a pre-Pauline hymn which Paul inserted at a crucial part of his letter. We have discussed this probability in the commentary.

The tradition that Colossians is authentically Pauline stands on

[1] I may refer here, in support to this description, to my commentary on Ephesians in the *Broadman Bible Commentary*, vol. 11, 1971.

good ground. The later church fathers accepted it and there was no dispute over its authorship in the earlier decades. Marcion included it in his canonical list, and it found a place in the Muratorian canon. The letter itself confirms this, with Paul's name appearing both at the beginning (1:1) and end (4:18) of the letter.

The first substantial denial of Paul's authorship came in 1838 with the publication of T. Mayerhoff's *Der Brief an die Kolosser*. He rejected the letter mainly because of its alleged dependence on Ephesians (a view recently ventilated by F. C. Synge, *Philippians and Colossians*, [1951], pp. 51–57, who takes Ephesians to be genuine and Colossians a pale and inadequate imitation) and its non-Pauline ideas. F. C. Baur and the Tübingen school discredited the apostolic authorship in the belief that Colossians reflected acquaintance with second-century gnosticism.

Both these arguments are to be questioned. The relationship of Ephesians and Colossians does not warrant Synge's theory (supported by J. Coutts, *New Testament Studies* 4, [1957–58], pp. 201–207), and recent investigation by A. F. J. Klijn (op. cit. pp. 101–2, 208–217) would lead to the conclusion that neither epistle is directly dependent on the other. The heresy combated in the letter is not the fully developed gnosticism of the second-century system but a proto-gnostic syncretism which may well have arisen in the apostolic age (at Corinth?) and for which there are parallels in nonconformist Judaism and the world of the recently discovered Nag Hammadi texts.

More serious objections to Paul's authorship have been launched in an attempt to drive a wedge between Colossians and the Pauline "capital epistles" (*Hauptbriefe*) of Romans, 1 and 2 Corinthians and Galatians. Part of this argument turns on some postulated differences of terminology. For instance, it is argued that the term "body of Christ" is used differently in 1 Corinthians-Romans, where its usage is figurative of the church, from Colossians in which the author speaks of the body as a cosmic reality (1:18,24; 2:19; 3:15) of which Christ is the head. But there are clear adumbrations of Paul's Colossian teaching in his second Adam typology. The teaching on baptism is held to be different in the two sets of documents. In Romans 6 the baptismal experience has a strongly moral emphasis and is set in a future eschatological frame, whereas Colossians lacks this eschatological tension and presupposes that baptism points back to a completed salvation-experience. But this judgment overlooks the meaning of 3:1-4 (see commentary and footnote 1 on p. 105).

Contemporary European scholars (Marxsen, Käsemann, Lohse) submit that the epistle belongs to the era of post-Pauline "early catholicism," chiefly on the ground of the transformation of "hope" from an existential and anticipatory posture into a present possession and a settled virtue,[1] the part played in the epistle by baptismal confession, the use of tradition embodied in the apostolate, and the first signs of a doctrine of apostolic succession in the case of Epaphras who (in 4:12) is treated as successor to Paul, like the presbyters in the Pastoral epistles. On the last mentioned point this understanding is hard to find in the text. Even if some provision were being made for the apostolic ministry to continue, we may question with J. H. Elliott[2] whether concern for ecclesiastical office and the prospect of the church's continued life in the world are indubitable marks of a later age of the church.

R. H. Fuller (*Critical Introduction to the New Testament*, 1966, p. 62) rightly concludes: "All the doctrinal differences can be adequately accounted for on the supposition that Colossians represents a later development of Paul's thinking in response to a more developed situation."

An intermediate position on the question of authorship is taken by Ch. Masson (*Epître aux Colossiens*, [1950] who postulates an authentic Pauline letter which has been interpolated with additional material by the author of Ephesians. Following Holtzmann's lead he concludes: "in its actual form (Colossians) is a revision and

[1] This is the conclusion reached by G. Bornkamm in his essay, "Die Hoffnung im Kolosserbrief," *Studien zum Neuen Testament und zur Patristik*, Festschrift E. Klostermann, 1961, pp. 56–64. His discussion is based on 1:5 in the context of 1:3–8, where "hope" is regarded as signifying not the subjective experience of the Christian (like "faith," "love") but the content of the whole gospel as a present, inviolable possession. It is the deposit of the faith which the Colossians have received as part of the divine "economy" (1:15) entrusted to the apostles and which presents a doctrinal position from which they must not depart (1:23). It is *spes quae speratur* rather than the normally accepted Pauline meaning of *spes qua speratur* (Rom. 4:18; 5:5; 8:24f.) which is either couched in an eschatological setting as the believer's hope of the parousia and the resurrection of the dead (1 Thess. 4:13, 5:8; Gal. 5:5), or has an existential reference to his present life of tension between the poles of "already ... not yet" (Rom. 8:20f., 12:12).

It is true that "hope" does carry this special meaning in Colossians, occasioned (we may believe) by the need to show that the church's trust in the gospel is secure here and now and is not to be lost by compromise with the heretics. Moreover, the eschatological dimension and the hope of the Lord's return are not absent (3:1–4). The present hour (4:5) is one of opportunity as Christians live "between the times" of the two Advents; and the prospect of future reward and judgment is held out (3:24—4:1).

[2] See his provocative article, "A Catholic Gospel: Reflections on 'Early Catholicism' in the New Testament," *Catholic Biblical Quarterly*, 31,2, 1969, pp. 213-223.

development of the primitive epistle of Paul to the Colossians by the author of Ephesians who, publishing both letters under Paul's name, has related them closely together one to the other" (op. cit. p. 86). E. P. Sanders (*Journal of Biblical Literature*, 85, [1966], pp. 28-45) has tried to show the textual foundation for such a view as a side-issue of his form-critical study of the epistle. But our doubts over this method are considerable and our impression agrees with that of J. Moffatt who once called its forerunner (perhaps unkindly) "filigree-criticism" (*Introduction*, p. 157). Where few external controls are available, it must remain a subjective exercise to separate out a genuine Pauline basic document from our canonical text and to regard the residue as editorializing accretions inserted tendentiously by a later hand.

Our knowledge of how Paul's letters were composed is limited. This epistle witnesses indirectly to the use of an amanuensis (4:18), but we cannot say whether Paul gave liberty to a secretary (Timothy? 1:1) to write up the final letter from his rough draft, taken down by dictation. On that assumption however, the unusual literary style of the epistle could be explained, along with the presence of some terms not found elsewhere in Paul (some 25 words, on Marxsen's count; Lohse, p. 134 has 28 words listed). These rare words, moreover, are largely technical or quasi-technical terms, which Paul may well have borrowed from his opponents, especially if he is quoting their actual language or using phrases suitable in debate. In addition he does incorporate the hymnic period (1:15-20) where a proportion of the special vocabulary is found.

Finally, the absence of some of the characteristic Pauline stylistic features especially in the use of particles may be set down to the nature of the letter.[1] While it is a polemical document, it is not written in a combative style, as is Galatians (Gal. 4:20; 5:12).

---

[1] As a document embodying distinctive material in a liturgico-hymnic style and traditional material of a didactic nature related to a specific occasion (this is E. Percy's contention: *Die Probleme*, p. 43), Colossians is a type of pastoral letter different from 1 Corinthians or Philippians.

The argument that the style of Colossians is non-Pauline needs some inspection. E. Percy, op. cit. pp. 36ff. concludes from an examination of the stylistic features (pp. 18-35) that there is no ground for denying Pauline authorship. So Kümmel, *Introduction*, p. 241. E. Lohse, *Kommentar*, p. 140, grants that arguments from language and style are inconclusive in settlement of the issue; he regards the theology of Colossians as decisively non-Pauline (cf. *New Testament Studies*, 15, 1969, pp. 211-220).

Interestingly, A. Q. Morton's computer findings show that, on the test-case of occurrences of *kai* (=and) Colossians and 1 Thessalonians have the same readings over the same number of sentences. He uses the overall result to doubt the Paulinity of both epistles but this seems to be *reductio ad absurdum* with a vengeance. See *Christianity and the Computer*, 1964, p. 92.

Paul felt keenly his pastoral responsibility for the churches of Galatia (Gal. 1:6; 4:12-20). But the Colossian letter, addressed to a congregation he knew only at a distance,[1] is by contrast more dispassionately reasoned and detached. It "pursues its course like a quiet stream without going off in a diversion" (Jülicher). This special occasion required a specialized vocabulary, and gave Paul's scribe a simpler task to compose in a more leisurely, systematic and reflective style.

---

[1] This impersonal relationship may explain a feature noted by E. Schweizer, "Zur Frage der *Echtheit* des Kolosser-und Epheserbriefes," *Zeitschrift für die NTliche Wissenschaft* 47, 1956, p. 287, that the appellative Paul uses often of his readers "my brothers" in the accepted epistles, is not present in Colossians and Ephesians. But the term "brothers" is found in the opening salutation of Colossians(1:2).

ABBREVIATIONS

Arndt-Gingrich	*A Greek-English Lexicon of the New Testament* etc. Cambridge, 1957.
AV	Authorised Version = King James' Version, 1611.
ET	English translation.
ExpT	*The Expository Times* (Edinburgh).
LXX	The Old Testament in Greek, the Septuagint.
Moulton-Milligan	*The Vocabulary of the Greek Testament*, London, 1914–30.
MSS	Manuscripts.
n.d.	no date of publication given.
NEB	The New English Bible, 1970 ed.
NTS	*New Testament Studies* (Cambridge).
Percy	E. Percy, *Die Probleme der Kolosser-und Epheserbriefe*, 1946.
Q	Qumran (1Q = Qumran cave 1; 1QH = *Hymns of Thanksgiving* from cave 1; 1QM = *War Scroll* from cave 1; 1QS = *Community Rule* from cave 1; 1Qp Hab = the *pesher* [commentary] on Habakkuk from cave 1).
RSV	Revised Standard Version, 1946 and 1952.
RV	Revised Version, 1881 and 1885.
Strack-Billerbeck	*Kommentar zum Neuen Testament aus Talmud und Midrasch*, Munich, 1922 ff.
TDNT	*Theological Dictionary of the New Testament* (ET by G. W. Bromiley of the following work, Grand Rapids, 1964 ff.).
TWNT	*Theologisches Wörterbuch zum Neuen Testament* (ed. G. Kittel; now G. Friedrich, Stuttgart, 1933 ff.).
Vermes	*The Dead Sea Scrolls in English*, translated by G. Vermes. Harmondsworth, 1962.

BIBLIOGRAPHY OF COMMENTARIES

Beare, F. W. *The Epistle to the Colossians*. Interpreter's Bible 11, New York/Nashville, 1955.

Benoit, P. *Les épîtres de saint Paul aux Philippiens, aux Colossiens, etc.* La sainte Bible, Paris, 1949.

Bruce, F. F. *Commentary on the Epistles to the Ephesians and Colossians* (with E. K. Simpson). New International/London Commentary, London/Grand Rapids, 1957.

Carson, H. M. *The Epistles of Paul to the Colossians and Philemon*. Tyndale New Testament Commentaries, London/Grand Rapids, 1960.

Conzelmann, H. *Die kleineren Briefe des Apostels Paulus Neue Testament Deutsch 8*. Göttingen, 1965.

Dibelius, M.—Greeven, H. *An die kolosser, Epheser, an Philemon. Handbuch zum Neuen Testament, 12*. Tübingen, 1953.

Johnston, G. *Ephesians, Philippians, Colossians and Philemon*. The Century Bible, London, 1967.

Lightfoot, J. B. *St. Paul's Epistles to the Colossians and Philemon*. London, 1879.

Lohmeyer, E. *Die Briefe an die Philipper, an die Kolosser und an Philemon*. Meyer Kommentar 9 (additional notes by W. Schmauch, 1964), Göttingen, 1953.

Lohse, E. *Die Briefe an die Kolosser und an Philemon*. Meyer Kommentar (new edition), Göttingen, 1968.

Masson, Ch. *L'épître de saint Paul aux Colossiens*. Commentaire du Nouveau Testament 10, Neuchatel/Paris, 1950.

Moule, C. F. D. *The Epistles of Paul the Apostle to the Colossians and to Philemon*. The Cambridge Greek Testament Commentary, Cambridge, 1957 (cited as Moule).

Moule, H. C. G. *Colossian Studies*. London, 1902 (cited as H. C. G. Moule).

Scott, E. F. *The Epistles of Paul to the Colossians etc.* Moffatt New Testament Commentary, London, 1930.

Synge, F. C. *Philippians and Colossians*. Torch Bible Commentary, London, 1951.

Thompson, G. H. P. *The Letters of Paul to the Ephesians, to the Colossians and to Philemon*. Cambridge Bible Commentary, Cambridge, 1967.

Note:
Since the manuscript left the author's hands, at least three notable studies

on the Colossian letter have appeared. For the general reader, R. E. O.
White has written a lucid commentary in the Broadman Bible Commentary (Nashville and London) volume 11. With somewhat more
technical interest shown but with admirable clarity J. L. Houlden's
Pelican Commentary series edition of the Prison Letters (Harmondsworth)
sheds a great deal of light on the epistle's message. For the student who
wishes to know the latest state of the question about the epistle's composition, background and argument as these are seen through the eyes
of recent German scholarship there is Johannes Lähnemann's very full
treatment, *Der Kolosserbrief* (Studien zum Neuen Testament, 3:
Gütersloh).

It is a pleasure to call attention to a careful treatment of "The Religious
Life-Setting of the Epistle to the Colossians" by a former student, James
Bradley, in *Studia Biblica et Theologica*, vol. ii, ed. E. K. Behrens,1972,
pp. 17–36.

BIBLIOGRAPHY OF OTHER BOOKS
AND ARTICLES

Anderson, C. P. "Who wrote 'the Epistle from Laodicea'?", *Journal of Biblical Literature*, 85, 1966, pp. 436–440.

Argyle, A. W. " 'Outward' and 'Inward' in Biblical Thought," *Exp Times* 68, 1956–57, pp. 196–9.

Baggott, L. J. *A New Approach to Colossians*. London, 1961.

Bandstra, A. J. *The Law and the Elements of the World: An Exegetical Study in Aspects of Paul's Teaching*, Kampen and Grand Rapids (n.d. about 1964).

Barrett, C. K. *From First Adam to Last*, London, 1962.

Beasley-Murray, G. R. "Baptism in the Epistles of Paul", *Christian Baptism*, ed. A. Gilmore, London, 1959.

—— *Baptism in the New Testament*, London, 1962.

Benoit, P. "Qumran and the New Testament," *Paul and Qumran*, ed. J. Murphy-O'Connor, London, 1968.

Best, E. *One Body in Christ*, London, 1955.

Bethge, E. *Dietrich Bonhoeffer*, London, 1970.

Bieder, W. *Die kolossische Irrlehre und die Kirche von heute*, (Theologische Studien, 33), Zürich, 1952.

Blanchette, O. A. "Does the *Cheirographon* of Col. 2, 14 represent Christ himself?", *Catholic Biblical Quarterly* 23, 1961, pp. 306–12.

Blass, F.—Debrunner, A.—Funk, R. W. *A Greek Grammar of the New Testament*, Cambridge and Chicago, 1961.

Bornkamm, G. "Die Häresie des Kolosserbriefes," *Das Ende des Gesetzes*[3]. Paulus-studien. Gesammelte Aufsätze, Band I., Munich, 1961.

—— "Das Bekenntnis im Hebräerbrief," *Studien zu Antike und Urchristentum*. Gesammelte Aufsätze, Band II., Munich, 1959.

—— "Die Hoffnung im Kolosserbrief—zugleich ein Beitrag zur Frage der Echtheit des Briefes," *Studien zum Neuen Testament und zur Patristik*, Festschrift E. Klostermann TU 77, Berlin, 1961.

—— "Baptism and New Life in Paul," *Early Christian Experience*, London, 1969.

Borsch, F. H. *The Christian and Gnostic Son of Man*, London, 1970.

Bousset, W. *Die Schriften des Neuen Testaments*, Göttingen, 1929.

Bowen, C. R. "Are Paul's prison letters from Ephesus?", *American Journal of Theology* 24, 1920, pp. 112–135,277–287.

Bruce, F. F. "St. Paul in Rome, 3. The Epistle to the Colossians," *Bulletin of the John Rylands Library*, 48, 2. Spring 1966, pp. 268–85.

Burney, C. F. "Christ as the *Arche* of Creation," *Journal of Theological Studies*, o.s. 27, 1926, pp. 160–177.

Carrington, P. *The Primitive Christian Catechism. A Study of the Epistles*, Cambridge, 1940.

Chadwick, H. " 'All Things to All Men'," *New Testament Studies*, 1, 1954–55, pp. 261–275.

Coppens, J. " 'Mystery' in the Theology of Saint Paul and its Parallels at Qumran," *Paul and Qumran*, ed. J. Murphy-O'Connor, London, 1968, pp. 132–158.

Coutts, J. "The Relationship of Ephesians and Colossians," *New Testament Studies*, 4, 1957–58, pp. 210–207.

Cox, H. *The Feast of Fools*, Cambridge, Mass. 1969.

Cullmann, O. *Early Christian Worship*, London, 1953.

—— "The Kingship of Christ and the Church in the New Testament," *The Early Church*, London, 1956, pp. 105–137.

Dahl, N. "Anamnesis: Mémoire et Commémoration dans le christianisme primitif," *Studia Theologica* 1, 1947, pp. 69–95.

Daube, D. "Participle and Imperative in 1 Peter," in *The First Epistle of St. Peter* by E. G. Selwyn, London, 1946, pp. 467–488.

Davies, W. D. *Paul and Rabbinic Judaism*,[2] London, 1955.

—— "Paul and the Dead Sea Scrolls," *The Scrolls and New Testament*, ed. K. Stendahl, London, 1958, pp. 157–182.

Deissmann, A. *Light from the Ancient East*, ET London, 1927.

Delling, G. *Die Taufe im Neuen Testament*, Berlin, 1963.

Dodd, C. H. *The Bible and the Greeks*, London, 1935.

Duncan, G. S. *St. Paul's Ephesian Ministry*, London, 1929.

Dunn, J. D. G. *Baptism in the Holy Spirit*, London, 1970.

Elliott, J. H. "A Catholic Gospel: Reflections on 'Early Catholicism' in the New Testament," *Catholic Biblical Quarterly*, 31, 1969, pp. 213–23.

Ellis, E. E. " 'Those of the Circumcision' and the early Christian Mission," *Studia Evangelica* iv, TU 102, 1968, pp. 390–99.

—— *The Gospel of Luke* (Century Bible), London, 1966.

Flemington, W. F. *Baptism in the New Testament*, London, 1948.

Flew, R. N. *The Idea of Perfection in Christian Theology*, Oxford, 1934.

Foerster, W. "Die Irrelehrer des Kolosserbriefes" in *Studia Biblica et Semitica. Festschrift Th.C. Vriezen*, Wageningen, 1966, pp. 71–80.

Francis, F. O. "Humility and Angelic Worship in Col. 2:18," *Studia Theologica*, xvi, 1962, pp. 109–134.

—— "Visionary Discipline and Scriptural Tradition at Colossae," *Lexington Theological Quarterly* II. 3, 1967, pp. 71–81.

Fuller, R. H. *A Critical Introduction to the New Testament*, London, 1966.

Gabathuler, H. J. *Jesus Christus. Haupt der Kirche—Haupt der Welt. Der Christushymnus Kolosser 1, 15–20 in der theologischen Forschung der letzten 130 Jahre. Zürich, 1965.

Gibbs, J. G. *Creation and Redemption. A Study in Pauline Theology*, Leiden, 1971.

Grant, R. M. *Gnosticism and Early Christianity*, London, 1966.

Grässer, E. "Kol 3, 1–4 als Beispiel einer Interpretation secundum homines recipientes," *Zeitschrift für Theologie und Kirche* 64, 1967, pp. 139–168.

Guthrie, D. *New Testament Introduction. The Pauline Epistles*, London, 1961.

Hall, B. G. "Colossians II. 23," *ExpTimes* 36, 1924–25, p. 285.

Hanson, S. *The Unity of the Church in the New Testament. Colossians and Ephesians*, Uppsala, 1946.

Harris, J. R. *Side-lights on New Testament Research*, London, 1909.

—— "St. Paul and Aristophanes," *ExpTimes*, 34, 1922–23, pp. 151–156.

Hendry, G. S. "Mystery," *A Theological Wordbook of the Bible*, ed., A. Richardson, London, 1950, pp. 156f.

Hester, J. D. *Paul's Concept of Inheritance*, Edinburgh, 1968.

Holtzmann, H. J. *Kritik der Epheser-und Kolosserbriefe*, Leipzig, 1872.

Hunter, A. M. *Paul and his Predecessors²*, London, 1961.

—— *Interpreting Paul's Gospel*, London, 1954.

—— *Teaching and Preaching the New Testament*, London, 1963.

Jeremias, J. *Infant Baptism in the First Four Centuries*, ET, London, 1960.

Jervell, J. *Imago Dei: Gen. i. 26f. im Spätjudentum, in der Gnosis und in den paulinischen Briefen*, Göttingen, 1960.

Johnston, L. "The Pauline Letters from Caesarea," *ExpTimes* 68, 1956–57, pp. 24.

Joüon, P. "Note sur Colossiens III. 5–11," *Recherches de Science Religieuse* 26, 1936, pp. 185–189.

Käsemann, E. *Leib und Leib Christi*, Tübingen, 1933.

—— "A Primitive Christian Baptismal Liturgy," *Essays on New Testament Themes*, London, 1964.

—— "Worship in Everyday Life: a note on Romans 12," *New Testament Questions of Today*, London, 1969.

Kehl, N. *Der Christushymnus im Kolosserbrief*, Stuttgart, 1967.

Klijn, A. F. J. *An Introduction to the New Testament*, Leiden, 1967.

Knox, J. *Philemon among the Letters of Paul²*, New York/Nashville, 1959.

Knox, W. L. *St. Paul and the Church of the Gentiles*, Cambridge, 1939.

Kuhn, K. G. "New Light on Temptation, Sin, and Flesh in the NT," *The Scrolls and the New Testament*, ed. K. Stendahl, London, 1958, pp. 94–113.

Kümmel, W. G. *Introduction to the New Testament*, ET, London, 1966.

Lampe, G. W. H. *The Seal of Spirit*, London, 1951.

Larsson, E. *Christus als Vorbild. Eine Untersuchung zu den paulinischen Taufe-und Eikontexten*, Uppsala, 1962.

Leaney, A. R. C. "Colossians II. 21–23," *ExpTimes* 64, 1952–53, p. 92.

Lightfoot, J. B. *St. Paul's Epistle to the Galatians*, London, 1874.

Lock, W. "Hymn," *A Dictionary of the Bible*, ed. J. Hastings, vol ii, Edinburgh, 1899, pp. 440f.

Lohse, E. "Christologie und Ethik im Kolosserbrief," *Apophoreta. Festschrift E. Haenchen,* Berlin, 1964, pp. 156–168.
—— "Pauline Theology in the Letter to the Colossians," *New Testament Studies,* 15, 1969, pp. 211–220.
—— "Die Mitarbeiter des Apostels Paulus im Kolosserbrief," *Verborum Veritas. Festschrift Gustav Stählin,* Wuppertal, 1970, pp. 189–194.
Lyonnet, S. "Saint Paul et le gnosticisme: la lettre aux Colossiens," *The Origins of Gnosticism,* Leiden, 1967, pp. 538–551.
—— "Col 2,18 et les mystères d'Apollon Clarien," *Biblica* 43, 1962, pp. 417–35.
MacRae, G. W. "The Coptic Gnostic Apocalypse of Adam," *Heythrop Journal* 6, 1965, pp. 27–35.
Marshall, I. H. *Kept by the Power of God,* London, 1969.
Marshall, L. H. *The Challenge of New Testament Ethics,* London, 1946.
Manson, T. W. *Studies in the Gospels and Epistles,* ed. M. Black, Manchester, 1962.
Martin, R. P. *The Epistle of Paul to the Philippians,* London, 1959.
—— "An Early Christian Hymn (Col. 1:15–20)," *The Evangelical Quarterly* 36. 4, 1964, pp. 195–205.
—— "Aspects of Worship in the New Testament Church," *Vox Evangelica* II, 1963, pp. 6–32.
—— *Worship in the Early Church,* London, 1964.
—— *Carmen Christi: Philippians, II. 5–11 in Recent Interpretation and in the Setting of early Christian Worship,* Cambridge, 1967.
—— *The Epistle to the Ephesians.* Broadman Bible Commentary, London/ Nashville, 1971.
Martin, W. J. "1 Corinthians 11: 2–16; an Interpretation," in *Apostolic History and the Gospel,* ed. W. W. Gasque and R. P. Martin. Exeter/ Grand Rapids, 1970, pp. 231–41.
Marxsen, W. *Introduction to the New Testament,* ET, London, 1968.
Mayerhoff, E. T. *Der Brief an die Kolosser,* Berlin, 1838.
Metzger, B. M. *The Text of the New Testament,* Oxford, 1964. ²1968.
Mitton, C. L. *The Epistle of James,* London, 1966.
Moffatt, J. *Introduction to the Literature of the New Testament*³, Edinburgh, 1918.
Morton, A. Q. *Christianity and the Computer,* London, 1964. (with McLeman, J.).
Moulton, J. H. *Grammar of New Testament Greek,* vol. I, Edinburgh, 1908.
Nauck, W. "Salt as a Metaphor in Instruction for Discipleship", *Studia Theologica* 6, 1952, pp. 165–178.
Nock, A. D. "The Vocabulary of the New Testament," *Journal of Biblical Literature* 52, 1933, pp. 131–139.
Oke, C. C. "A Hebraistic Construction in Colossians I. 19–22," *ExpTimes* 63, 1951–52, pp. 155f.

Percy, E. *Die Probleme der Kolosser-und Epheserbriefe*, Lund, 1946.

Pfitzner, V. C. *Paul and the Agon Motif* (Supplements to Novum Testamentum), Leiden, 1967.

Pollard, T. E. *Johannine Christology and the Early Church*, Cambridge, 1970.

Ramsay, W. M. *The Cities and Bishoprics of Phrygia*, Oxford, vol. 1, part 2, 1897.

—— *The Teaching of Paul in Terms of the Present Day*, London, 1913.

Reicke, B. "Zum sprachlichen Verständnis von Kol 2, 23," *Studia Theologica* 6, 1952, pp. 39–52.

—— "Caesarea, Rome, and the Captivity Epistles," in *Apostolic History and the Gospel*, Festschrift F. F. Bruce, edd. W. W. Gasque and R. P. Martin, Exeter/Grand Rapids, 1970, pp. 277–86.

Reumann, J. "*Oikonomia*—Terms in Paul in comparison with Lucan *Heilsgeschichte*," *New Testament Studies* 13, 1966–67, pp. 147–167.

Robinson, B. W. "An Ephesian Imprisonment of Paul," *Journal of Biblical Literature*, 29, 1910, pp. 181–89.

Robinson, J. A. T. *The Body*. A study in Pauline Theology, London, 1952.

Robinson, J. M. "Die Hodajot-Formel in Gebet und Hymnus des Frühchristentums," in *Apophoreta*. Festschrift E. Haenchen, Berlin, 1964, pp. 194–235.

Rowley, H. H. *The Unity of the Bible*, London, 1953.

Sanders, E. P. "Literary Dependence in Colossians," *Journal of Biblical Literature*, 85, 1966, pp. 28–45.

Sanders, J. T. *The New Testament Christological Hymns*, Cambridge, 1971.

Schmithals, W. *The Office of Apostle in the Early Church*, ET, Nashville, 1969.

Scott, C. A. A. *Christianity according to St. Paul*, Cambridge, 1932.

—— *Saint Paul: the Man and the Teacher*, Cambridge, 1936.

Scott, R. B. Y. "Wisdom in Creation: the '*Amon* of Proverbs viii. 30" *Vetus Testamentum* 10, 1960, pp. 213–223.

Schnackenburg, R. *Baptism in the Thought of St. Paul*, ET, Oxford, 1964.

Schweizer, E. "Zur Frage der Echtheit des Kolosser-und Epheserbriefe," *Zeitschrift für neutestamentliche Wissenschaft*, 47, 1956, p. 287.

—— *Lordship and Discipleship*, ET, London, 1960.

—— *The Church as the Body of Christ*, Richmond, Va., 1964.

—— "The Church as the Missionary Body of Christ," *New Testament Studies*, 8, 1961–62, pp. 1–11.

—— "Die 'Elemente der Welt' Gal. 4,3,9; Kol. 2,8,20," *Verborum Veritas*. Festschrift Gustav Stählin, Wuppertal, 1970, pp. 245–259.

Selwyn, E. C. *St. Luke the Prophet*, London, 1901.

—— "The Carefulness of Luke the Prophet," *The Expositor*, 7, 1909, pp. 547–558.

Tannehill, R. C. *Dying and Rising with Christ*. A Study in Pauline Theology. Berlin, 1967.

Thrall, M. E. *Greek Particles in the New Testament*, Leiden, 1962.

Turner, N. *A Grammar of New Testament Greek*, vol. III, Edinburgh, 1963.

—— *Grammatical Insights into the New Testament*, Edinburgh, 1965.

Vermes, G. "Baptism and Jewish Exegesis: New Light from Ancient Sources," *NTS* 4. 1957–58, pp. 308–19.

Williams, A. Lukyn "The cult of Angels at Colossae," *Journal of Theological Studies*, o.s. 10, 1909, pp. 413–38.

Wilson, R. McL. "Gnosis, Gnosticism and the New Testament," *The Origins of Gnosticism*, Leiden, 1967, pp. 511–527.

—— *Gnosis and the New Testament*, Oxford, 1968.

Yamauchi, E. "Qumran and Colosse," *Bibliotheca Sacra* 121, 1964, pp. 141–152.

INDEX OF MAIN SUBJECTS TREATED

INDEX OF MODERN AUTHORS

INDEX OF PRINCIPAL REFERENCES TO
SCRIPTURAL PASSAGES

A. OLD TESTAMENT

B. NEW TESTAMENT